IMAGES
of America

YANCEY COUNTY

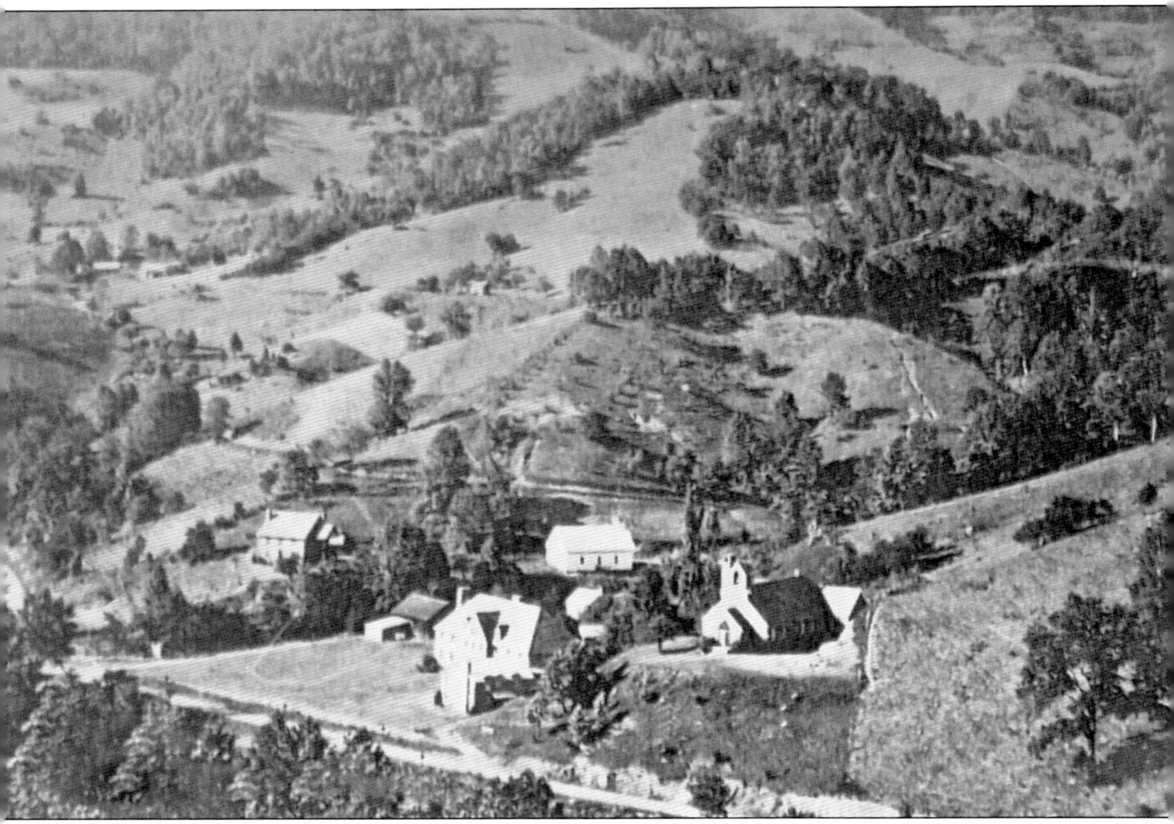

Higgins, North Carolina, fronts Highway 19 West, and this view depicts the Presbyterian church, parsonage, staff house, and the former Markle Building, which served as a hospital and clinic until the 1960s. In the background stands the Higgins Free Will Baptist Church. (Courtesy of Dorothy McMahan.)

On the Cover: Raleigh Radford (center), local postmaster and store owner in the community, stands amid one of the old bridges on Cane River. Also pictured are W.M. Wray (second from left) and Lee Evans. (Courtesy of Nancy Randolph Silvers.)

IMAGES
of America

YANCEY COUNTY

Elaine McAlister Dellinger
and Kiesa Kay

ARCADIA
PUBLISHING

ISBN 978-0-7385-8760-8

Published by Arcadia Publishing
Charleston, South Carolina

Printed in the United States of America

Library of Congress Control Number: 2011920417

For all general information, please contact Arcadia Publishing:
Telephone 843-853-2070
Fax 843-853-0044
E-mail sales@arcadiapublishing.com
For customer service and orders:
Toll-Free 1-888-313-2665

Visit us on the Internet at www.arcadiapublishing.com

In loving memory of my father, Warren Burdett McAlister (1921–1983); my mother, Birdie Elizabeth Honeycutt McAlister (1912–2000); and my only sibling, Shirley McAlister Buchanan (1941–1993); each one taught me so much about family values and heritage. Lastly, to my loving husband, Charles Lee, who has been with me through so much and continues lending his helping hand and support without fail.

—Elaine McAlister Dellinger

For my children, Ameli "Katie" Cyr and Benjamin Cyr, and to Gordon "Joe" Quinlan, who shared the journey.

—Kiesa Kay

Contents

Acknowledgments

This book would not be possible without the generous memories of our contributors. We want to thank our consultants, Melanie Stallings, an eagle-eyed librarian with a penchant for precision, and James Byrd, an expert on local history for whom the Mountain Heritage High School library was named and a good friend who provided continued support and assistance in proofreading the manuscript. We also thank Lindsay Harris Carter, Charles Dellinger, Gordon Quinlan, Janice Barnett, Samantha Phipps, Patti Smith, Michelle McCluskey, Judy Carson, and David Biddix for kind words at crucial moments. The Yancey History Association, led by Jake Blood, has been an important resource. This book is possible only through the kind consideration of our contributors, who devoted time and shared their dearest family memories. We could use only a fraction of the photographs that were collected, but we appreciate every contribution.

Photographs appear courtesy of Charlotte Anglin, Roy Lee Anglin, Helen Threadgill Baden, Evelyn Hope Bailey, Gwen Bodford, Madge Brookshire, Carolyn Wheeler Bryant, James Byrd, Thelma Carmack, Barbara Cole, Linda Peterson Cox, Charles L. Dellinger, Elaine McAlister Dellinger, Tom P Dellinger, Virgie Duncan, Barbara Ford, Vickie Fortune, Elaine Gales, Ronnie Griffith, Mildred Gibbs Harris, Genevieve Harrison, June McCandless Jerome, Tom Kaluzynski and Linda Kinnane, Mike Ledford, Rebecca Proffitt McCall, Amy Hopson McCurry, David McAlister, Wayne and Phyllis McKinney, Dorothy McMahan, Judie Bailey Miller, Robin Owen, Tim Penland, Jane Whitson Peterson, Bennie Phillips, Ruth Pope, Sarah Woody Proffitt, Carol and Joe Renfro, Joseph Sasek family archives, Mike Shelton, Nancy Randolph Silvers, Dixie Styles, Grant Ward, Earl Webb, Shirley Barnett Whiteside, the Yancey History Association, Virginia York, and Betty Lou Young.

INTRODUCTION

Yancey County's beauty and agricultural bounty provided sustenance for many years before the formation of the county. The rich archaeological heritage dates from before 3000 BC, and two significant digs are occurring within the county today. The boundaries between counties were fluid for a time, but in November 1833, stars fell in a powerful meteor shower that lit the night sky, and the next month, Yancey County was born. The county took its name from Bartlett Yancey, a powerful politician of the times who promoted establishing counties and education in Western North Carolina. He worked with "Yellow Jacket" John Bailey and others to create the town of Burnsville by donating land.

Many families who arrived here during the Revolutionary War simply came to the mountains and never wanted to leave. Nestled between the lovely Cane and Toe Rivers, Yancey County contained everything a family needed to thrive: natural beauty, an abundance of wild foods like ramps and herbs of all kinds, fine bottomland for farming, and delicious spring water. With all of the laurels, trilliums, and rhododendrons in bloom, the county can resemble an unabashed Eden. At the end of the 19th century, Yancey County took first premium at the state fair in sweet potatoes, apples, cabbages, and dried fruit.

The War Between the States brought strife throughout the region, as Yancey men became soldiers for both the Union and the Confederacy. The Battle of Burnsville is reenacted annually to commemorate those rugged times. When the war ended, neighbors resumed their coexistence.

The beginning of the 20th century brought several changes. Logging became increasingly commonplace. One sawmill handled 75,000 feet of lumber daily in the Black Mountains of Yancey County. More than 10,000 acres were sold for $10 to $15 an acre, and the great-grandfather trees began crashing to earth. The county had 60 varieties of trees felled to be sold as timber, including chestnut, oak, poplar, maple, and spruce. The county land had an average of 5,000 feet of timber per acre, which amounted to a billion feet in the county limits, and in those days before environmental activism, the trees became a financial resource, a source of jobs, and the material for heating and housing.

The logging intensified with the world wars, too, when European production became less accessible. Trees from Yancey County supplied ship floors and more across the globe.

A great flood slammed the Toe River Valley in 1916, but farming continued, and in 1925, the average farm was 64.8 acres. The land offered up its bounty, and Yancey apples won 14 awards at a Paris exposition.

Education mattered deeply to the mountain families, not as a way out of the mountains but as a way to bring even more pleasure to everyday life. The noted explorer Meriwether Lewis taught for a time in Burnsville. Sam and Jennie Bennett donated the property for a building site for Yancey Collegiate Institute in the early 1900s. By 1936, five high schools graced the county. This tradition has continued through the years, handed down from generation to generation. Shirley Barnett Whiteside became the first to integrate the schools in Yancey County in 1960. In 2008, her son, the noted minister Bill Whiteside, became the first African American on the school board. The county also boasts a unique private boarding school, the Arthur Morgan School, in the Celo area.

Annie Wray Bennett wrote that Yancey had around 300 square miles, or 109,720 acres, with 30,000 in natural forest reserve; 100,000 in second growth; and 60,000 laid to farms. Mining and industry infiltrated the area, too. By 1942, olivine was being pulled from the land, along with mica and soapstone.

Tourism began when Mount Mitchell became known as the highest mountain east of the Mississippi, and the forested mountains attracted hikers, including Mrs. Charles Hutchins (Effie), who broke the world's long-distance hiking record in 1927. Hutchins's record was broken soon afterward by a woman who claimed to consume an ancient Native formula and hot chocolate to keep up her strength.

The land remains home to all manner of birds, deer, foxes, wild turkeys, and black bears. The rivers run with wild trout, frisky beavers, and an abundance of several varieties of fish, plus the rare elktoe mussel. Waterfalls on both private and public lands enhance the peace that pervades the area even to this day.

The town boasted one of the best Negro League baseball teams in the country, the Burnsville Eagles. George Lee Griffith, a wonderful player, had offers to go professional after the color barrier broke, but he chose to stay in Yancey with his family and friends. He initiated the ball field in the county, which was named in his honor half a century later. Another native son, Glenn Gardner, joined a big-league team in the 1930s.

One thing that has distinguished Yancey County for 150 years has been the desire of families to stay here and to stay together, so that the people of each generation know not only the history but also the actual land and people of their homeland. When it came time to choose profession or home, time and again, true Yancey families have chosen to nourish their roots instead of cutting them. Yancey's children have grown up with several generations together in a multi-dimensional family environment based on strong values of love, trust, and living off the land. Some communities, though, have disappeared altogether, like the magical Lost Cove community.

Patriotism and strong spiritual values characterize Yancey County, and it has a strong musical heritage, too. Lesley Riddle accompanied A.P. Carter throughout the Appalachians to collect songs, and there is an annual Riddlefest to commemorate his contributions not only to the culture of this county but to all of country music.

Folks who come to visit often stay for the rest of their lives, including doctors, physicists, and classical pianists. The renowned song collector and fiddler Bruce Greene hails from here. Some folks stay for only an indelible moment, such as William Jackson of Jacks Creek, who went back home to become known as the greatest harpist in all of Scotland and founder of the legendary Ossian. The area has also become known for its intrepid glass blowers, such as Billy and Katherine Bernstein and the irrepressible Rob Levin.

"If I wrote about what's happened here, I'd call my book *They Killed the Buffalo*," said Sam Loftis, a local taxidermist. He sees a surge away from the old ways and culture. His uncle offered work to several men during the Depression, and together, a team of men built a beautiful cabin tucked deep in the woods with forged iron on the doors and a chimney made of all the minerals and stones found naturally in this region.

Evelyn Hope Bailey, Parkway Playhouse historian, recounts the changes even in the last few decades. Before television and computers, kids would make their own fun, creating plays and performing them in the yard, complete with costumes and homemade scripts. The Parkway Playhouse used to have a delightful mural made by a Celo student, but it got painted over—and changes continue.

Through all the changes, though, Yancey County remains a place where the creeks sing and crickets dance as stars fall through the clear night sky.

One

Many Blessings

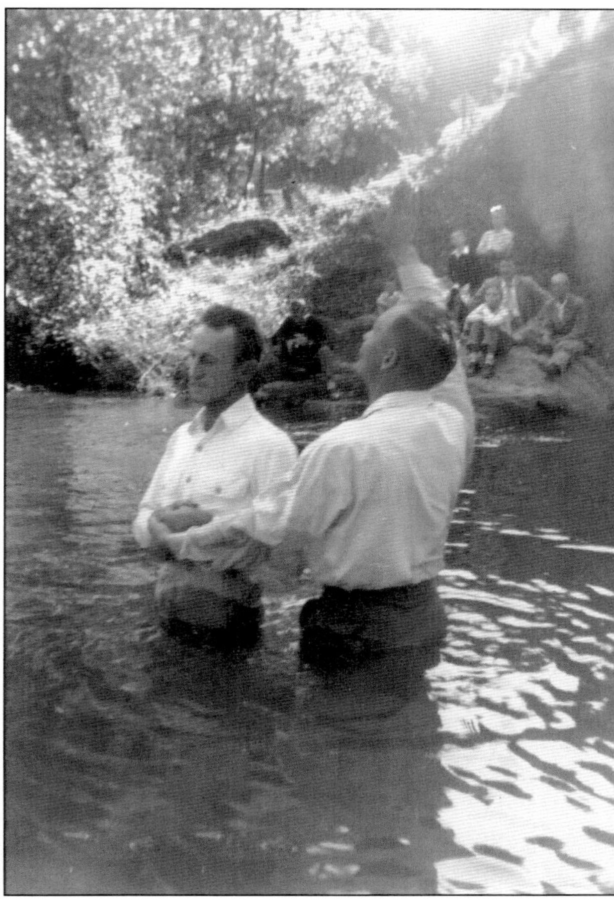

James Theodore Hughes, born in the Shoal Creek community in 1915, is being baptized in the river. (Courtesy of Robin Owen.)

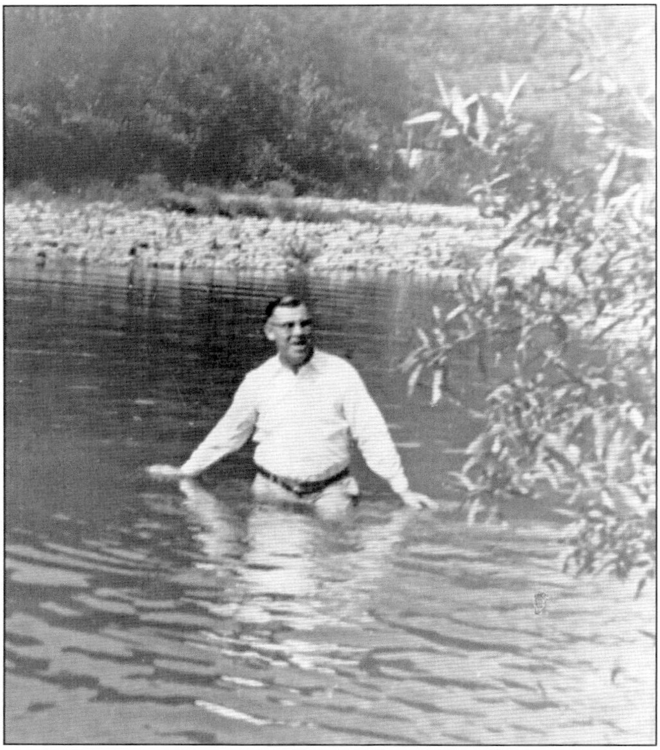

Preacher Ebb Wheeler, a well-beloved Free Will Baptist minister, performed many baptisms in the river in the 1940s and 1950s. Many Yancey residents have strong religious convictions and believe "Not by works of righteousness which we have done, but according to His mercy He saved us, by the washing of regeneration, and renewal of the Holy Spirit" (Titus 3:5). Baptisms bring times of celebration to the community. (Courtesy of Wayne and Phyllis McKinney.)

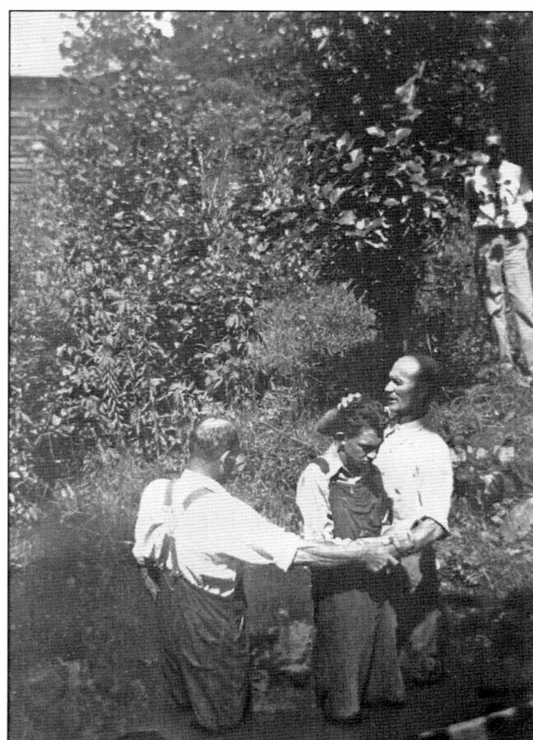

In the hollow at Arthur and Lucy Webb's place by Battle Branch Road in Green Mountain, a creek has been dammed up for this special baptism. A full third of Yancey citizens are Baptist, and county citizens of other faiths also find the rivers and creeks to be places of spiritual renewal and rebirth. (Courtesy of Earl Webb.)

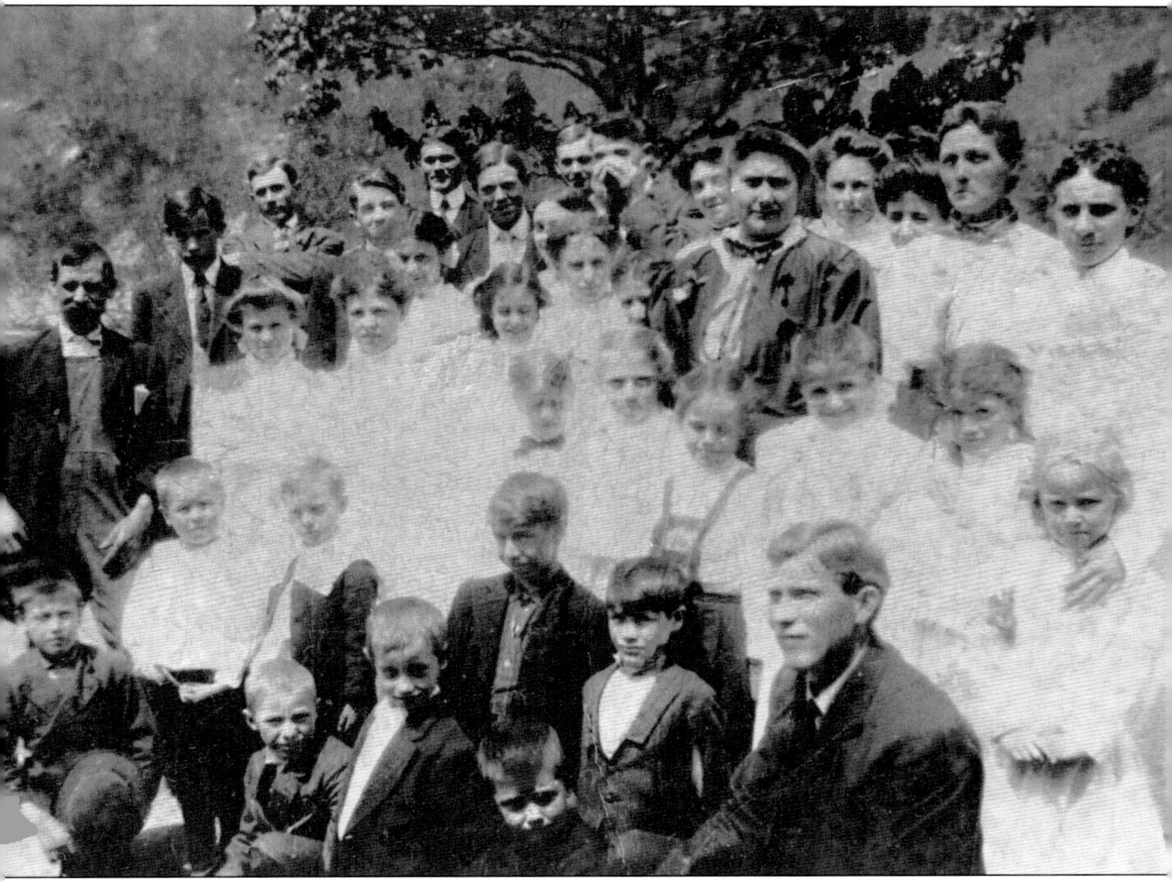

Shown here at Mouth of Pigeon Roost in 1908 are Boyd Warrick, Clayton McCurry, Park Bradshaw, Holt Bradshaw, George Warrick, Marcus Bradshaw, Charlie Byrd, Lawson Gouge, Robert Byrd, Vickie Byrd, Emma Byrd, Golda Warrick, Flora Whitson, James Madison Byrd, Nettie Whitson, Nola Gouge, Geneva Bradshaw, Etta Horton Bradshaw, Blanche Bradshaw, ? Jackson, Bertha Bradshaw, Smith Warrick, Bernie Bradshaw, Malachi Byrd, Henry Lewis, Sam Bailey, Bob Renfro, Dr. Isaac Bradshaw, Rose McCourry, Rissie Byrd, and others. (Courtesy of James Byrd.)

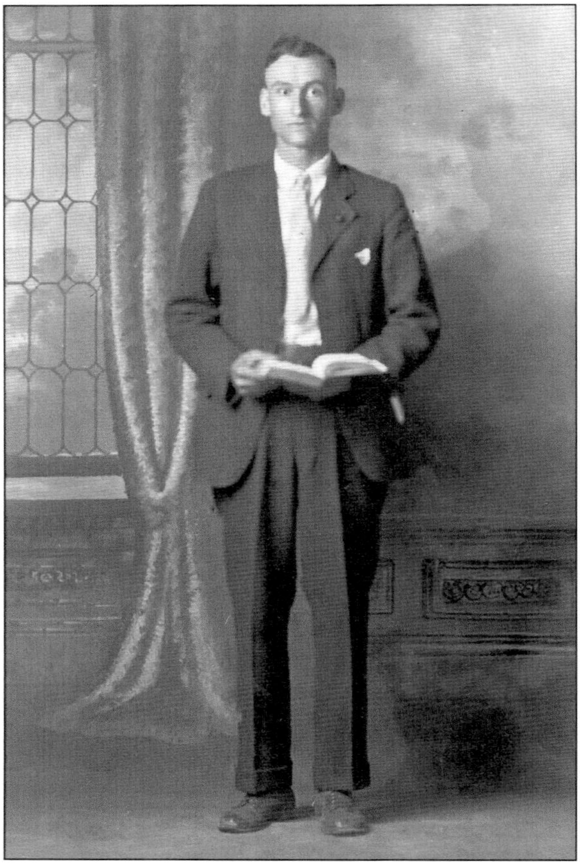

The Reverend Charles Hayden Honeycutt was ordained into the ministry and a member of the Jacks Creek Baptist Association. Hayden married Viola Branch of South Toe. Their daughter, Geneva, married Bud Bates. (Courtesy of Elaine McAlister Dellinger.)

This church group gathered in the Ramseytown area. Ramseytown has always been a bit isolated because of its rough terrain. It borders Tennessee and has several churches, always the hub of the community. (Courtesy of Elaine McAlister Dellinger.)

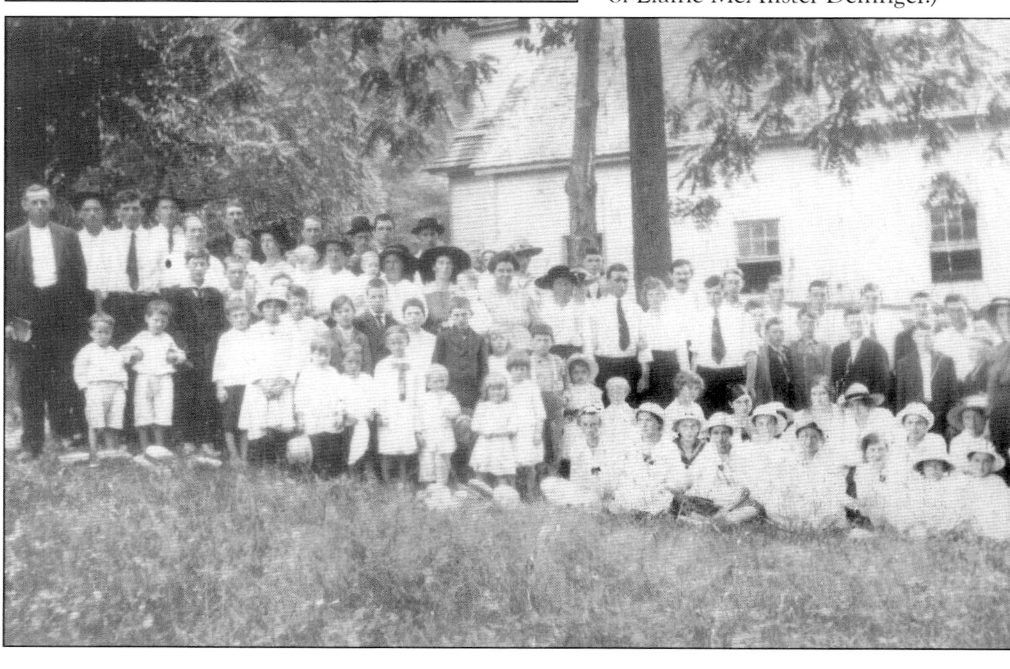

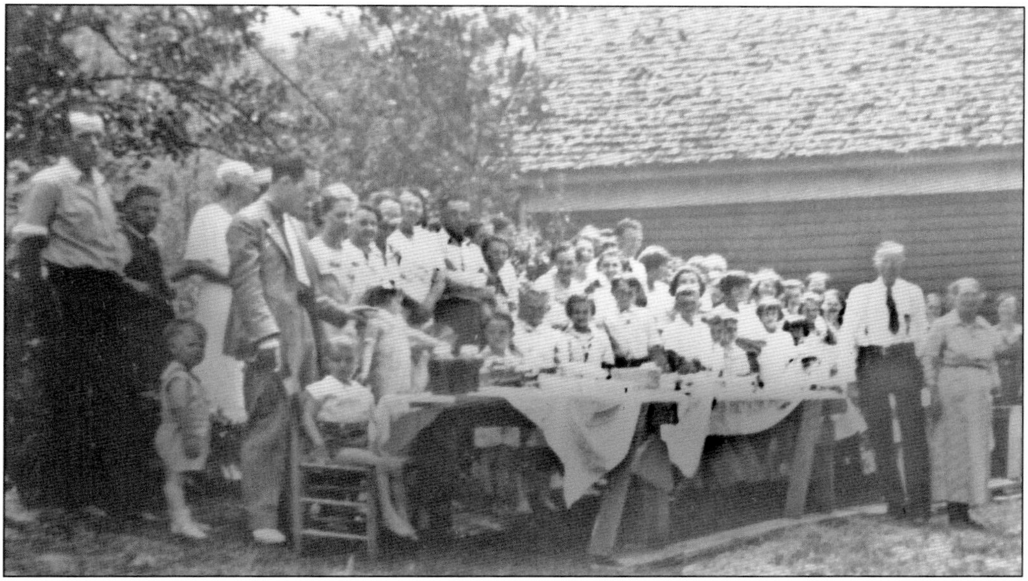

After decorations, families celebrated with large dinners, and the outdoor picnic tables sagged from the bounty of home-baked Appalachian specialties. (Courtesy of Betty Lou Young and Linda Cox.)

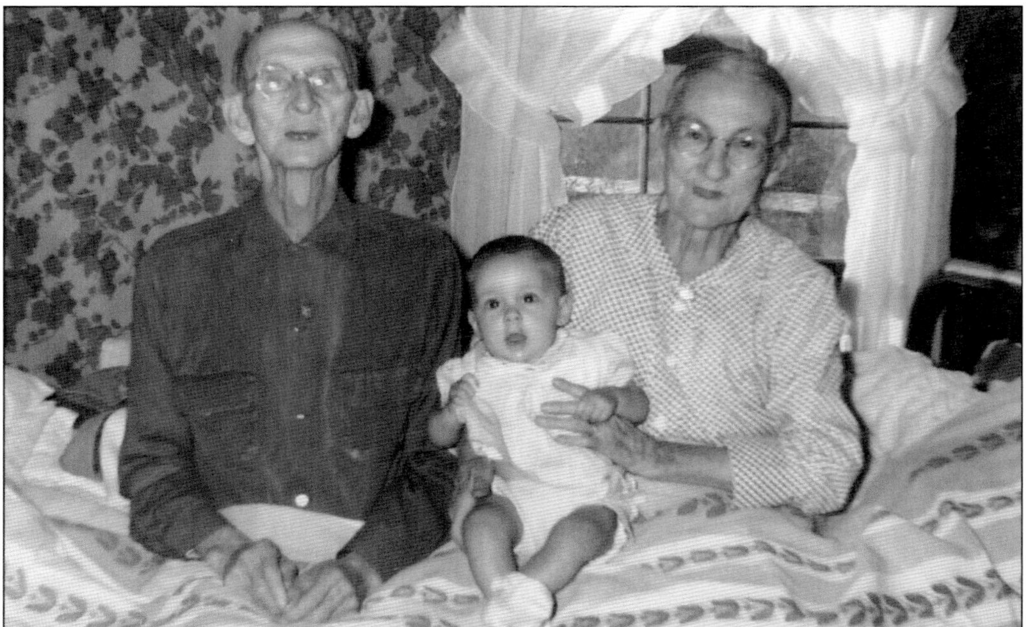

Families started several churches in Yancey County to meet the spiritual needs of the community, and church members supported one another through prayer and good works. Lora Jane Bailey Honeycutt was one of the charter members of the Bald Mountain Free Will Baptist Church and was well known and respected by many in the church. Seen here from left to right are William Andrew Honeycutt, great-granddaughter Tammy Buchanan, and Lora Jane Bailey Honeycutt. (Courtesy of Elaine McAlister Dellinger.)

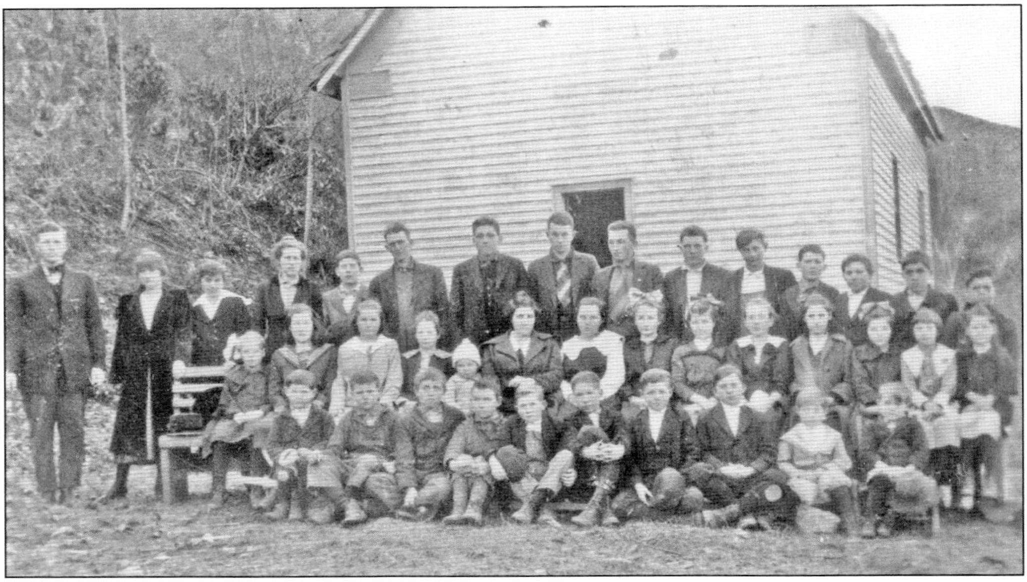

Faith groups tried to provide a place for everyday learning as well as spiritual quests. The Baker's Creek Baptist Church housed the school. This 1949 class on Baker's Creek included, among others, (first row) Shirley Black, Genette King, Glenn Roland, Barbara Melton, Gene Elkins, and Earnest Ayers; (second row) Genella Anglin, Ivory Melton, Dean King, Charles Roland, Arville Baker, Howard Roland, Jeralene Byrd, and Roy Anglin; (third row) Nadine McIntosh, Evalee King, Maphria Wilson, and Norris McCandless. (Courtesy of Roy Lee Anglin.)

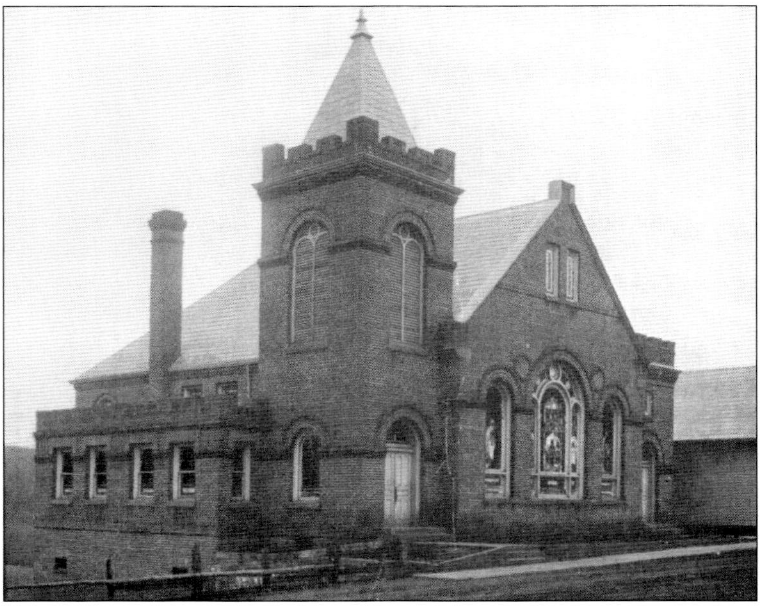

The 1920s Burnsville First Baptist Church stood tall on Main Street in the spot where the Yancey Baptist Association building currently stands. Some of the brick was used to restore the Rush Wray Museum, and its stained glass windows can be seen in other local churches as well. The church is gone but not forgotten. (Courtesy of Barbara Ford.)

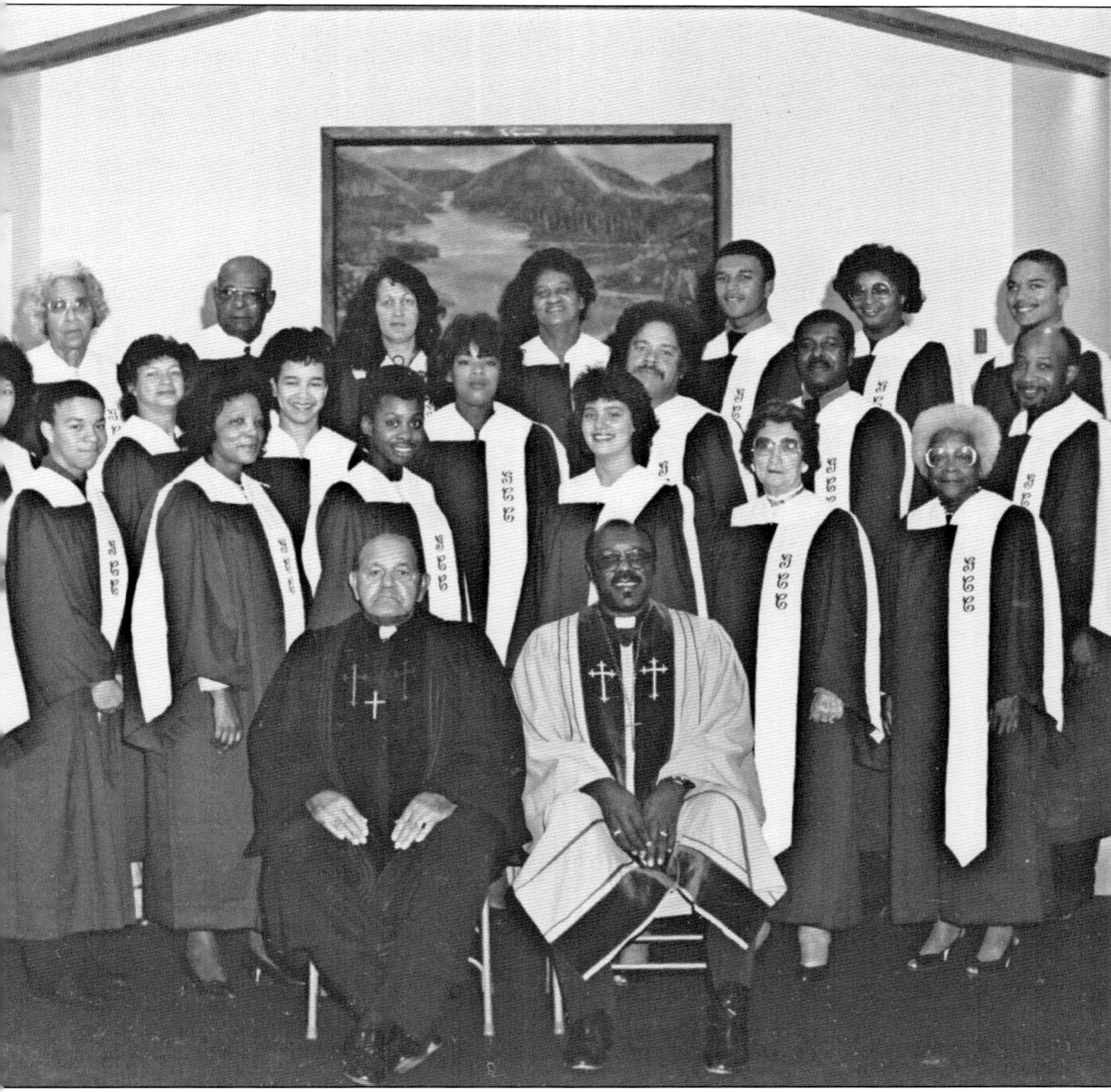

The Griffith Chapel Choir has been a source of civic pride for many years. The church bought its building back from the AME Church and raised enough money to pay off the mortgage through the choir's singing. They have been invited to sing at prestigious events throughout the country, thanks to beautiful voices like that of choir director Roberta Whiteside. From left to right, pictured here are (first row) Kevin Watkins, Rose Staley, Charisse ?, Christie Griffith, Selelia Griffith, Virginia Griffith, the Reverend Grady Riddle (seated left), and the Reverend James Staley (seated right); (second row) Cathy Henson, Patsy Griffith, Sonya Shade, Janice Barnett, Stevie Griffith, Leon Smith, and Ray Williamson; (third row) Mamie Wilson, Charles Young, Kittie Smith, Peggy Wilson, Carlos Smith, Sandy Pertella, and Bill Whiteside. (Courtesy of Shirley Whiteside.)

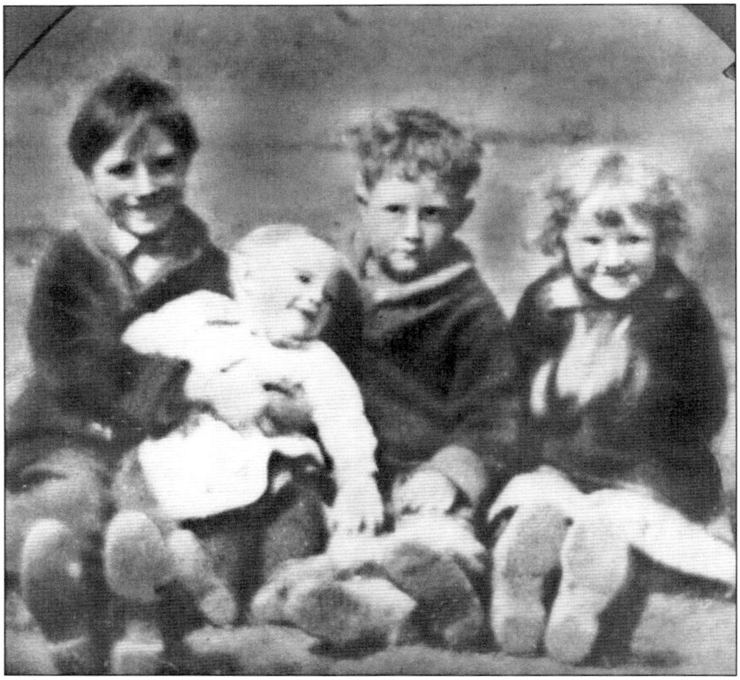

From left to right, Liston, Keith, and Jack Penland, sons of John and Bessie Penland, sit next to their cousin Edna Mitchell Metcalf (1919–1927). Little Edna was holding hands with Liston when she was hit and killed by a drunk driver as they walked with her family toward their home in Woodfin after having just visited her grandmother Margaret in the hospital. Family says Liston never talked of Edna again until after he suffered a stroke just two weeks before he died. (Courtesy of Tim Penland.)

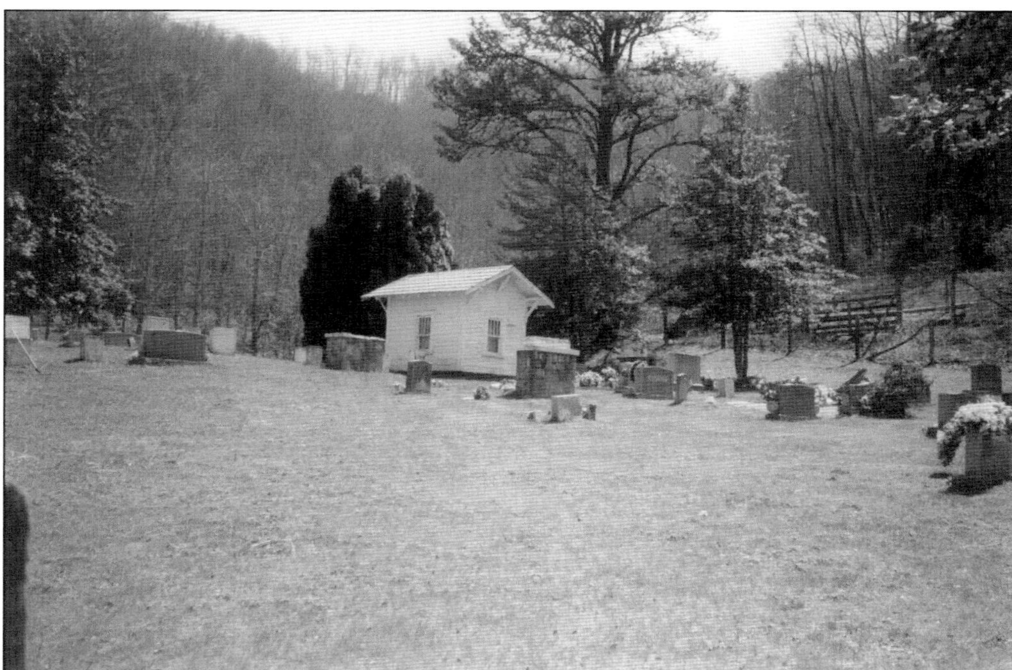

The playhouse on Edna Metcalf's grave, built by her father, John Metcalf, used to contain all of the little girl's toys. The floor is covered in sand. It sits among the tombstones, with her tombstone safely inside it. Edna's parents placed her grave facing east, as is traditional, but situated their own graves to face hers. Historian Gwen Bodford has recorded more than 730 cemeteries in the county, including this one. (Courtesy of Gwen Bodford.)

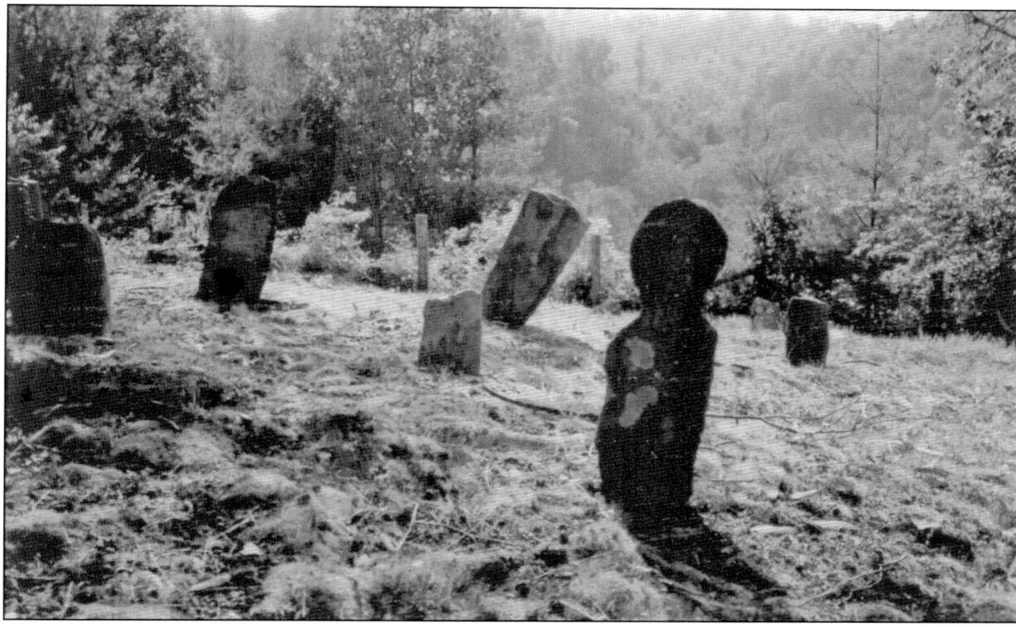

Meinshr stones are gravestones in the shape of a man. This tradition goes back to the Old World, where the people believed the effigy would ward off evil spirits. This stone is one of about three in the Old Zion Church Cemetery in the Green Mountain or Pig Pen area. Some of the graves in this same cemetery follow a different custom of keeping the graves mounded up and swept clean of grass. (Courtesy of Elaine McAlister Dellinger.)

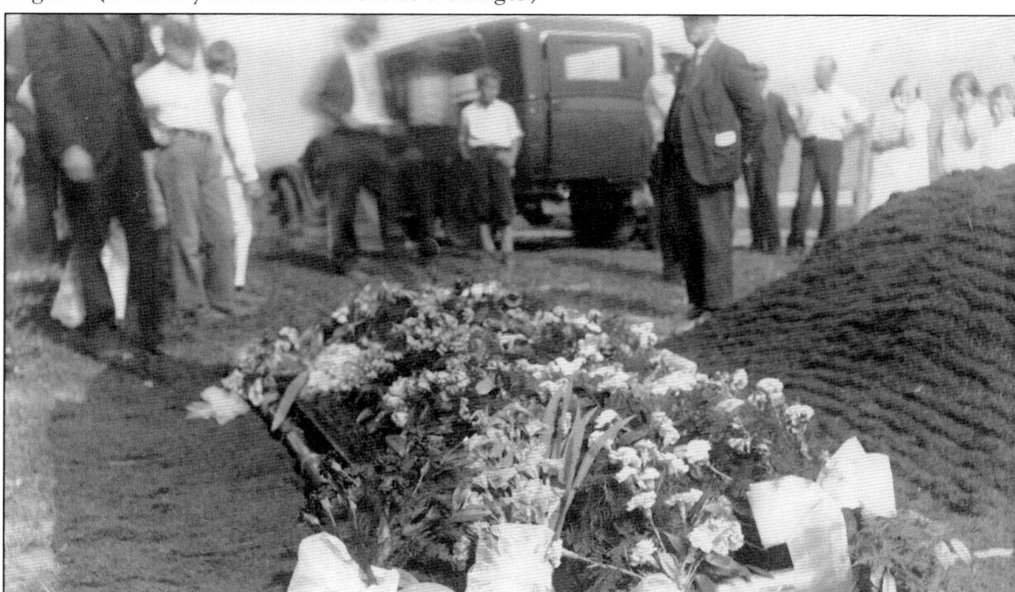

Fresh flowers, especially dahlias, traditionally cover the graves for funerals and Decoration Day. Lee Evans's funeral day was remembered somberly in Yancey. When the family returned home on the day of the funeral, the banker was there to foreclose on their farm. The only property left in the family was the 50-acre tract on what is now Walking Road at Bald Creek. (Courtesy of Nancy Randolph Silvers.)

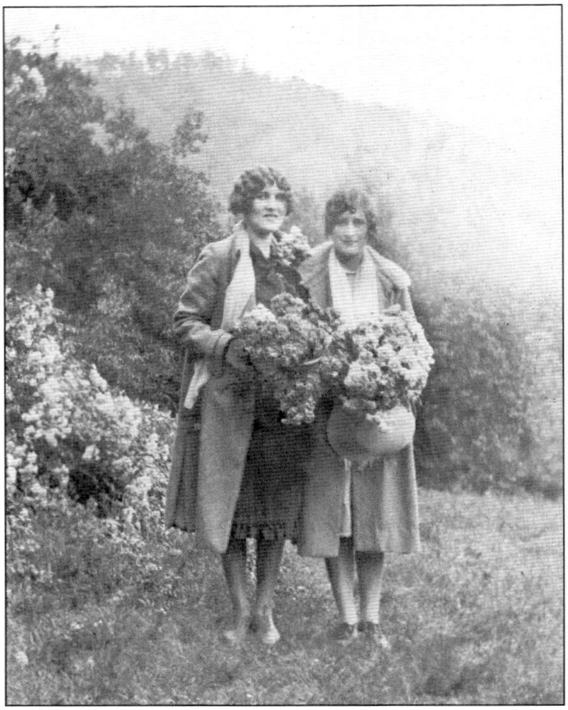

In 1924, Margie Renfro and Margaret Willa "Bill" Renfro continued the Decoration Day traditions at Byrd Branch in Upper Jacks Creek. Margie married her second husband, Lloyd Hogan, on a Saturday, and he was hit by a Coca-Cola truck and died that following Wednesday. Bill did hair and taught school, sometimes fording the creek with a mule to get to school to teach. Many families lost loved ones, and Decoration Day became a time to celebrate their lives and remember. (Courtesy of Carol and Joe Renfro.)

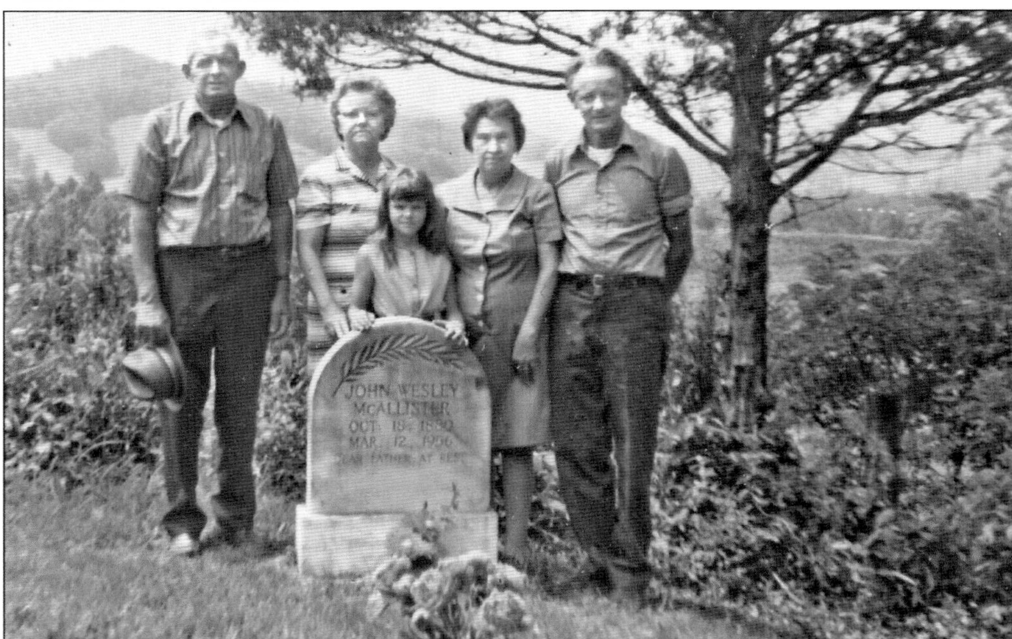

Yancey families continue to commemorate Decoration Day. Shown here at Cane River Baptist Church Cemetery are, from left to right, Charles Anglin and his wife, Edith McAlister Anglin; Vickie Buchanan, granddaughter of Warren and Birda; and Birda Honeycutt McAlister and her husband, Warren Burdett McAlister, standing behind the grave of John Wesley McAlister, father to Edith and Warren. (Courtesy of Elaine McAlister Dellinger.)

Two

Crossing Cane and Toe Rivers

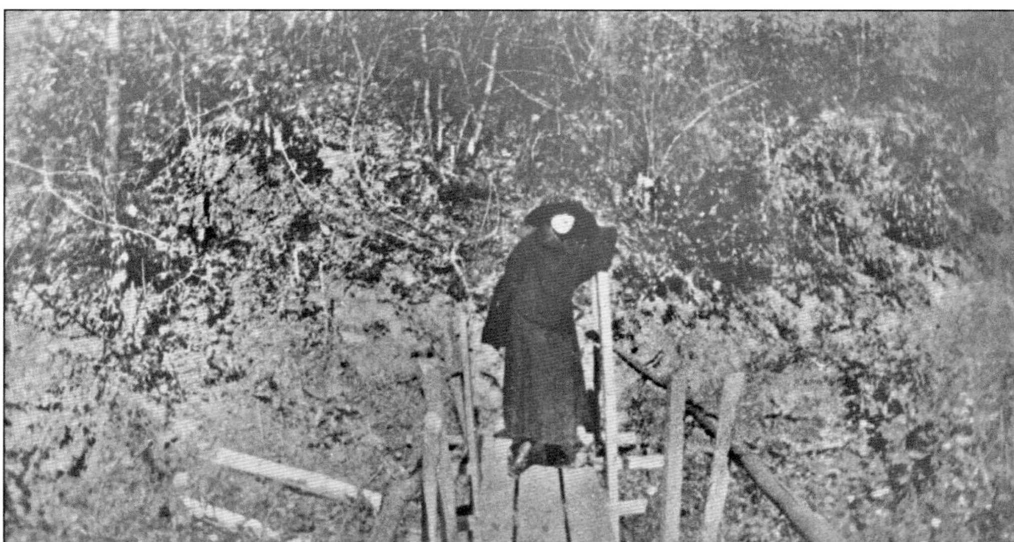

Just below the mouth of Bee Branch near Relief, a 1920s beauty crosses the swinging bridge. The Toe and Cane Rivers could not isolate Yancey County; first swinging bridges and ferries and later steel and concrete structures kept citizens and goods flowing to either side. (Courtesy of Wayne and Phyllis McKinney.)

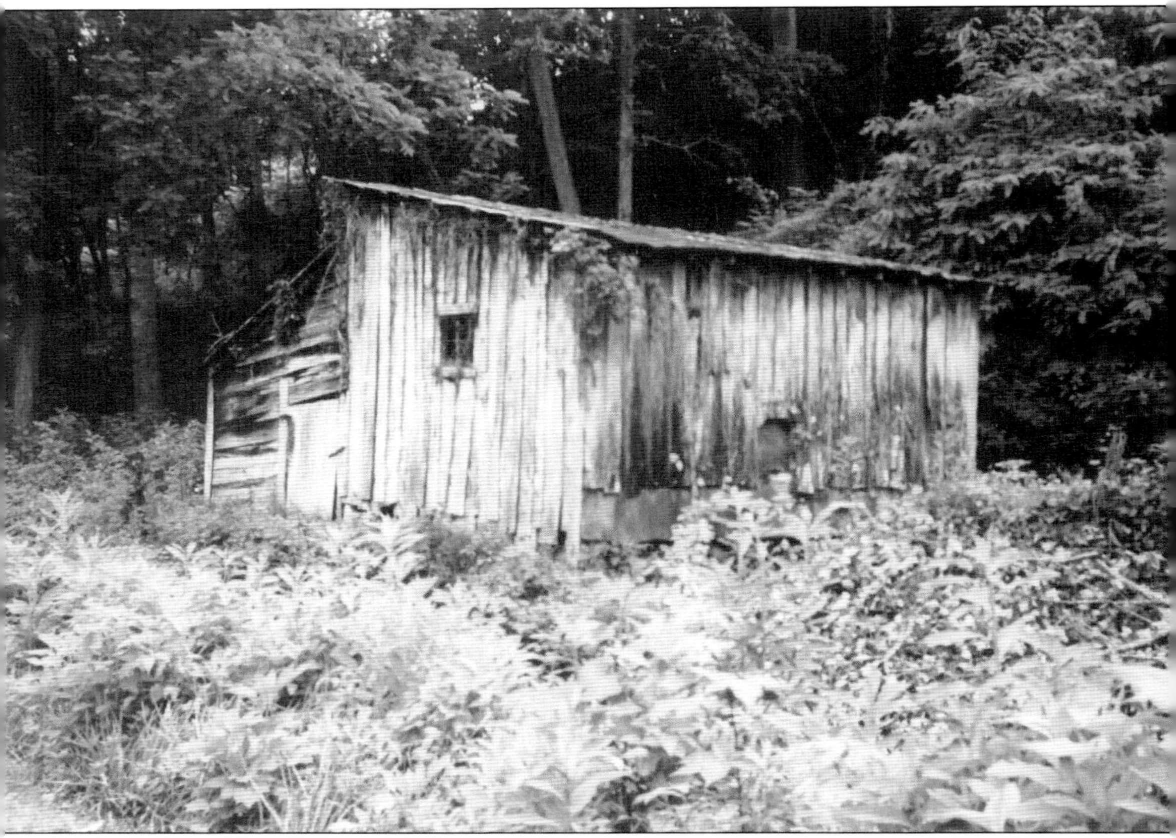

Only the remnants of a once-vital gristmill remain at the mouth of the creek adjacent to Hardscrabble Road at the point where it empties into the Cane River. This mill is one of the few still visible along Cane River. The mill had been owned and operated for many years by the Wilson Edwards family. The mill wheel was removed during the 1950s, as were so many others in the county. However, the wooden cogs and operating mechanism were removed around 2008. (Courtesy of Elaine McAlister Dellinger.)

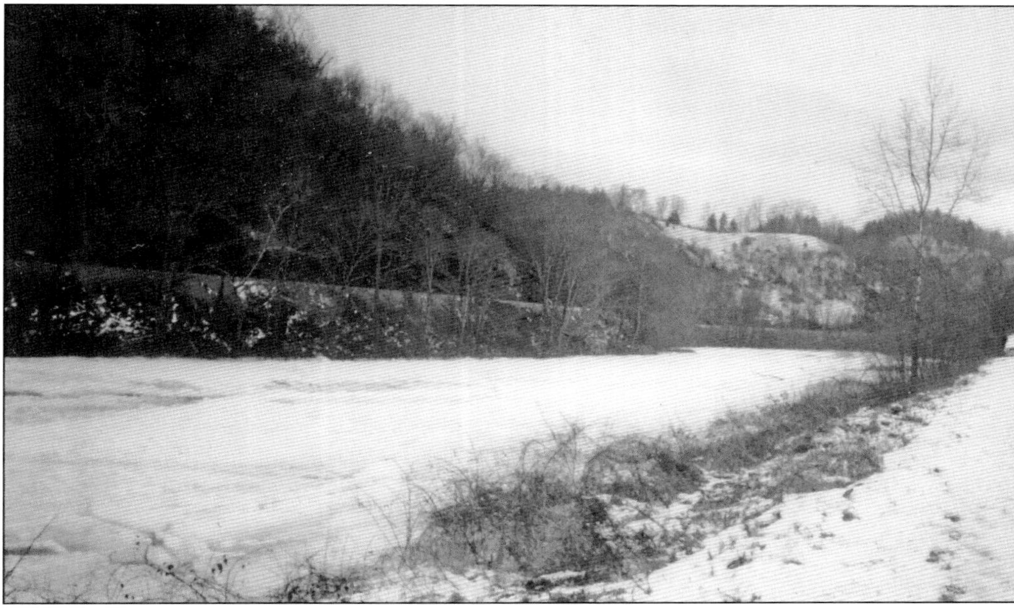

On those few harsh and bitter winters when the Toe River froze solid, folks could cross the river on foot. The river froze many times near Relief, even as recently as 1989. (Courtesy of Wayne and Phyllis McKinney.)

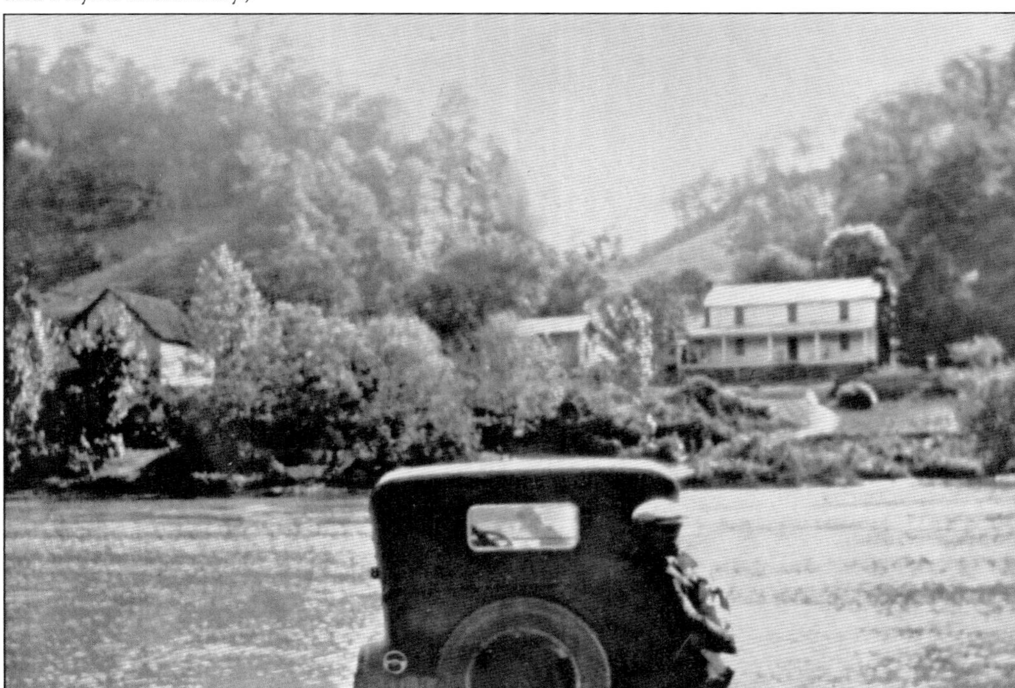

Before sturdy bridges were built, cars crossed the rivers by ferry, as in this 1939 photograph taken at Relief. The silhouette through the car window is I.B. Bailey, and the one on the right beside the car is Gus Bailey. The home of Marcus and Blanche Bradshaw is on the right; the building to the left was a subscription school. (Courtesy of Betty Lou Young and Linda Cox.)

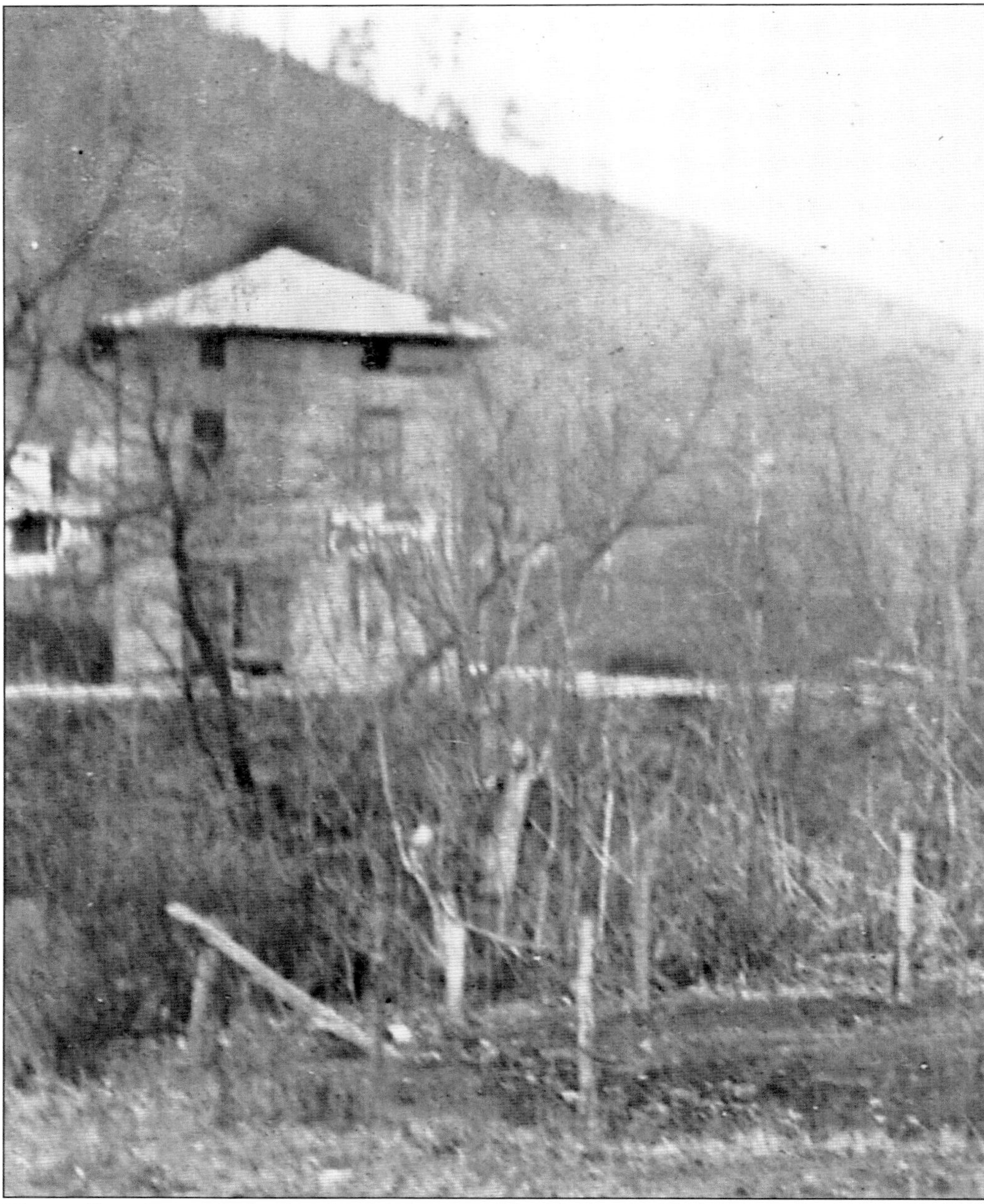

This mill on Lower Jacks Creek was constructed and operated before 1869 by Ike Bailey. Jack Tipton and Fred Peterson said the boys would dam up the millrace to swim, and Oliver Peterson, Fred's father, would have to get onto the boys time after time because they stopped the water flowing into the mill. (Courtesy of Betty Lou Young and Linda Cox.)

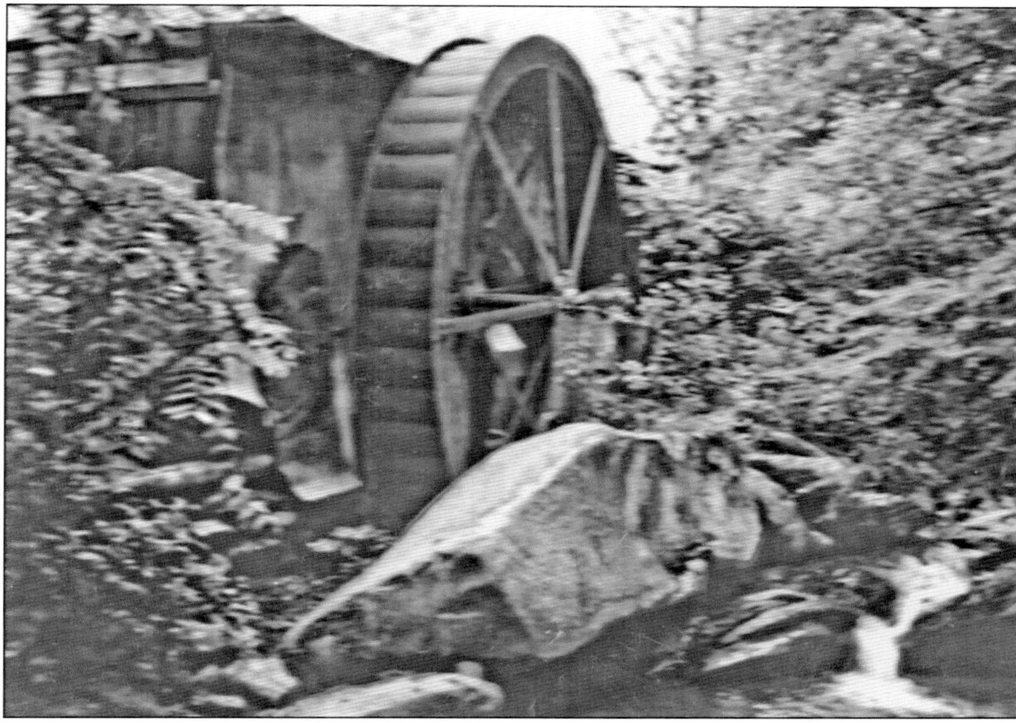

Waterwheels such as the Ike Bailey Mill one depicted here powered mills to grind grain throughout Yancey. (Courtesy of Betty Lou Young and Linda Cox.)

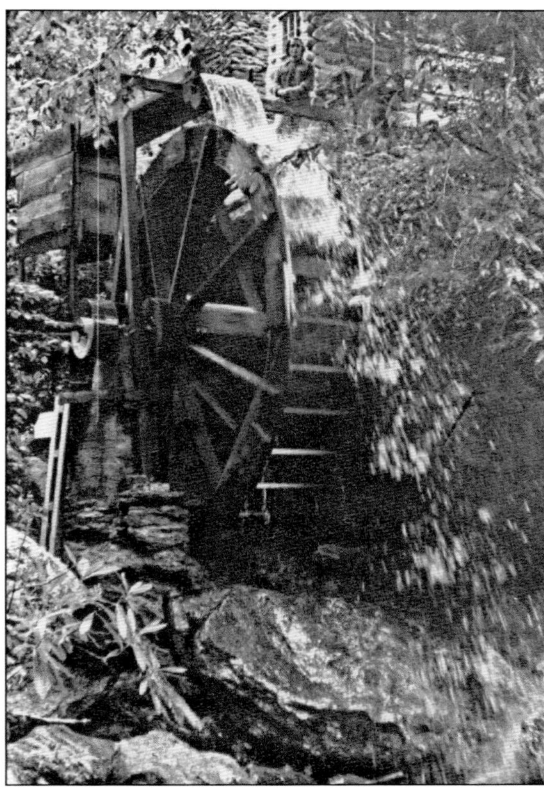

Cattail Water Mill, owned and operated by Will Hutchins, was located on the Cattail Creek and fed by a branch flowing into the Cattail Creek. The mill closed in the later part of the 1930s, when a larger mill was built in the nearby Pensacola community. (Courtesy of Helen Threadgill Baden.)

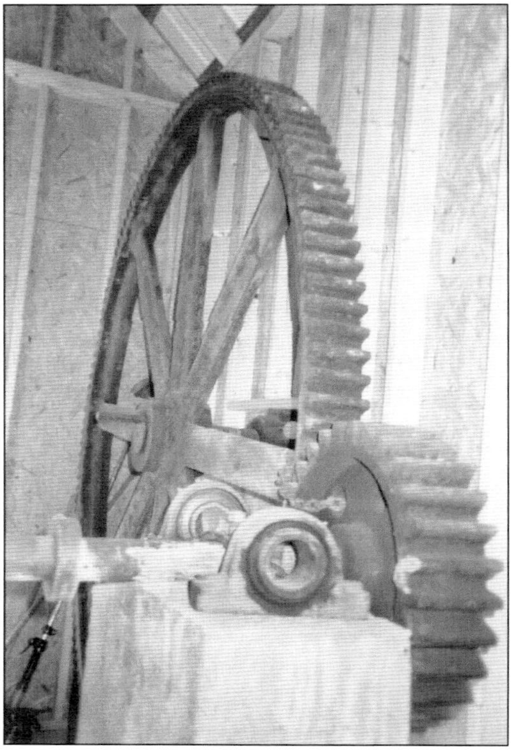

Here is an interior view of gears turned by the waterwheel of the Ike Bailey Mill. The larger wheel was connected to the water wheel on the outside of the building; it in turn moved the smaller gear, which drove the shaft that operated the mill wheel, which ground the grain. This mill was saved from destruction by Bill and Betty Young and moved to their home near Highway 197 North near Burnsville. (Courtesy of Betty Lou Young and Linda Cox.)

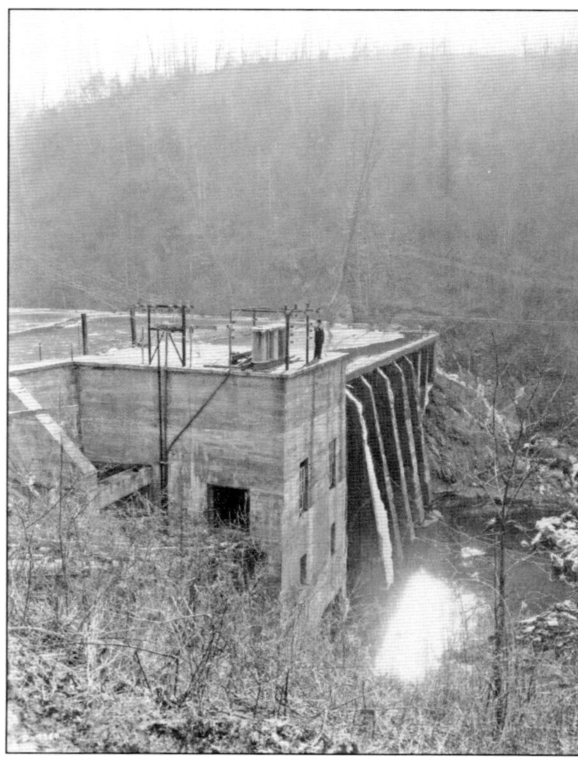

G.B. Woody stands atop the largest dam in Yancey County, called the Cane River Dam. This dam generated power for the county through hydropower, and G.B. Woody was its superintendent. When this dam was disassembled entirely in 2008, the Toe River Valley Watch made special care to ensure that the rare Appalachian Elktoe mussels went unharmed in the process. (Courtesy of Sarah Woody Proffitt.)

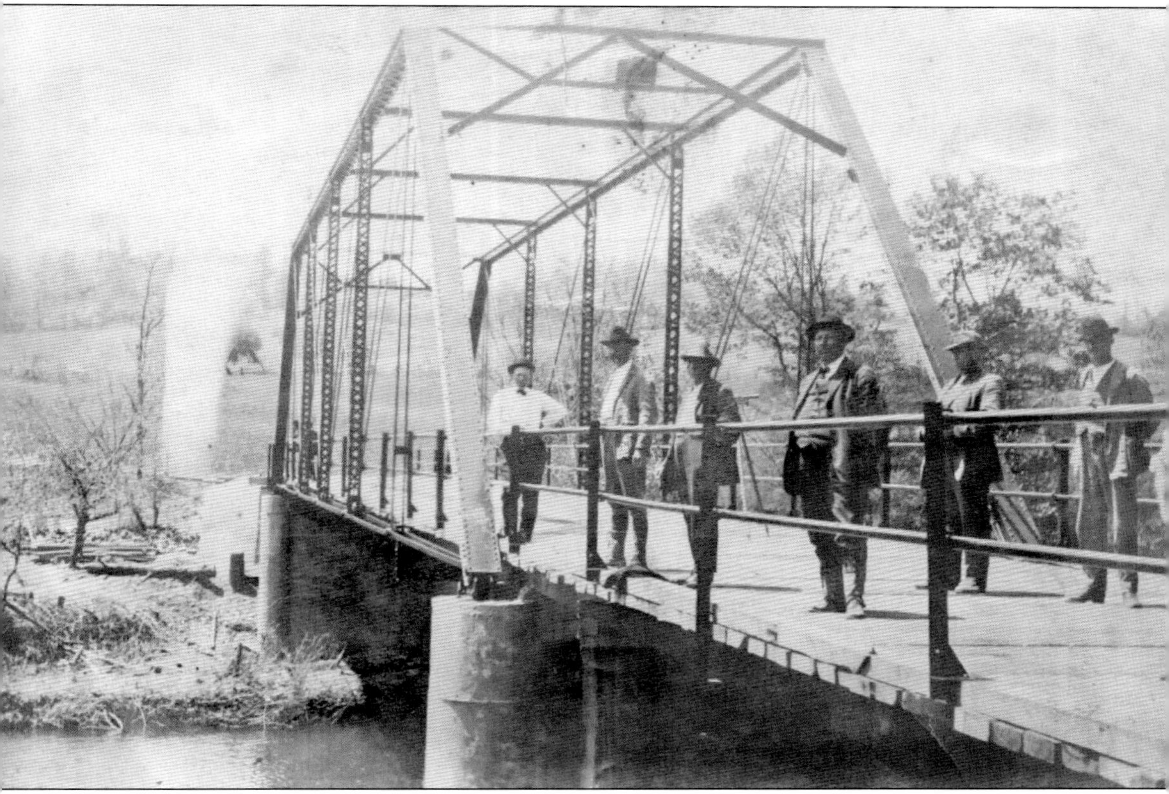

A group of men stand amid one of the old bridges which crossed the Cane River at present-day Whittington Road. Among those pictured are Raleigh Radford, the local postmaster and store owner (third man from the left), William Wray, Hiram Whittington, and others. (Courtesy of Nancy Randolph Silvers.)

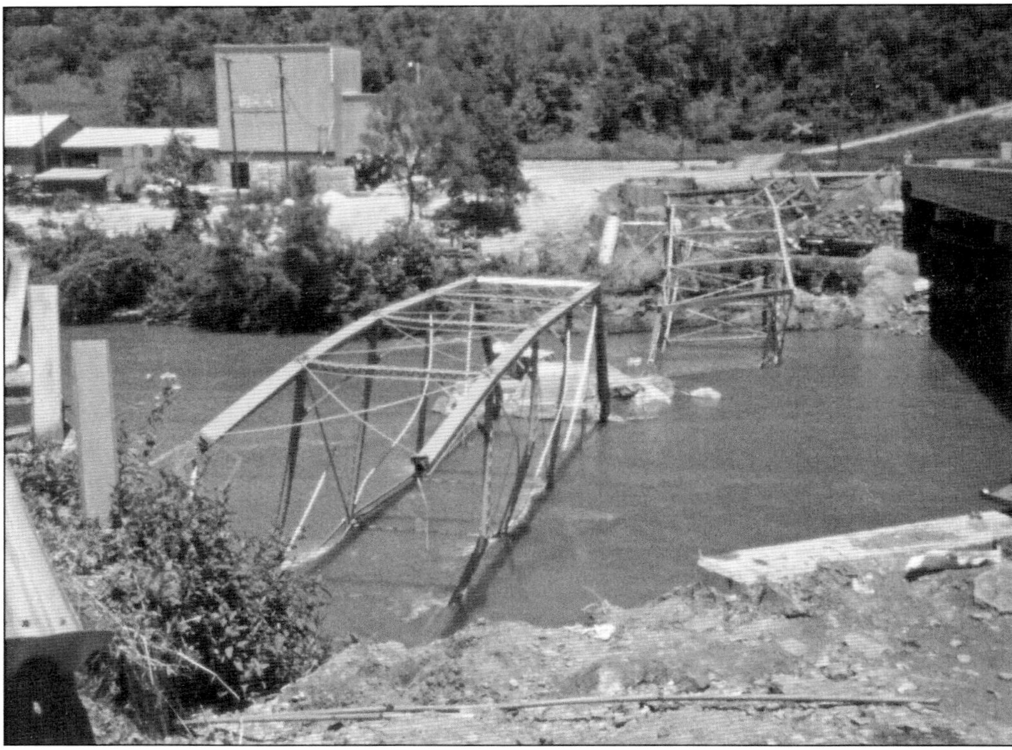

When cars and trucks became heavier, the old bridge in Green Mountain had to go, and a new concrete structure took its place. The new bridge can be seen at far right. (Courtesy of Jane Whitson Peterson.)

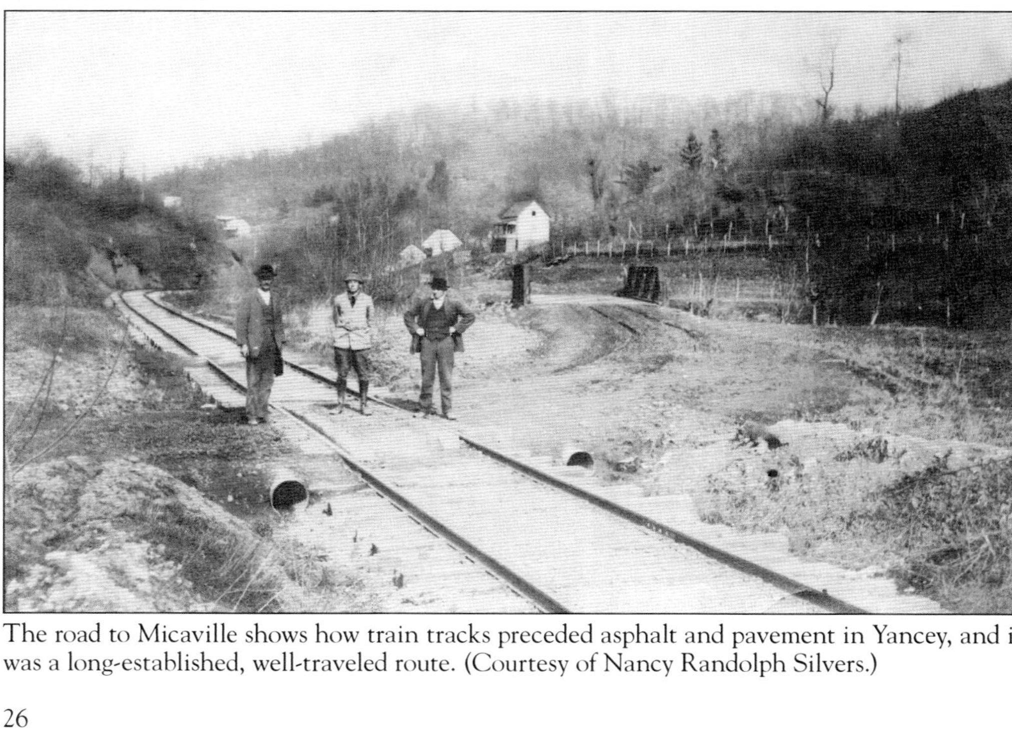

The road to Micaville shows how train tracks preceded asphalt and pavement in Yancey, and it was a long-established, well-traveled route. (Courtesy of Nancy Randolph Silvers.)

Three

Patriots in Our Midst

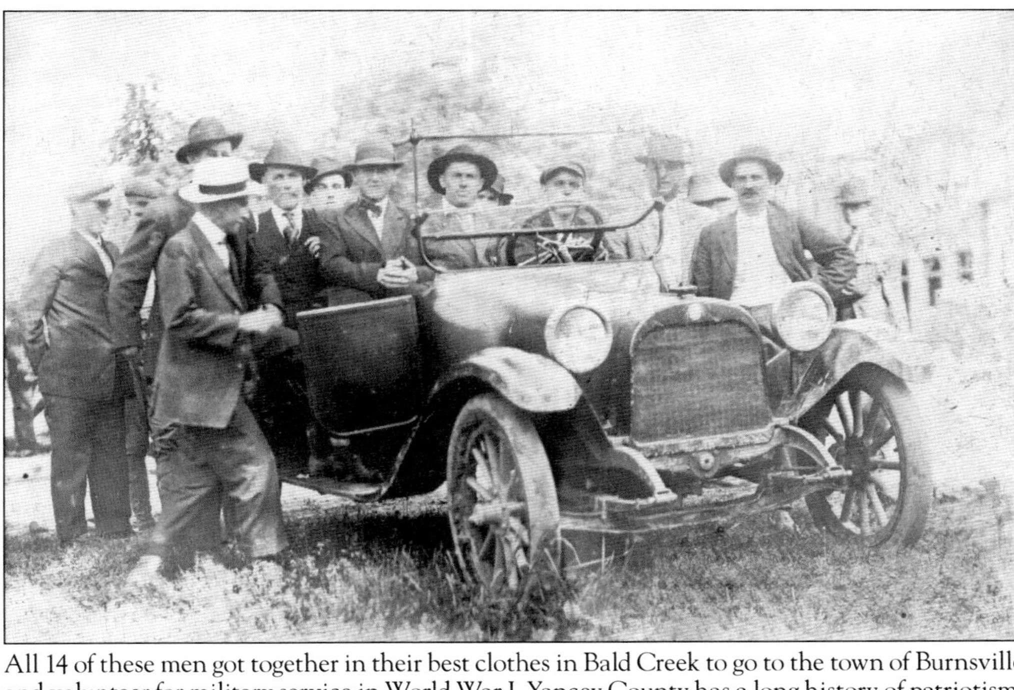

All 14 of these men got together in their best clothes in Bald Creek to go to the town of Burnsville and volunteer for military service in World War I. Yancey County has a long history of patriotism. (Courtesy of Carol and Joe Renfro.)

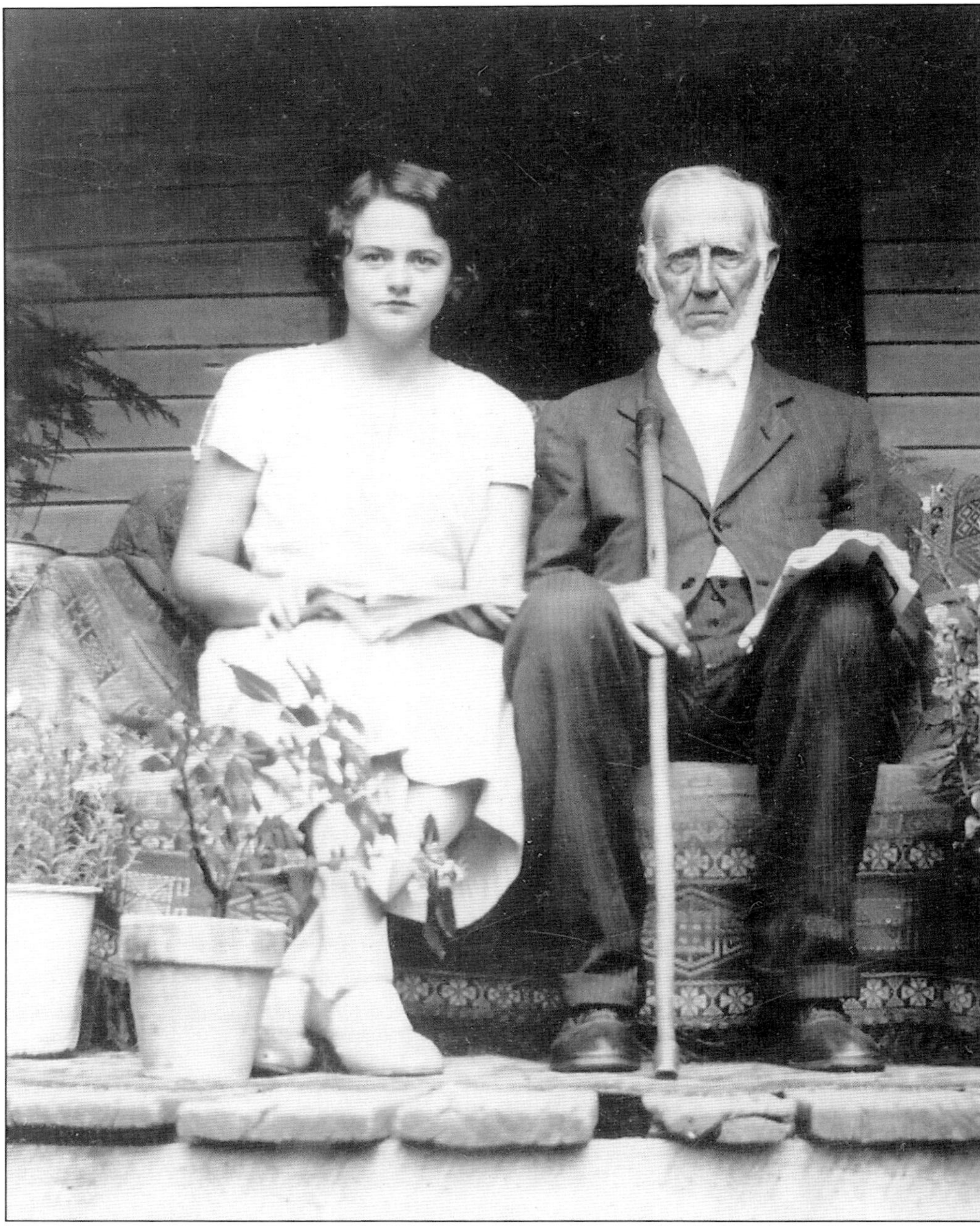

John Gilbert Wilson sits beside his niece, Jenny Horton. John fought for the Union in the War Between the States as a cavalry officer. He took his manservant Nate Ray with him when he left for war, and they fought side by side for the Union, comrades in arms. John drew a pension of $100, and later it was increased to $125. He married Lucinda Ray. (Courtesy of Virginia York.)

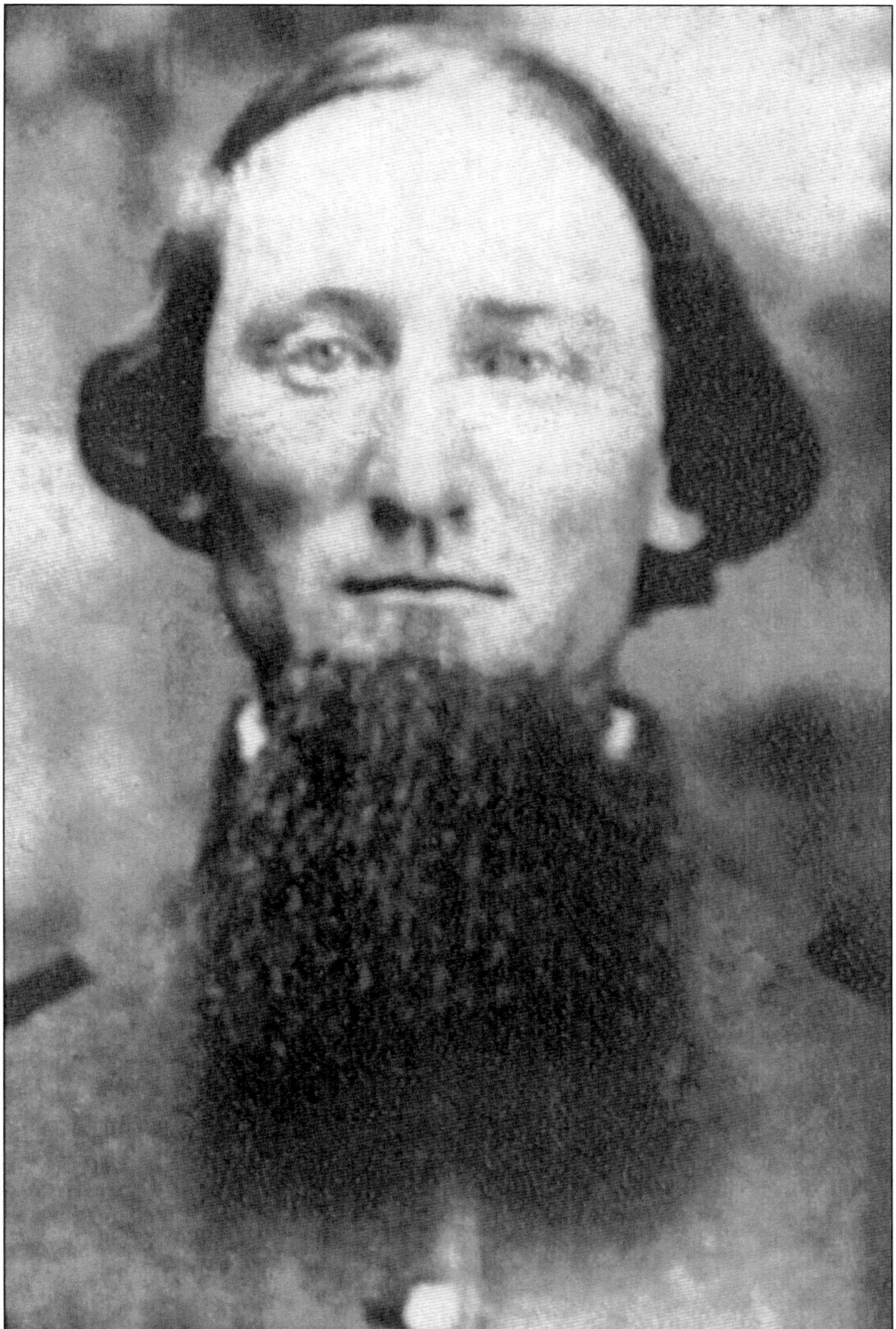

George Conley, a Confederate soldier, here wears his North Carolina–issue uniform. He lived on Seven Mile Ridge Road in Yancey County as well as in Mitchell County. He is the great-grandfather of James Byrd and Phyllis Byrd McKinney through their mother's mother, Lidia (Liza Ida) Conley, who was George Conley's daughter. (Courtesy of Wayne and Phyllis McKinney.)

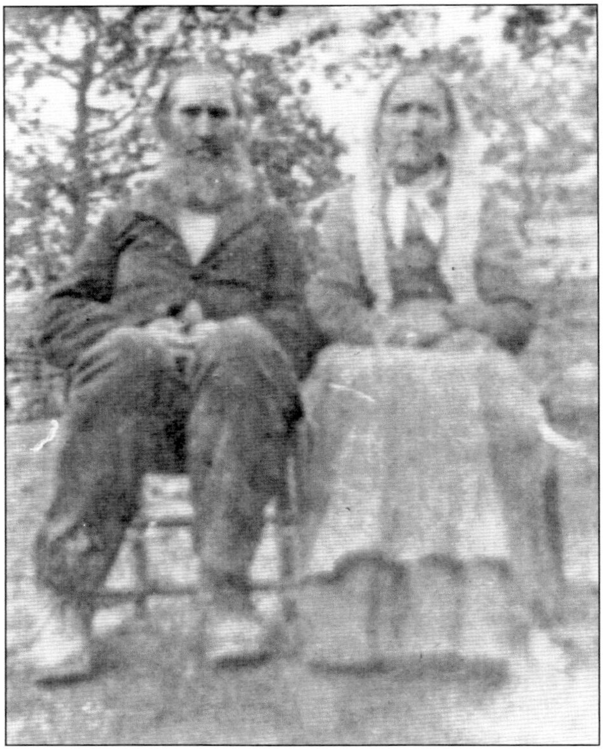

Ephraim Phillips married Sarah Edwards in 1846. Ephraim, born in 1826, served with the Confederacy in the War Between the States in Company K of the 29th North Carolina. He died of fever just weeks after returning from the war. (Courtesy of Madge Brookshire.)

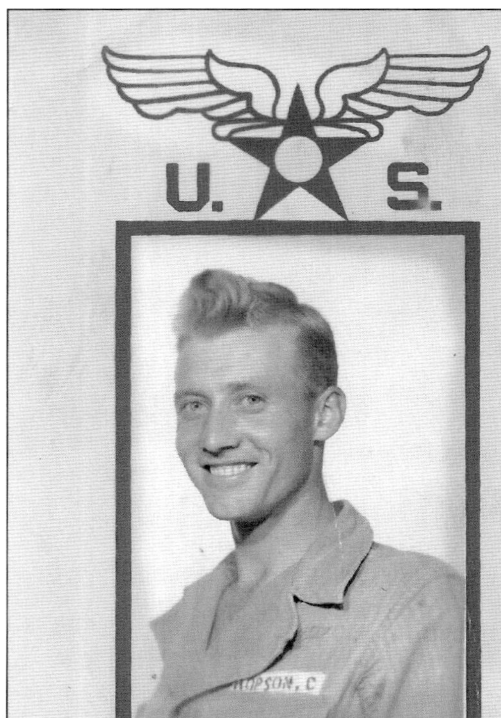

Charles Evan Hopson was a World War II B-17 bombardier. This photograph was taken on July 14, 1943, while he was stationed at Amarillo Field in Texas. The photograph was part of a patriotic postcard he had sent his mother and signed simply, "Love, your son." (Courtesy of Ona Jean Hopson.)

Landon Wilson, son of Harriet and Gene Wilson of the Pensacola area, served in World War I. Here he is standing near a cannon at Camp Jackson. He married Bonnie Roland, and they lived in Burnsville after the war. (Courtesy of Charles Dellinger).

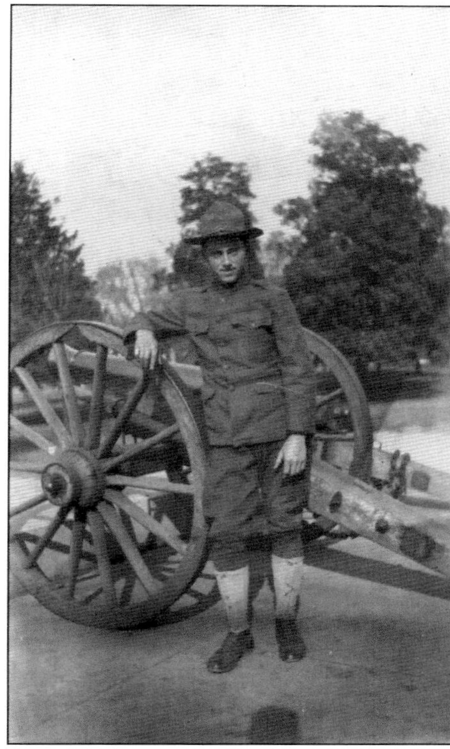

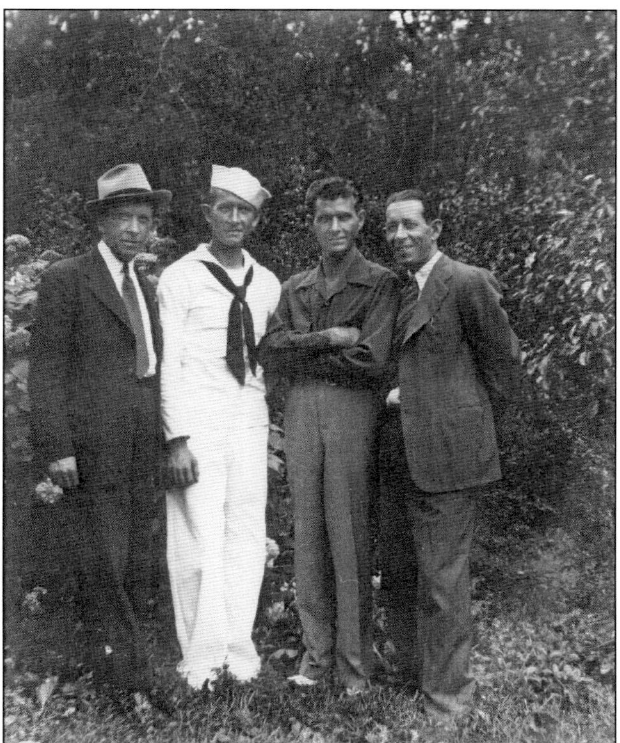

Carl and Don Renfro served in World War I; Carl made a fortune in real estate until the 1929 stock market crash. Seen here from left to right are Carl, Don, Charlie, and Zelze. (Courtesy of Carol and Joe Renfro.)

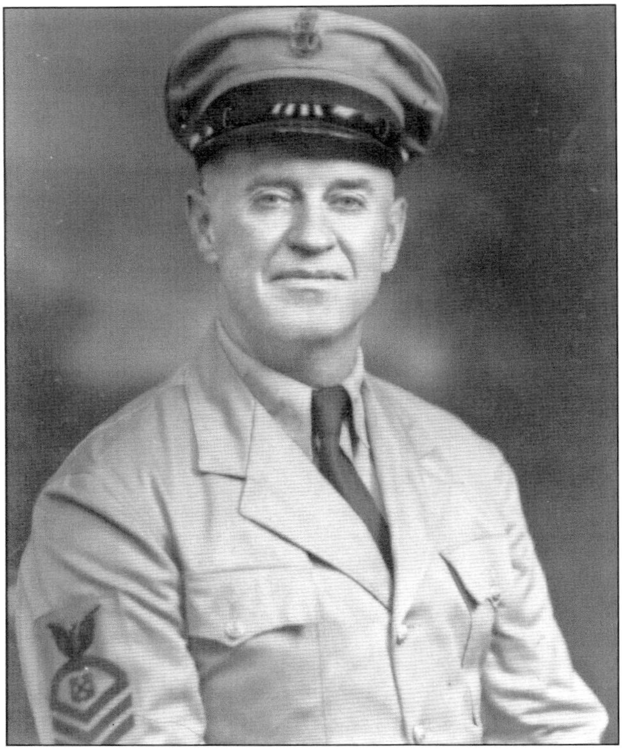

Carl McCandless was a US Navy bandleader for 36 years. During this time, he traveled the world, entertaining presidents, kings, and all manner of royalty. After he retired from the Navy, he played background music in Hollywood and on Broadway. (Courtesy of June McCandless Jerome.)

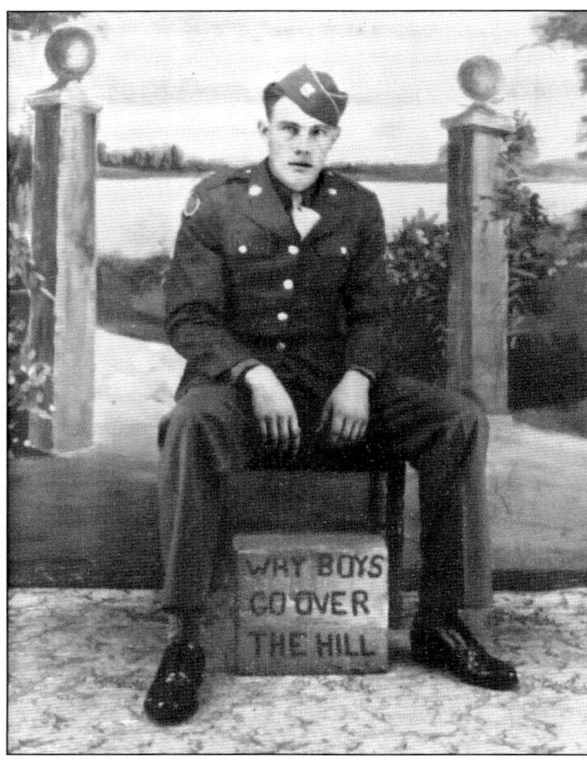

Keith Penland was a prisoner of war for 209 days during World War II and was a combat-wounded rifleman who received a Purple Heart. After the war, he returned to farm in Yancey. (Courtesy of Tim Penland.)

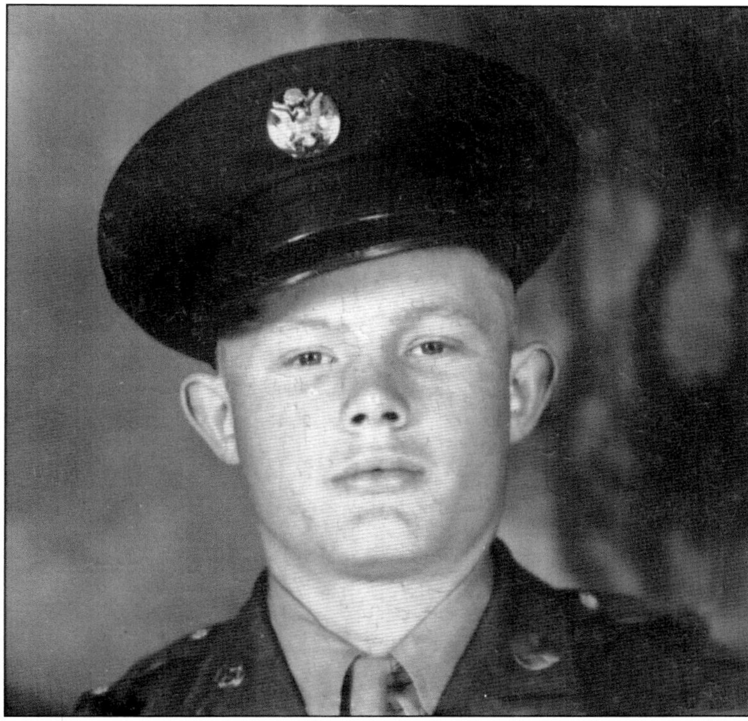

Crate Bailey received many honors for his military service. He was a prisoner of war and a recipient of the Purple Heart. His house stood beside Cane River in the Higgins-Egypt community. (Courtesy of Judie Bailey Miller.)

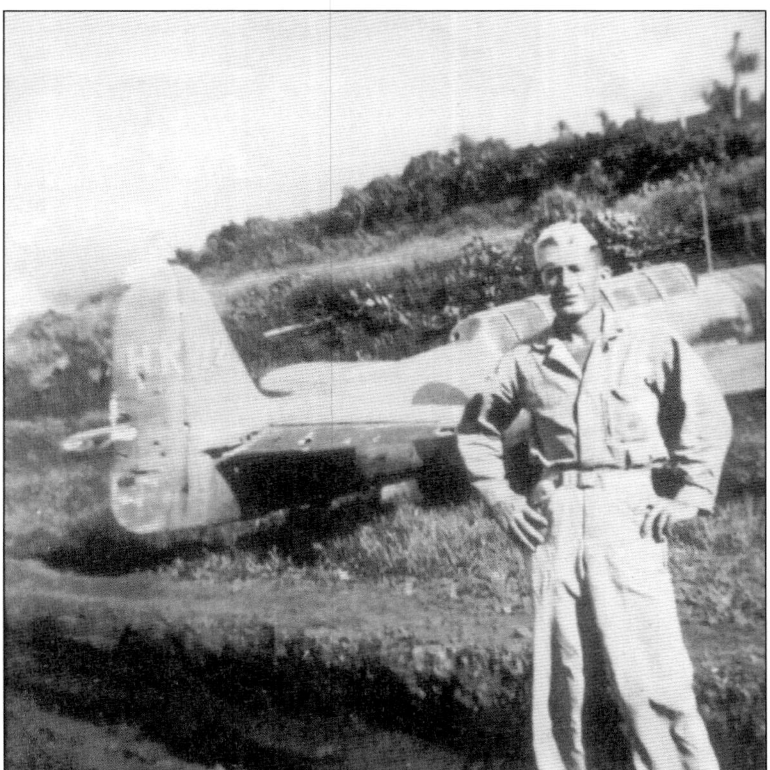

Robert Lee Dellinger, while serving in World War II in the Marines, traveled from Pensacola to be part of the attack on Iwo Jima. He was the son of Nathaniel Shelby and Martha Hutchins Dellinger of Burnsville. (Courtesy of Charles Lee Dellinger.)

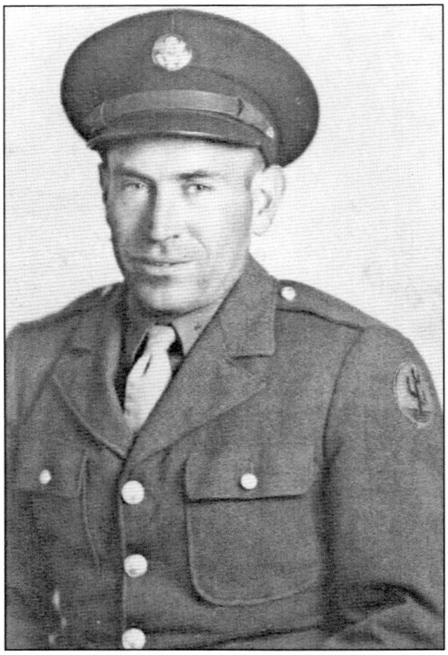

Larmer Byrd served during World War II, returning to the farm after his service ended. He married Maude Wheeler, and they lived on Parson's Branch. (Courtesy of James Byrd.)

Charles Lee Dellinger, E-5, is pictured here in Illesheim, Germany, in 1966 with a UH-1B Huey medical evacuation helicopter of the 421st Unit. He retired as an E-7 in the US Army Special Forces after serving the nation for 21 years, including two tours in Vietnam. He received many awards, including the Meritorious Service, multiple Bronze Stars with Oak Leaf Cluster, Air Medals, and others. (Courtesy of Charles Lee Dellinger.)

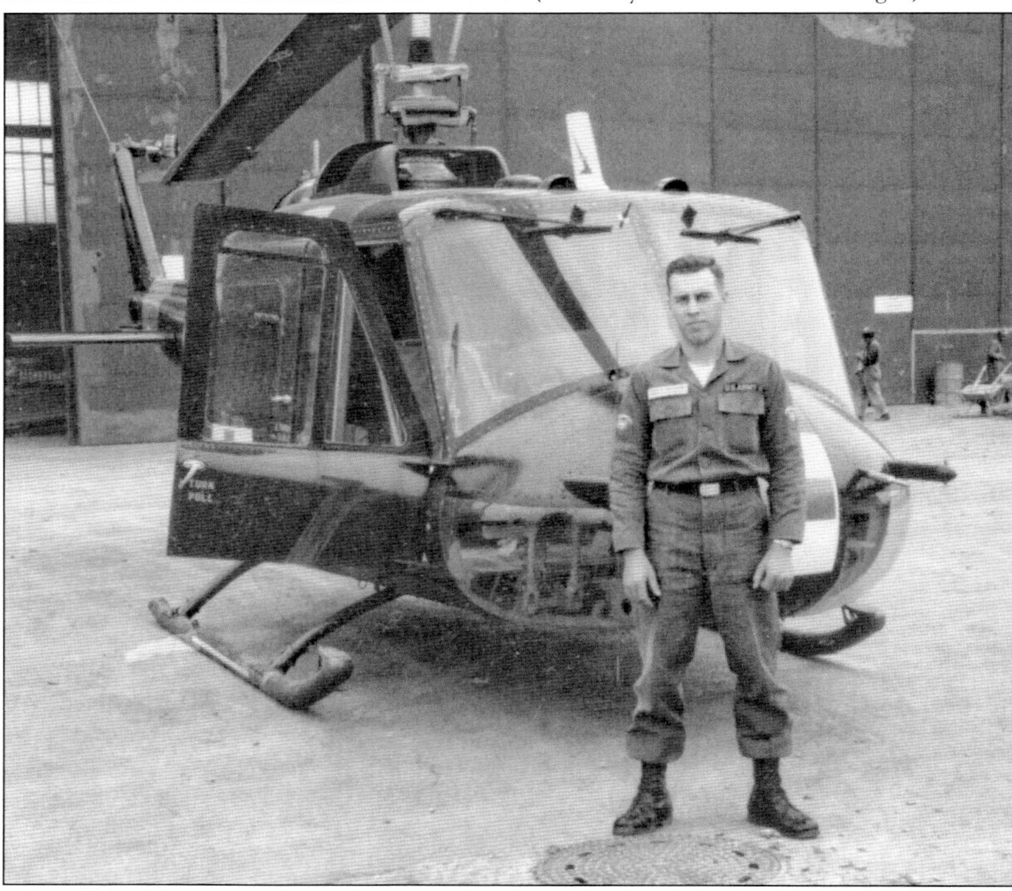

Four

Sweet Taters, Corn, and Tobacco

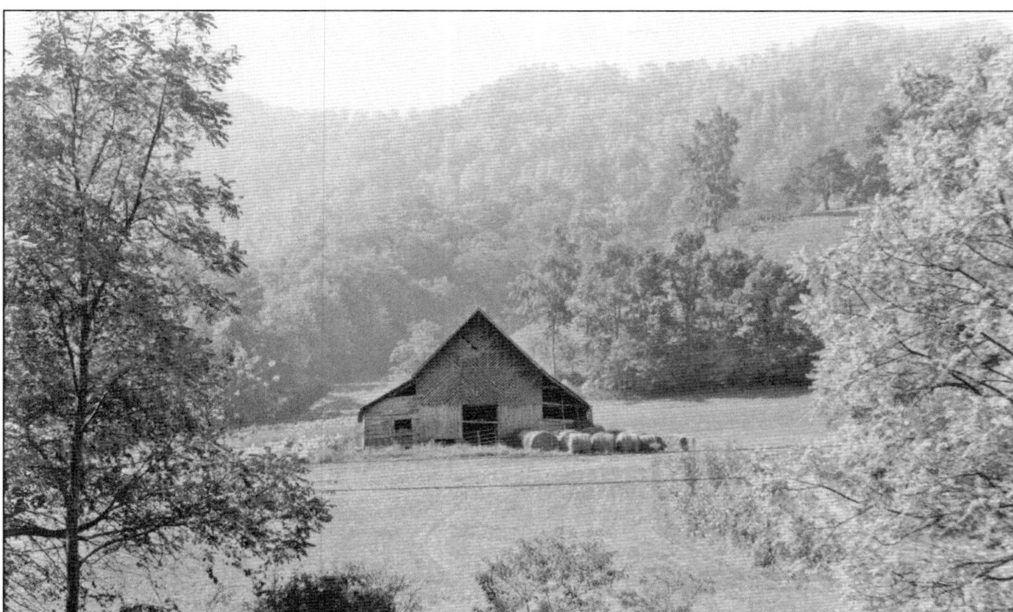

Barns are disappearing from the farmlands all across the county. Pictured here is the barn built by Hiram Albert Proffitt around 1871 on Possum Trot Road west of Burnsville—the date is based on when the family home adjacent to the barn had been built. Notice the typical modern rolls of hay, the tobacco patch to the side, and the view of the surrounding meadow with a cornfield in the foreground. Not much seems to have changed; the farm remains in the same family, which has farmed the land for more than 130 years, according to Hiram's great-granddaughter Becky Proffitt McCall. (Courtesy of Elaine McAlister Dellinger.)

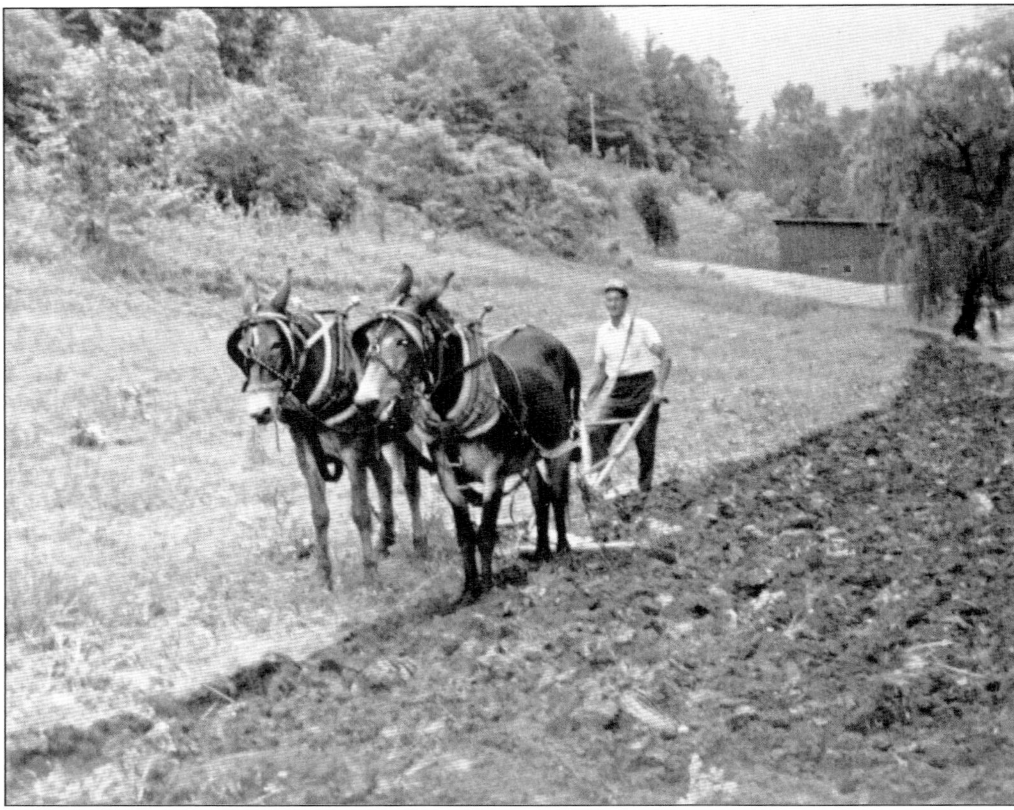

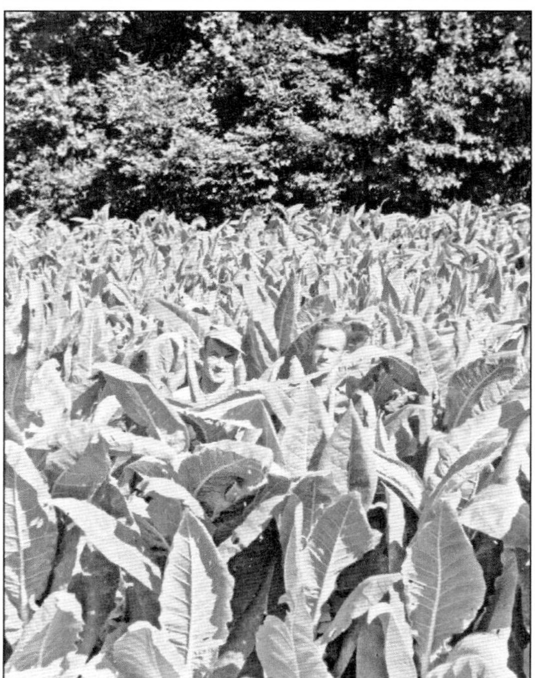

Farm life was hard but enjoyable; there was work from daylight until dark every season and then some. Here Wayne McKinney plows a patch of ground for a spring crop with his team of mules. (Courtesy of Wayne and Phyllis McKinney.)

Topping and suckering tobacco was the last phase of work until the crop was ready to be cut and put into the barn. Brothers Wayne and James McKinney can be seen near the middle of the picture. In the 1860 census, North Carolina raised 32,582,350 pounds of tobacco, and Yancey contributed significantly to that quantity. (Courtesy of Wayne and Phyllis McKinney.)

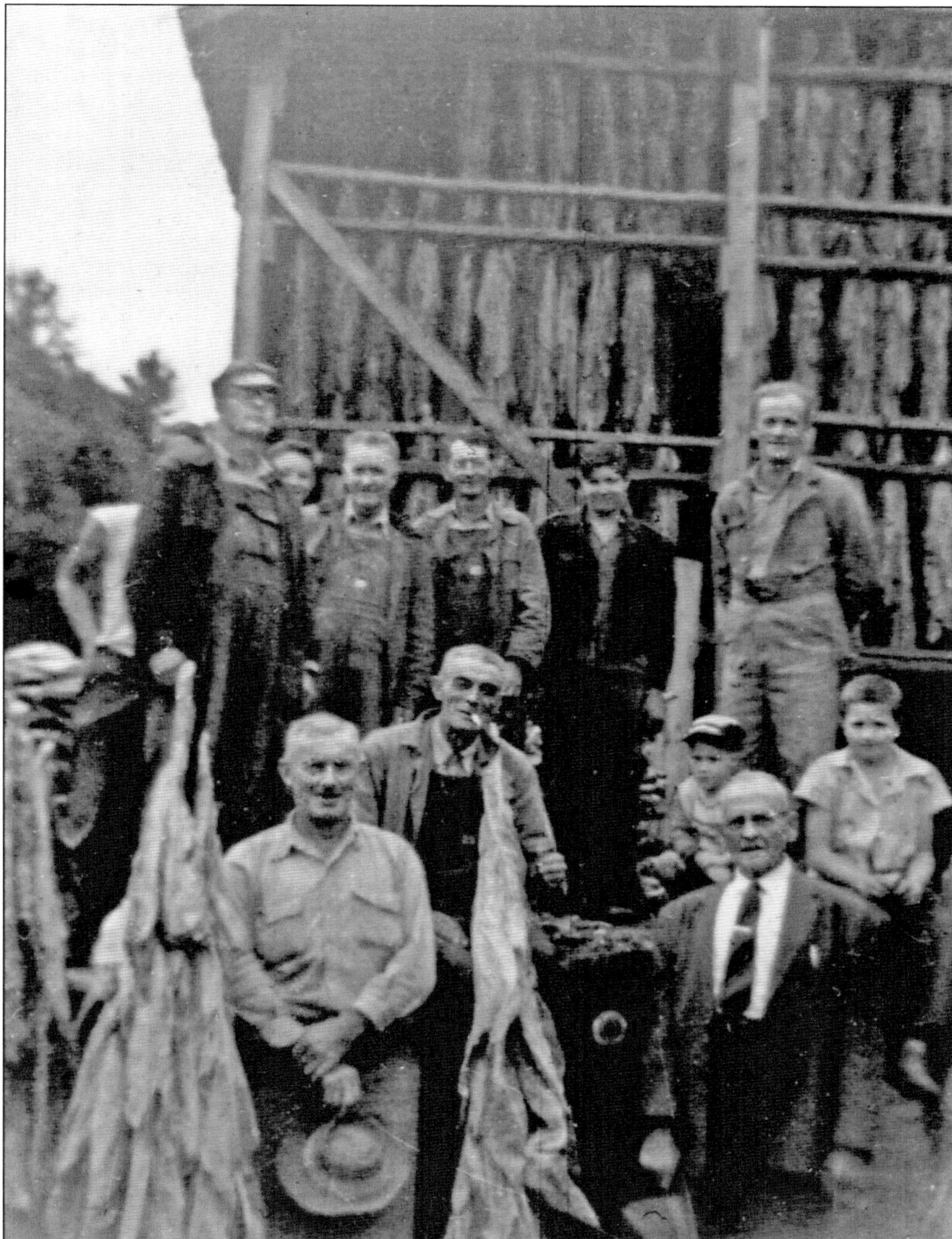

The South Bend Free Will Baptist Church needed a building, so these folks got together and put in a tobacco crop to make the money for building materials. They sold the tobacco and then built the church. On Samuel J. Byrd's farm on Upper Jacks Creek stand, from left to right, (first row) Levi Deyton, Clyde Duncan, the Reverend Ed Woody, Ike Peterson's son, and Dean Briggs; (second row) Earl Webb, Landon Briggs, an unidentified girl, Luther Renfro, Julie Tipton, J.D. Briggs, and Ike Peterson. The Reverend Frances Radford took the photograph. (Courtesy of Earl Webb.)

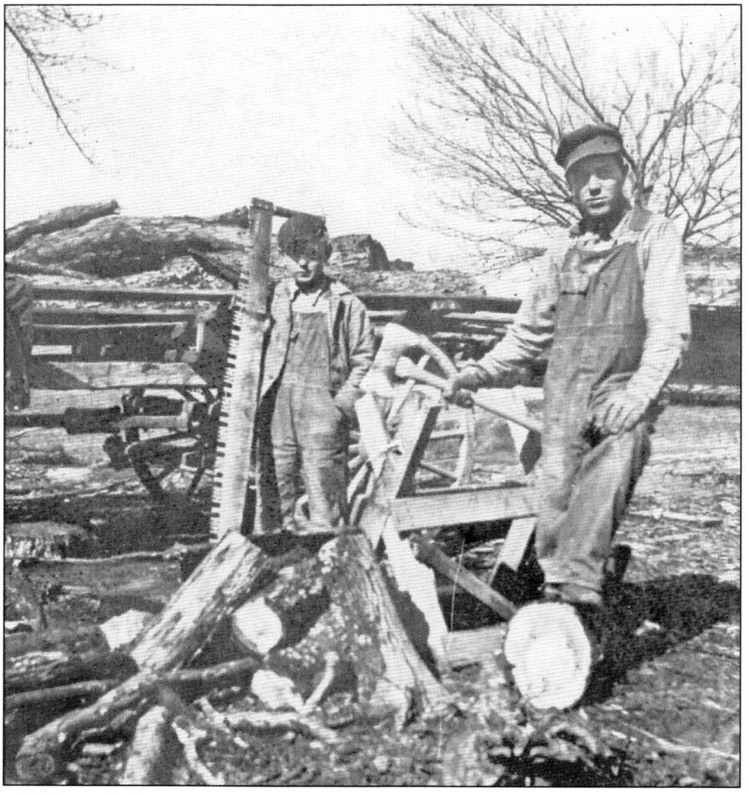

Levi Edwards (left) and Henry Edwards, the grandsons of James Madison and Ann Bailey Byrd, stand with a hand-hewn wagon, a crosscut saw, and a double-bitted ax in this 1920s photograph from the part of the county called Relief. (Courtesy of Wayne and Phyllis McKinney.)

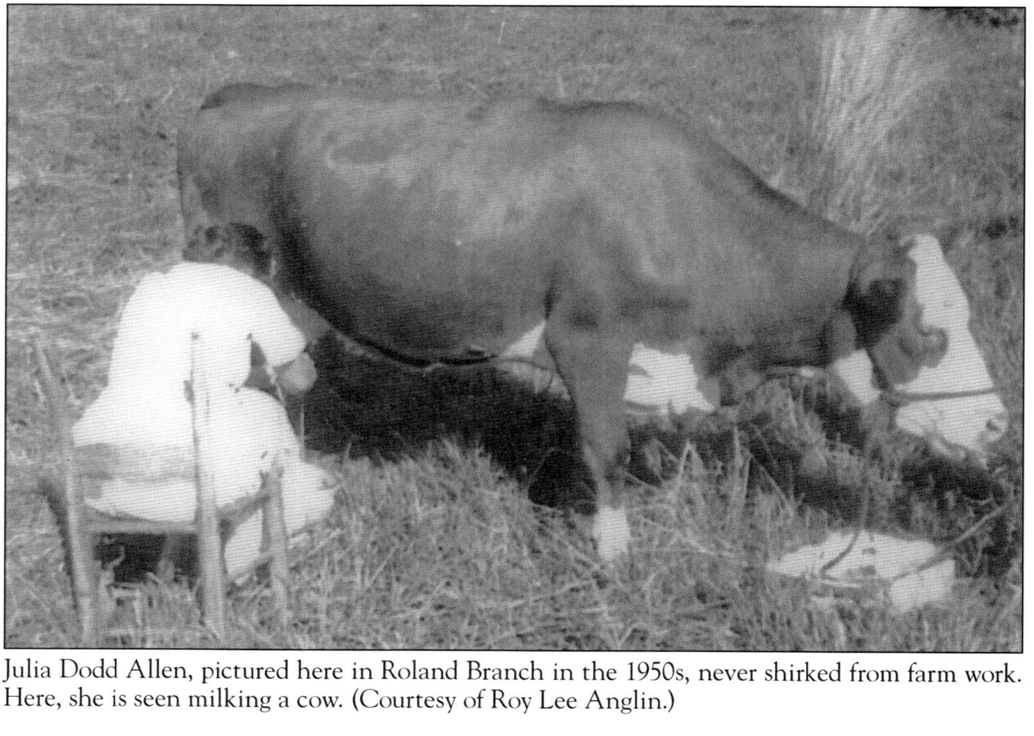

Julia Dodd Allen, pictured here in Roland Branch in the 1950s, never shirked from farm work. Here, she is seen milking a cow. (Courtesy of Roy Lee Anglin.)

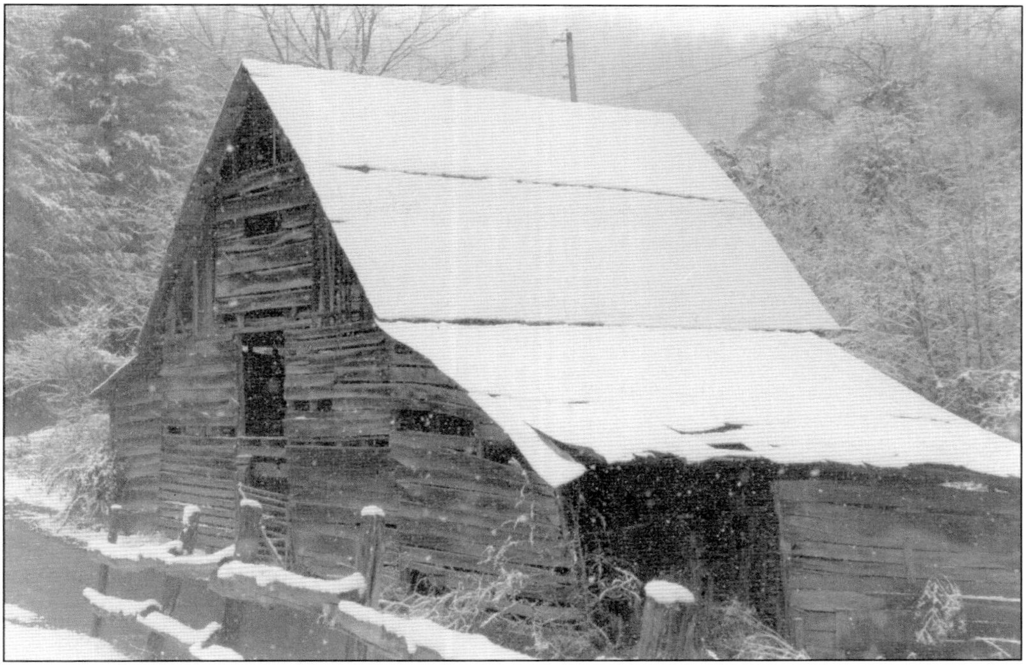

Ernest Proffitt, who was married to Minnie Edwards, grew chewing tobacco and cigarette tobacco. In keeping with long-standing tradition, he cured the leaves in this barn, located on Proffitt Branch in the Cane River area. (Courtesy of Elaine McAlister Dellinger.)

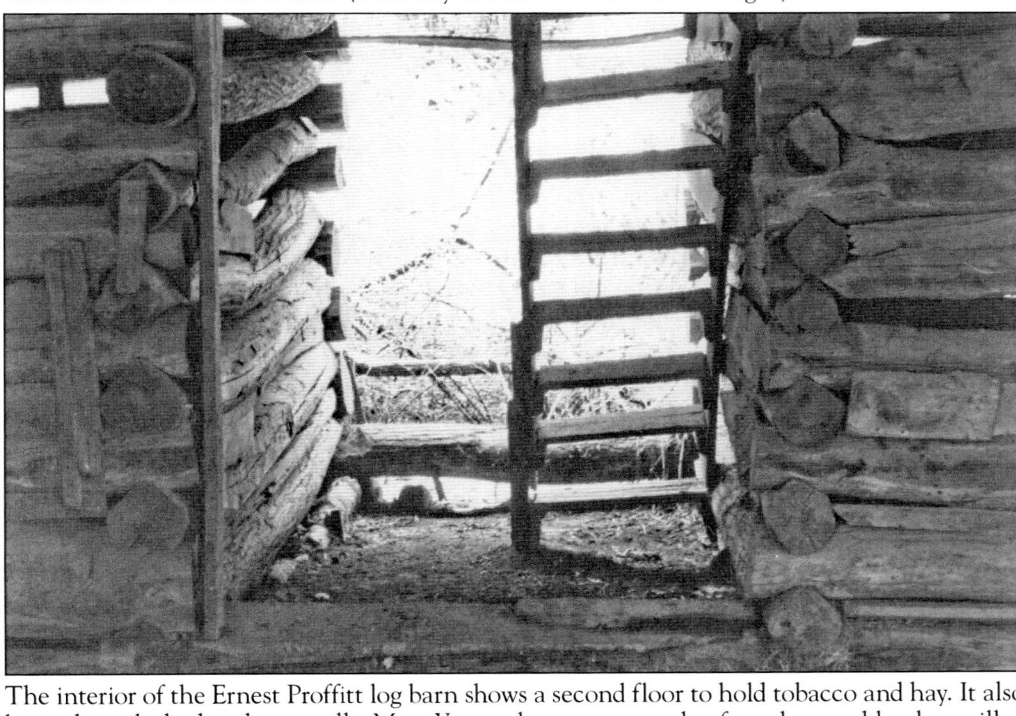

The interior of the Ernest Proffitt log barn shows a second floor to hold tobacco and hay. It also housed a crib shed and two stalls. Most Yancey barns were made of raw logs and lumber milled from trees on the land where they stood. (Courtesy of Elaine McAlister Dellinger.)

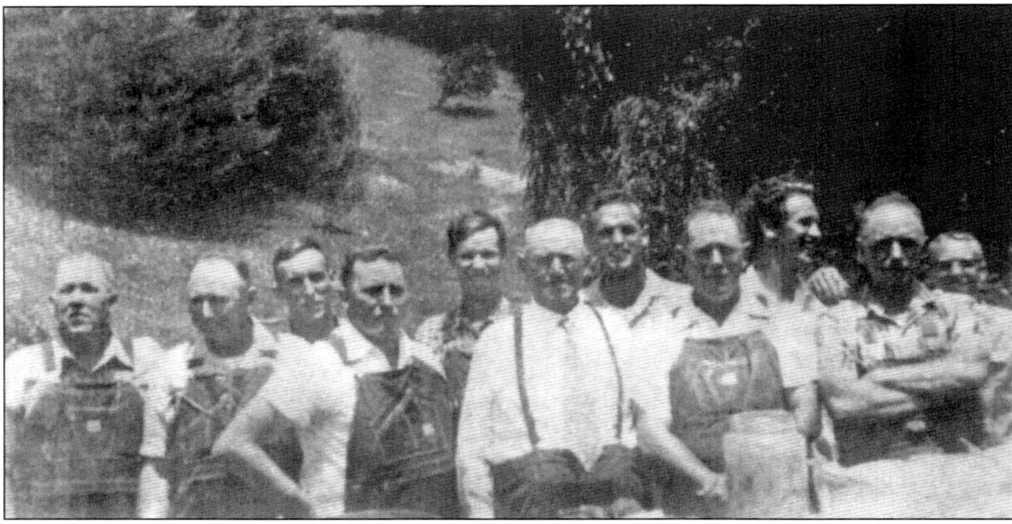

Silas Wesley Silvers and his sons raised sheep and tobacco on their land in Bald Creek. (Courtesy of Judie Bailey Miller.)

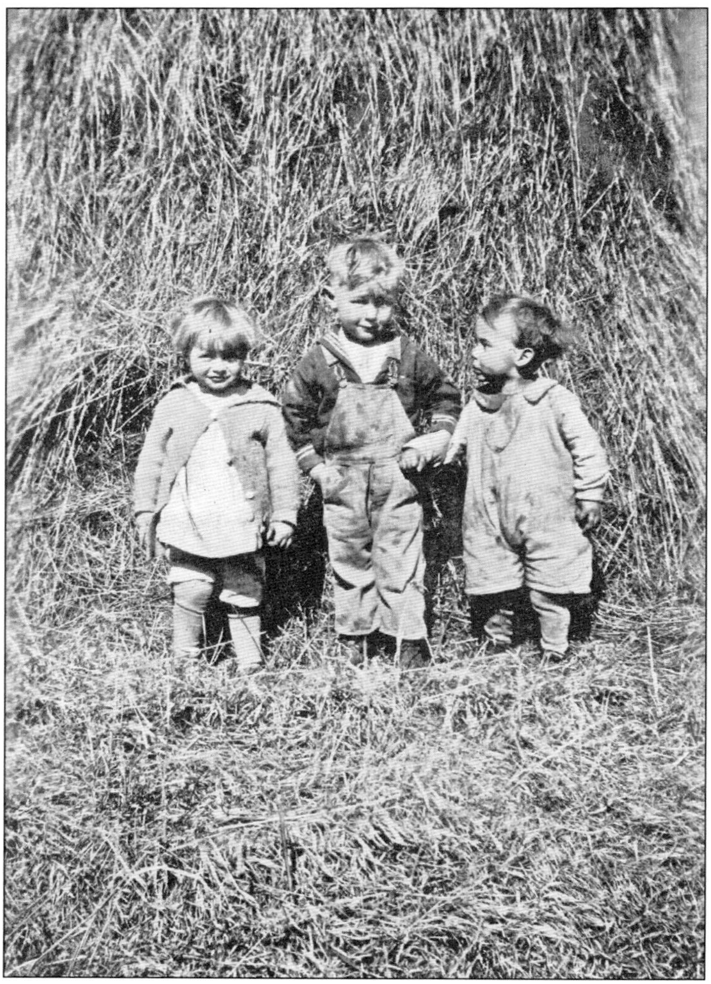

Robert Lake Harris and his two best friends played in front of the haystack on Shoal Creek. Farm children never lacked for adventure at any age. (Courtesy of Robin Owen.)

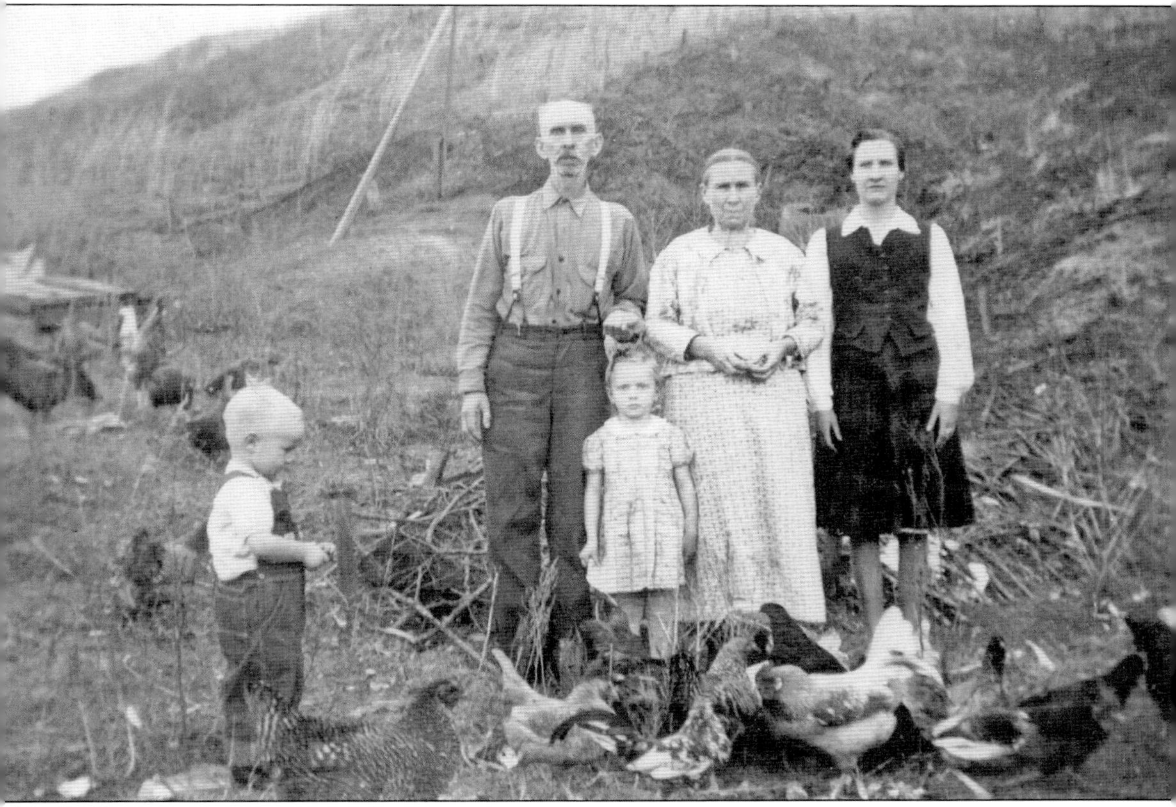

Seen here from left to right are Reece Honeycutt, his grandfather William Andrew "Andy" Honeycutt, his sister Opha Honeycutt, his grandmother Lora Jane Bailey Honeycutt, and his aunt, the Honeycutts' youngest daughter, Lillian. Lora Jane read tea leaves and predicted many events that later took place, and she was a founding member of the Bald Mountain Free Will Baptist Church. A true mountain woman, she made maple candy each year for the children so that they each had a whole molded teacup full of maple candy on Christmas morning. (Courtesy of Elaine McAlister Dellinger.)

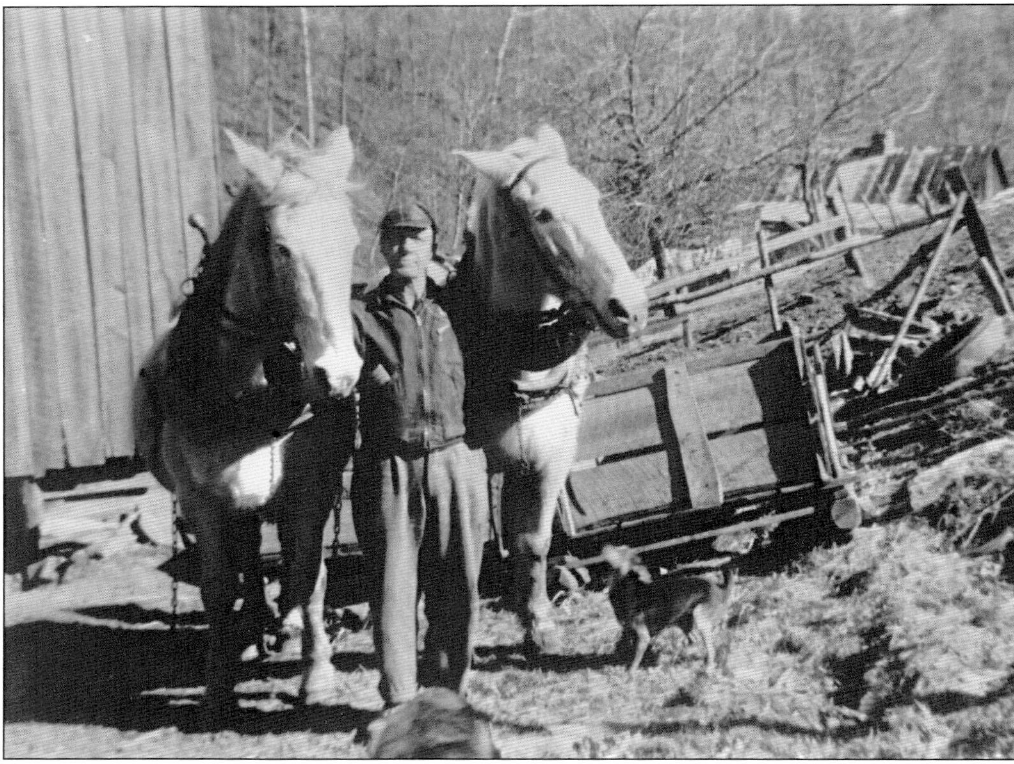

Jeter McCurry of Jacks Creek farmed with his plow and horses into the 1960s. (Courtesy of Amy Hopson McCurry.)

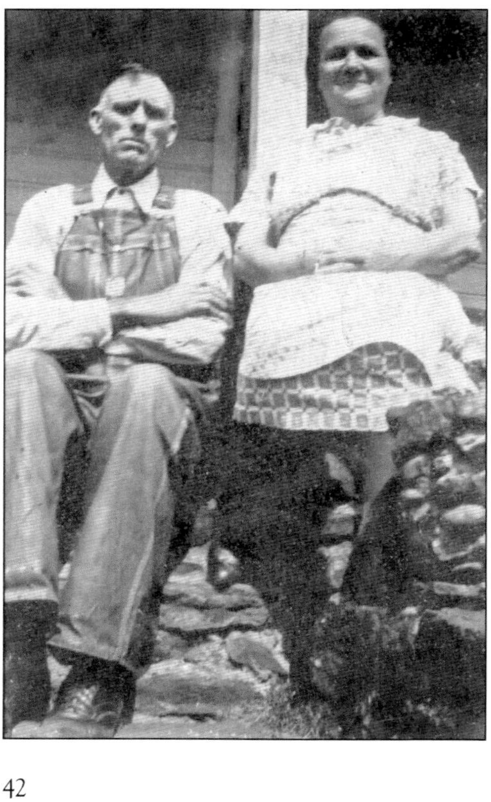

Jim Wheeler and his wife, Linda Hilemon Wheeler, sit on the front porch steps of their house, located on Cane River at Higgins, where some of the family still resides. (Courtesy of Carolyn Wheeler Bryant.)

Five

Blue Ridge, Bluegrass, and Baseball

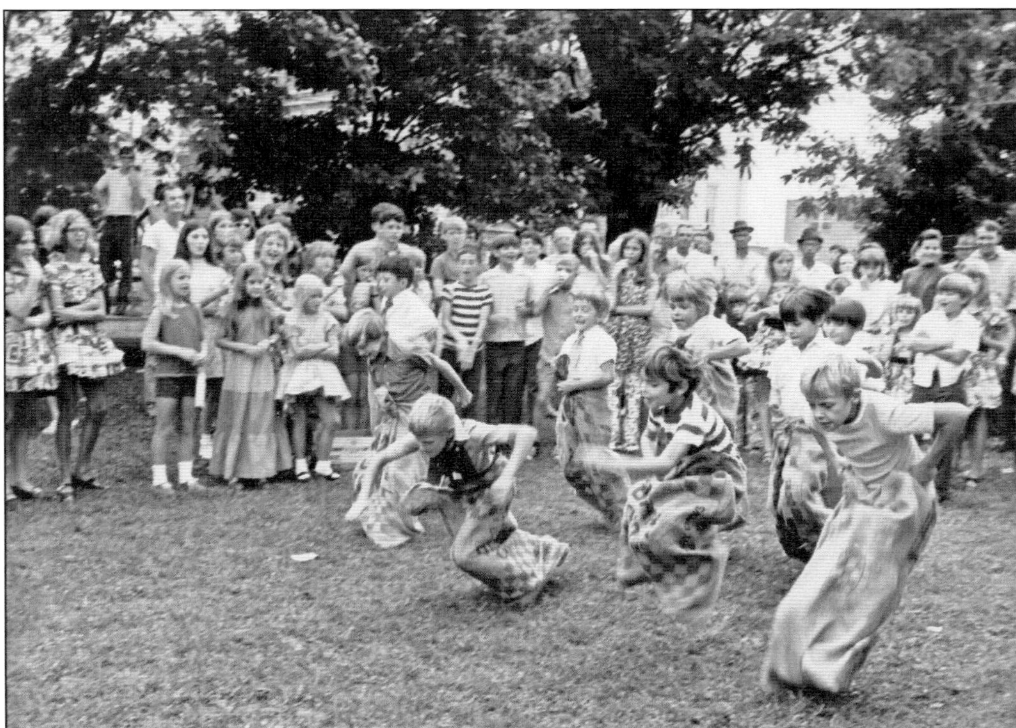

The Mount Mitchell Crafts Fair has been the biggest gathering in Yancey County for many years, featuring crafts and games. This 1970 sack race included Alan McKinney, hopping in a sack second from left. His father, Wayne, stands in the crowd between the trees in front of the old courthouse. (Courtesy of James Byrd and Phyllis and Wayne McKinney.)

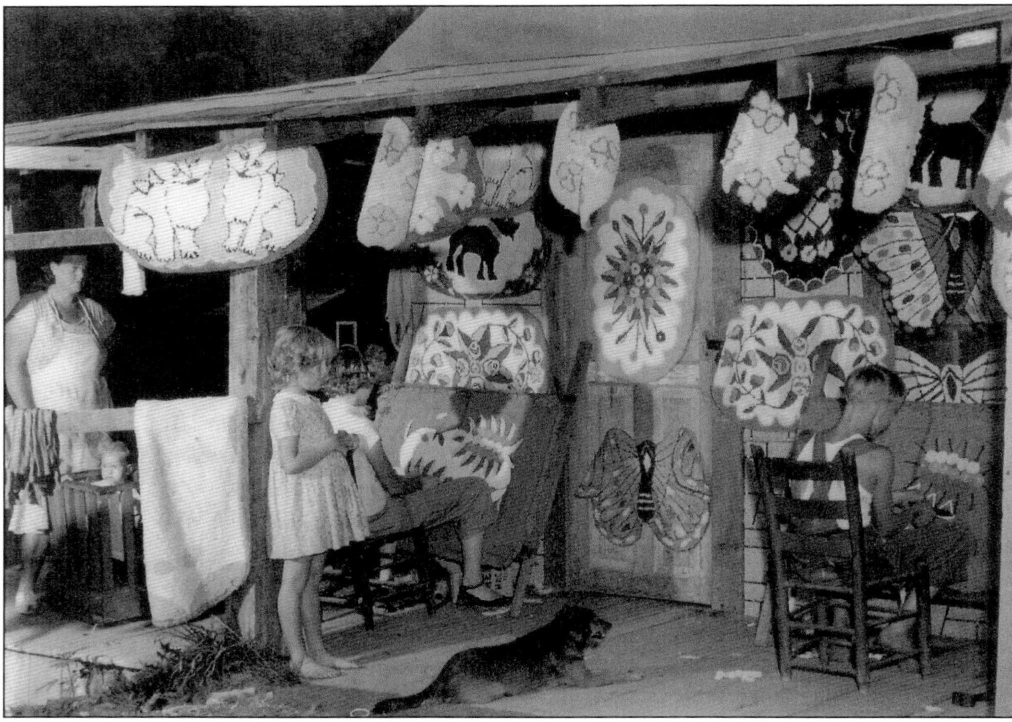

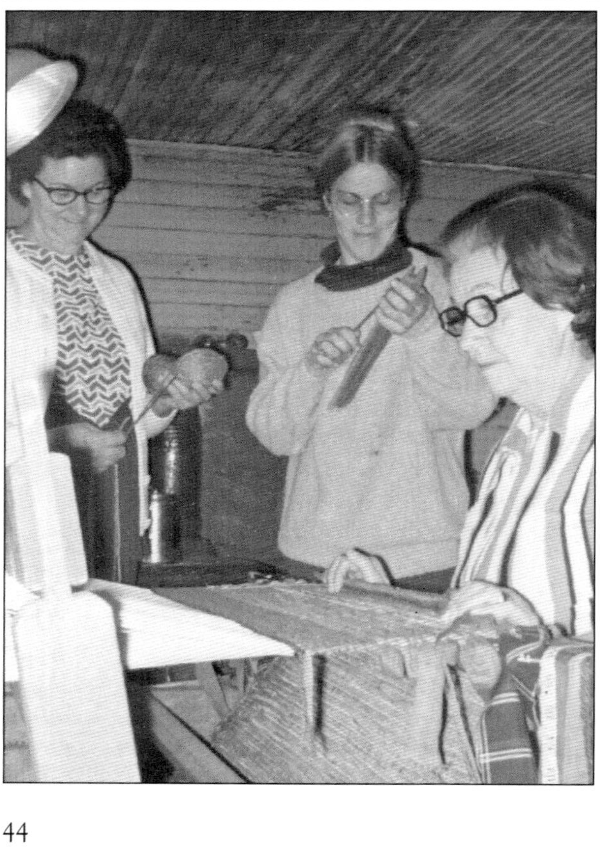

Amanda Silvers and her children, (from left to right) Gayle, Iva, Barbara, and Bruce, are shown here making hooked rugs. The Swiss community was known as Rug Town. Rug makers stretched burlap over a wooden frame made of narrow boards and tiny nails. To stencil a pattern on the burlap, they used dye made of one cup black dye with a gallon of kerosene. Stencils dried in 15 minutes. (Courtesy of Nancy Randolph Silvers.)

Seen here from left to right are June Miller, an unidentified person, and Birdie McAlister at the loom. In the 1960s and 1970s, these women gathered in the community as students or participants in a government marketing program where they met each week for classes in various handicrafts, which they would help in marketing. (Courtesy of Elaine McAlister Dellinger.)

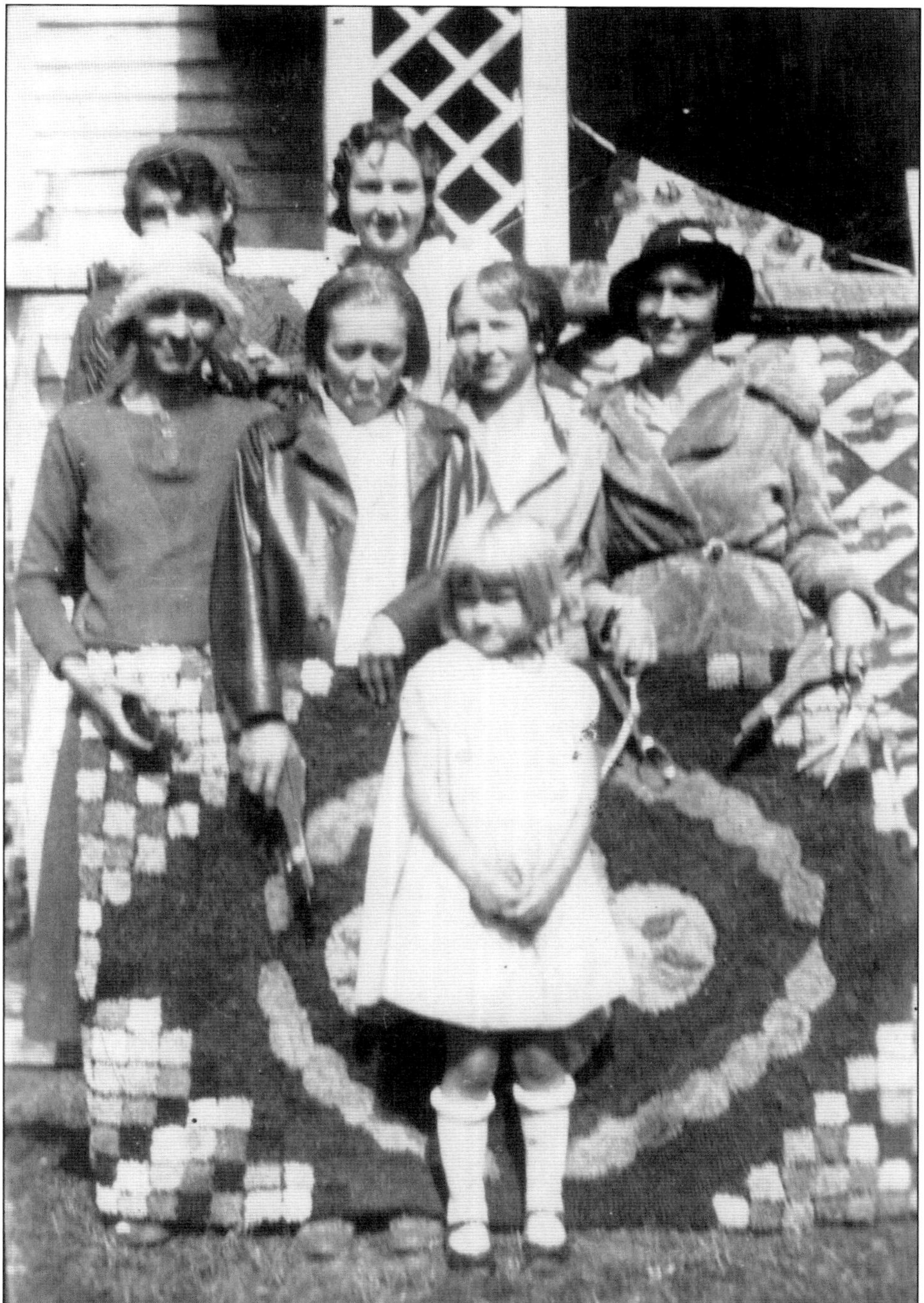

From left to right in front, sisters Ida Robertson, Polly Gardner, and Birdie McAlister and sister-in-law Jane Honeycutt pose with one of their daughters in Bald Creek. The two women in back are unidentified. The sisters hold the tools of the craft and a finished rug. They would work on the rugs in their homes after completing all the day's chores. Rug-making season lasted the winter, November through March, providing year-round income. Customers in New York, Kentucky, Pennsylvania, and Virginia bought rugs made in Yancey. (Courtesy of Elaine McAlister Dellinger.)

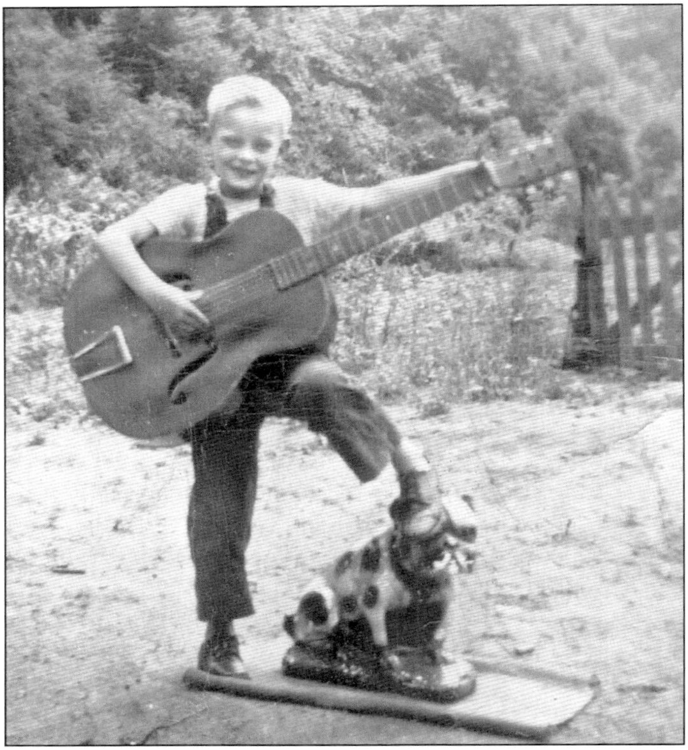

Donald Robertson, age seven, the son of Hicks and Ida Honeycutt Robertson of Hardscrabble community, enjoyed playing his guitar. He took ill and died a few months after this photograph was taken. (Courtesy of Elaine McAlister Dellinger.)

Isaac Cox, great-grandfather to Barbara Ford, plays guitar in the Crabtree area as his grandchildren listen. His wife ran the post office. The flag in this photograph has only 48 stars. (Courtesy of Barbara Ford.)

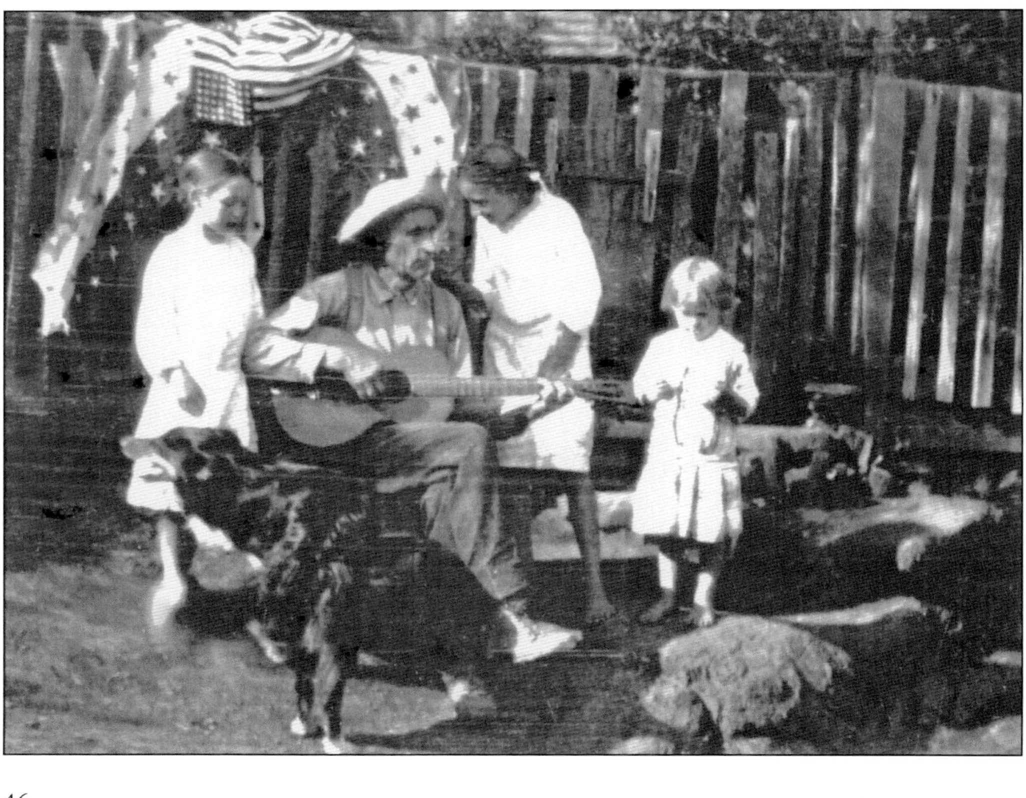

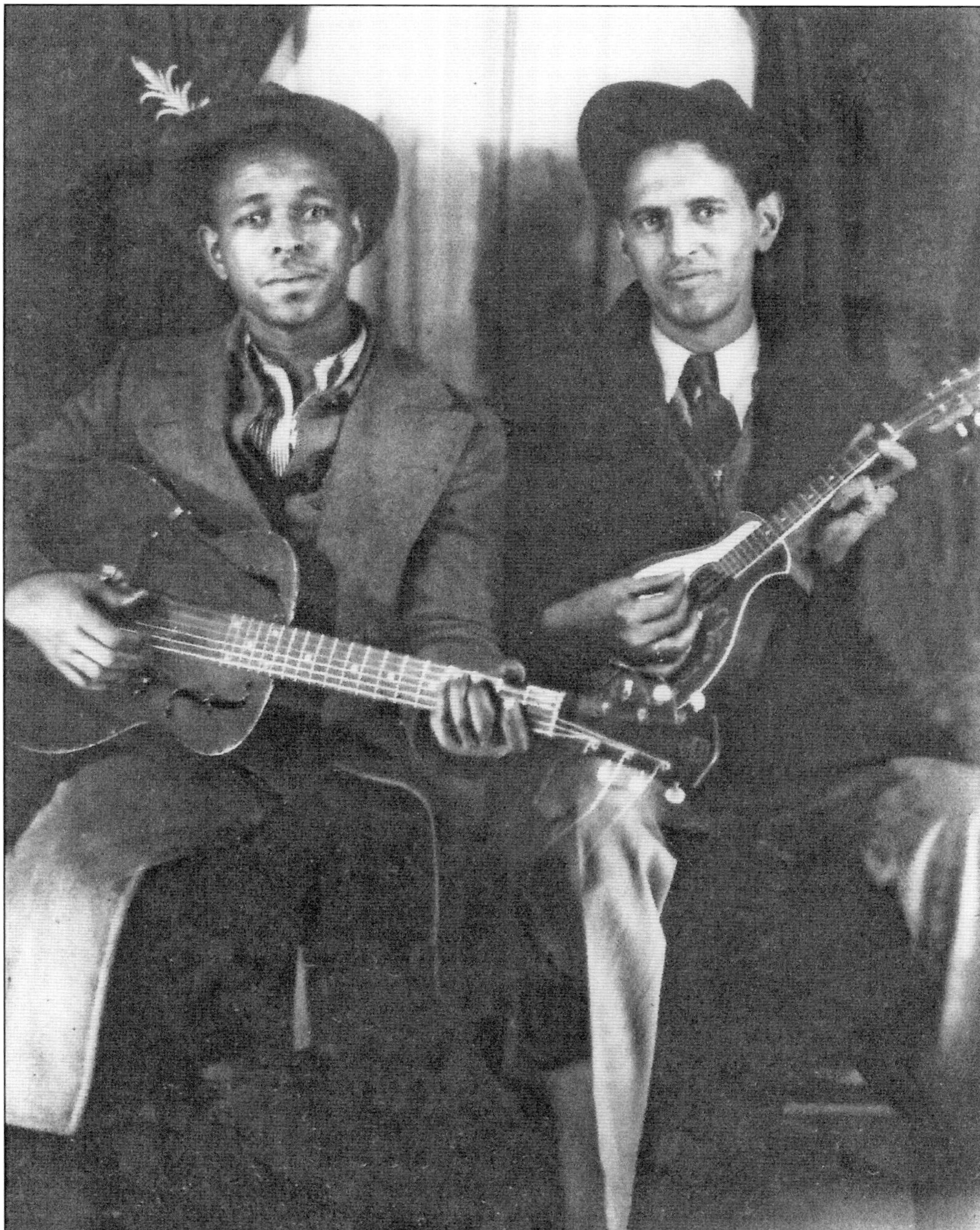

Lesley Riddle gathered songs throughout the Appalachians with A.P. Carter, and the Carter Family popularized many of his songs, including "Hello Stranger" and "I Know What It Means to Be Lonesome." Here is Lesley (right) with Walter Brown "Brownie" McGhee. Lesley was a brilliant songwriter and musician, but he fell on tough times and had to sell his guitar. He was a shoeshine man and crossing guard in 1965 when folksinger Mike Seeger rediscovered him and released a CD of his music, *Step by Step*. Yancey County honors Riddle with an annual Riddlefest and *Esley*, a play by Jeff Messer. (Courtesy of Jody Higgins.)

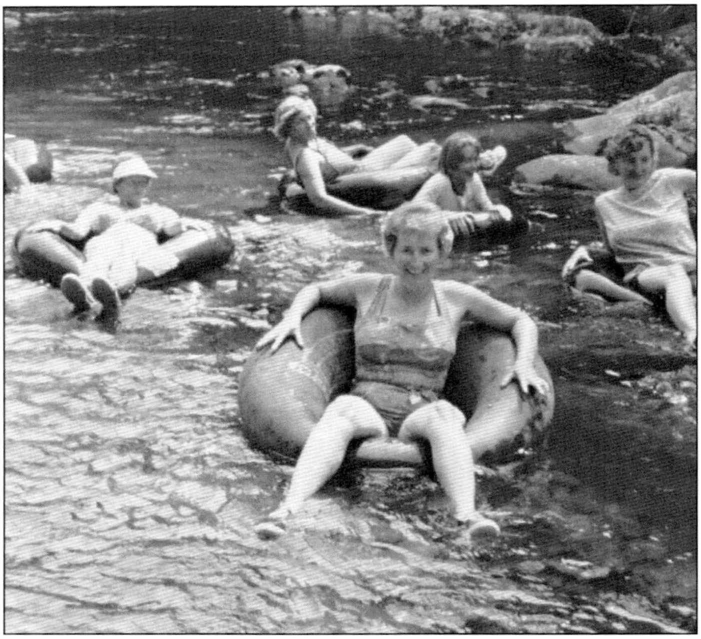

The Gibbs sisters played at the Carolina Hemlocks from the time they were little girls, and tubing is a pleasure they will never outgrow. Many Southern ladies and gentlemen still plunge into the Toe River when the temperatures climb, riding inner tubes or swimming in the swirling rapids. Here, Mildred Gibbs Harris is in front, and in back, from left to right, are Nina Gibbs Johnson, Grace Gibbs Simmons, Marie Gibbs Johnson, and Nell Gibbs Huskins. (Courtesy of Mildred Gibbs Harris.)

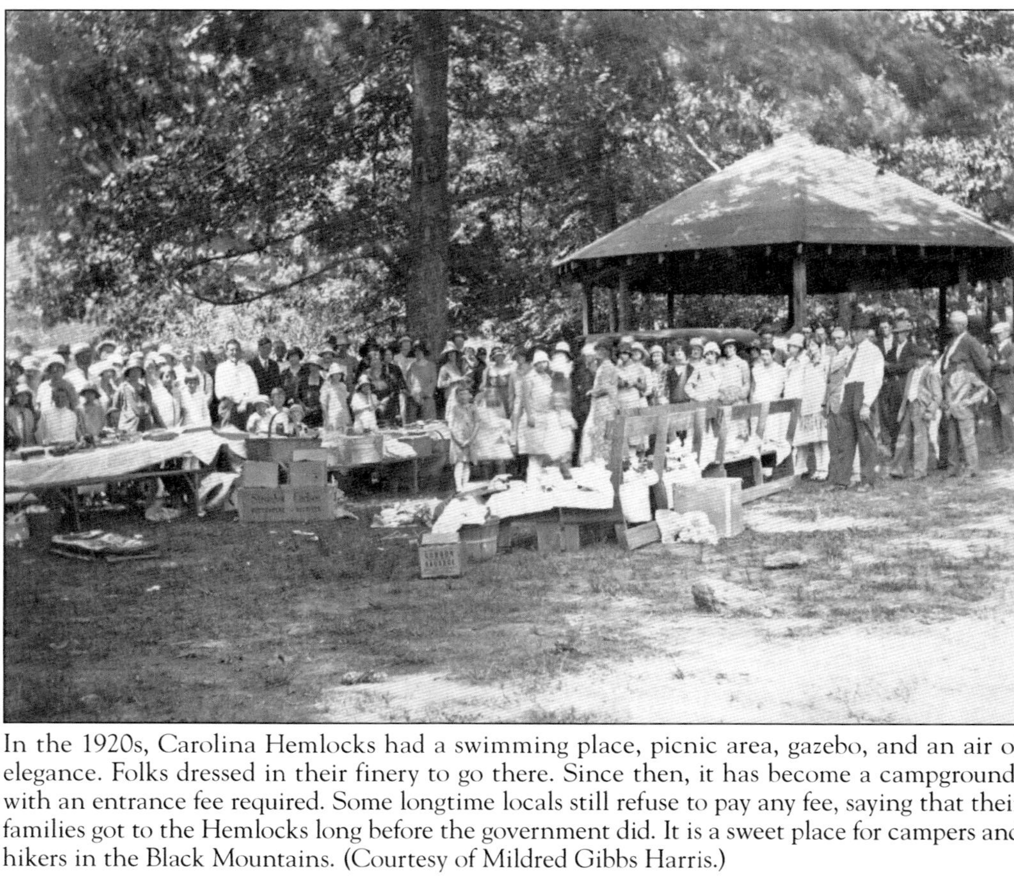

In the 1920s, Carolina Hemlocks had a swimming place, picnic area, gazebo, and an air of elegance. Folks dressed in their finery to go there. Since then, it has become a campground, with an entrance fee required. Some longtime locals still refuse to pay any fee, saying that their families got to the Hemlocks long before the government did. It is a sweet place for campers and hikers in the Black Mountains. (Courtesy of Mildred Gibbs Harris.)

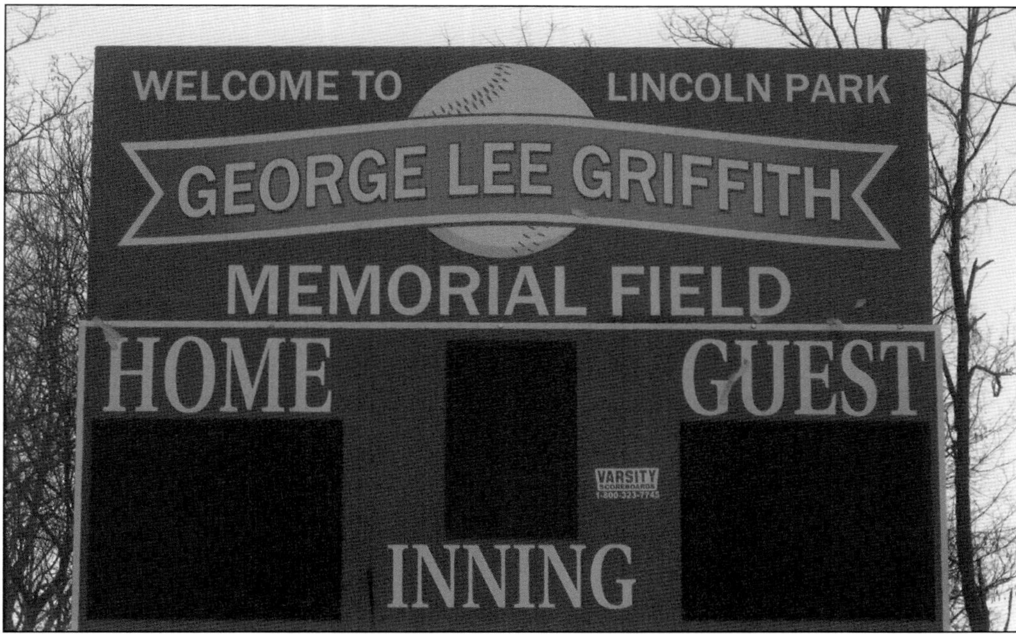

The Burnsville Eagles played baseball in the Negro Leagues. In a resolution in 2010, the county commissioners acknowledged the Burnsville Eagles for bringing fame, pride, and praise to Yancey County and fostering racial harmony. This sign was unveiled during the dedication ceremony for the ballpark that namesake George Lee Griffith had loved all his life. (Courtesy of Elaine McAlister Dellinger.)

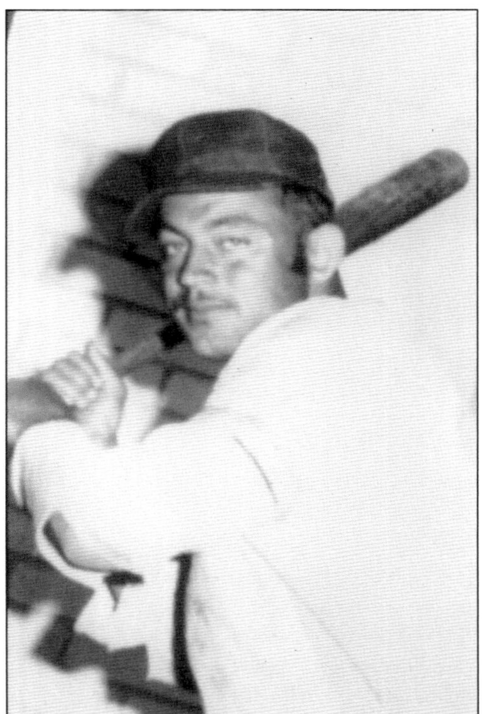

George Lee Griffith, a founding member of the Burnsville Eagles baseball team from the 1940s to the 1960s, brought the resources to the community to build a baseball field that could be used by anyone, and it has been called his field of dreams. The baseball field at Lincoln Park has been named the George Lee Griffith Memorial Field in his honor. He received offers to play professional ball, but he chose to stay in Yancey. (Courtesy of Jody Higgins.)

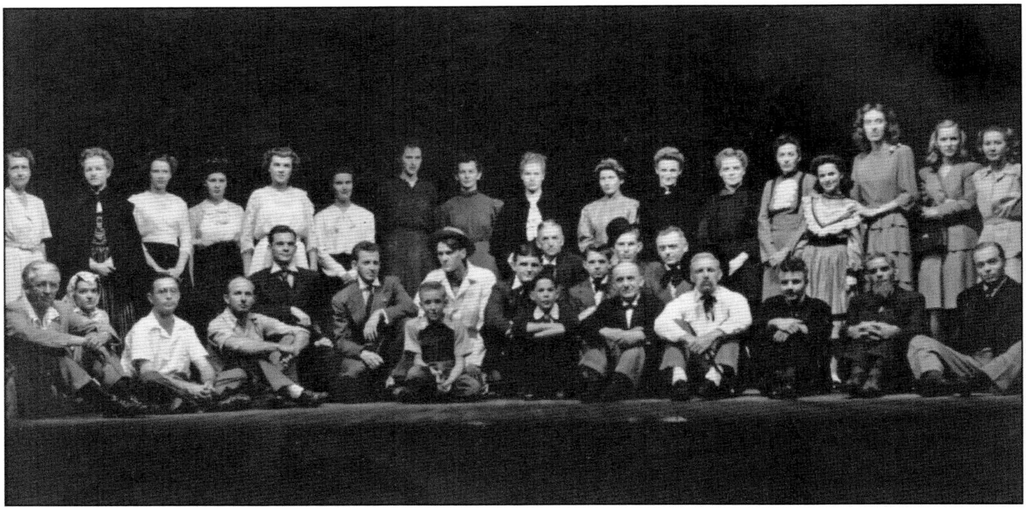

The Parkway Playhouse began in 1947 as the first of its kind in the South. Burnsville Playhouse, Inc., and School of Dramatic Arts opened in a converted Burnsville High School gym. Here is the cast of *Our Town*, with William Raymond Taylor, the theater's founder, seated at far left. Absent from the image is the star of that play and many others, W.C. "Mutt" Burton, who took the photograph. (Courtesy of Evelyn Hope Bailey.)

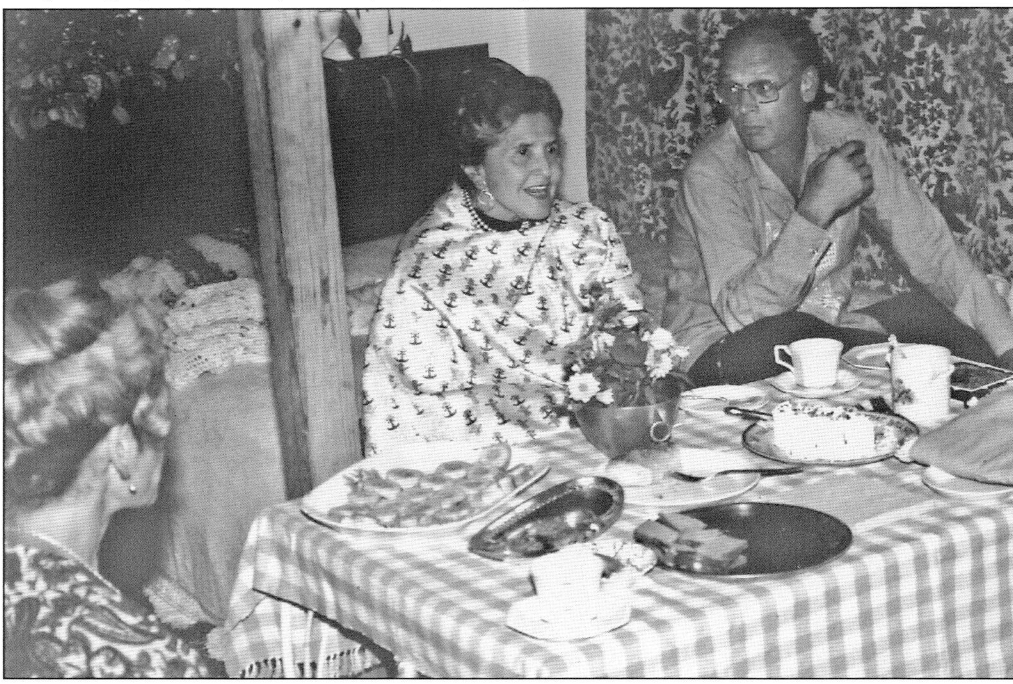

Enjoying afternoon tea at the William Dreyer home in Celo are, from left to right, Ruth Pope, Madame Lili Kraus, and William "Bill" Dreyer. Between her global travelling and performing as a classical pianist, Madame Kraus resided in Celo. She and her daughter, Ruth, had been in Japanese prisoner-of-war camps in World War II but emerged strong and resilient. Ruth initiated Music in the Mountains, a celebration of classical music. Bill Dreyer spent six years as the managing and artistic director of the Parkway Playhouse. (Courtesy of Joseph Sasek Family Archives.)

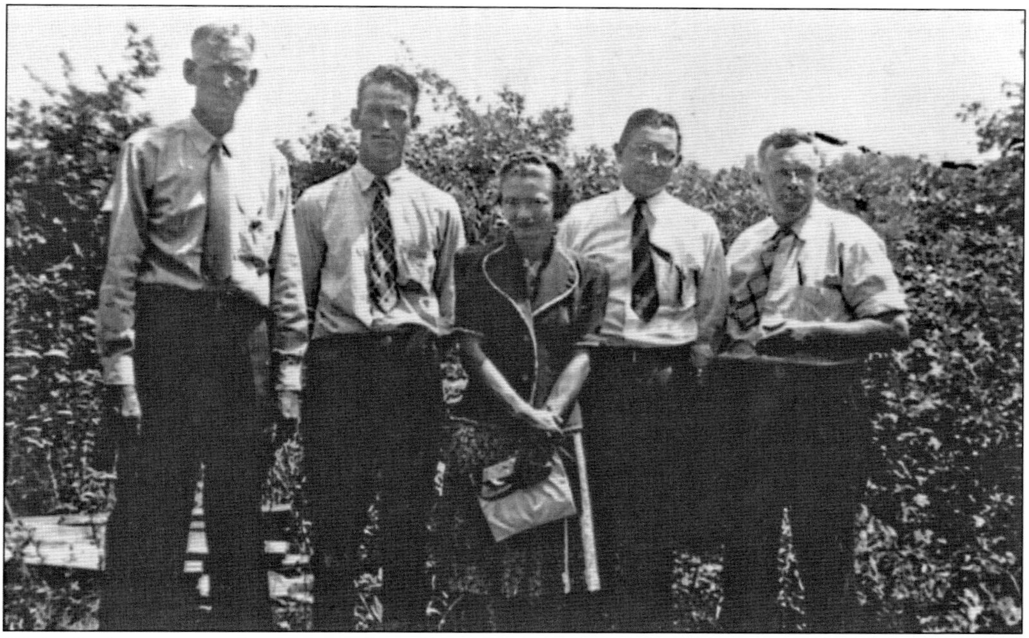

Welzie Robinson owned a store in Micaville and sang with the Travelers, a popular quartet frequently heard on radio. Seen here from left to right are the Travelers: Welzie Robinson, Dooley Wilson, pianist Leanne Robinson, Edd Gibbs, and I. Hurd. (Courtesy of Mildred Gibbs Harris.)

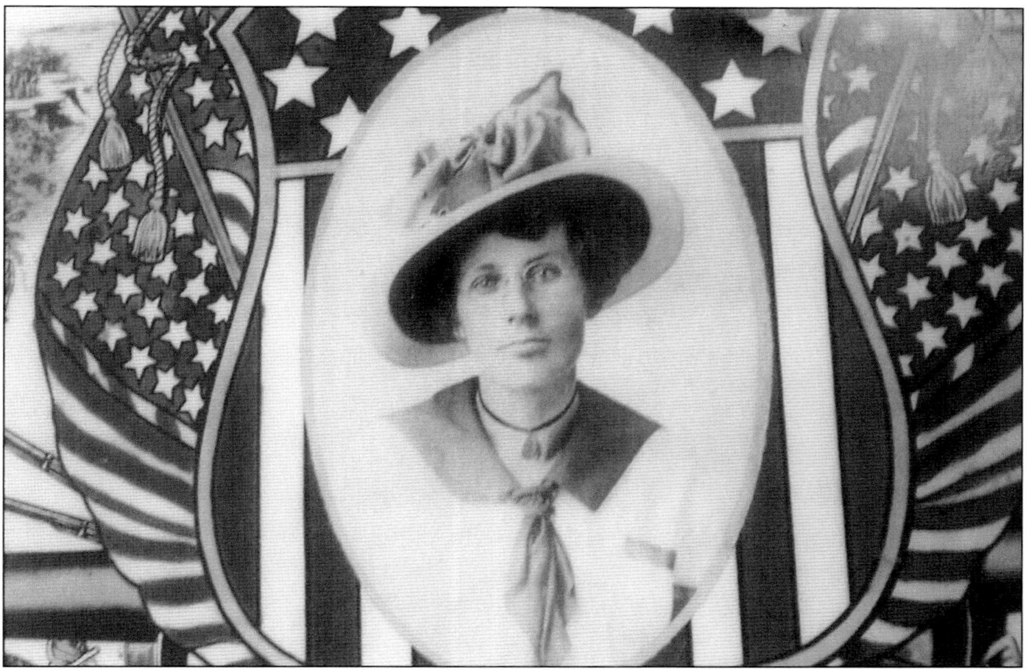

People took time out from their work for special themed photographs of the times. Patriotism was as big in the early 1900s as it is today, as seen here with Elizabeth Edney Beaver of the Upper Jacks Creek area near Iron College, all adorned with red, white, and blue. (Courtesy of Barbara Cole.)

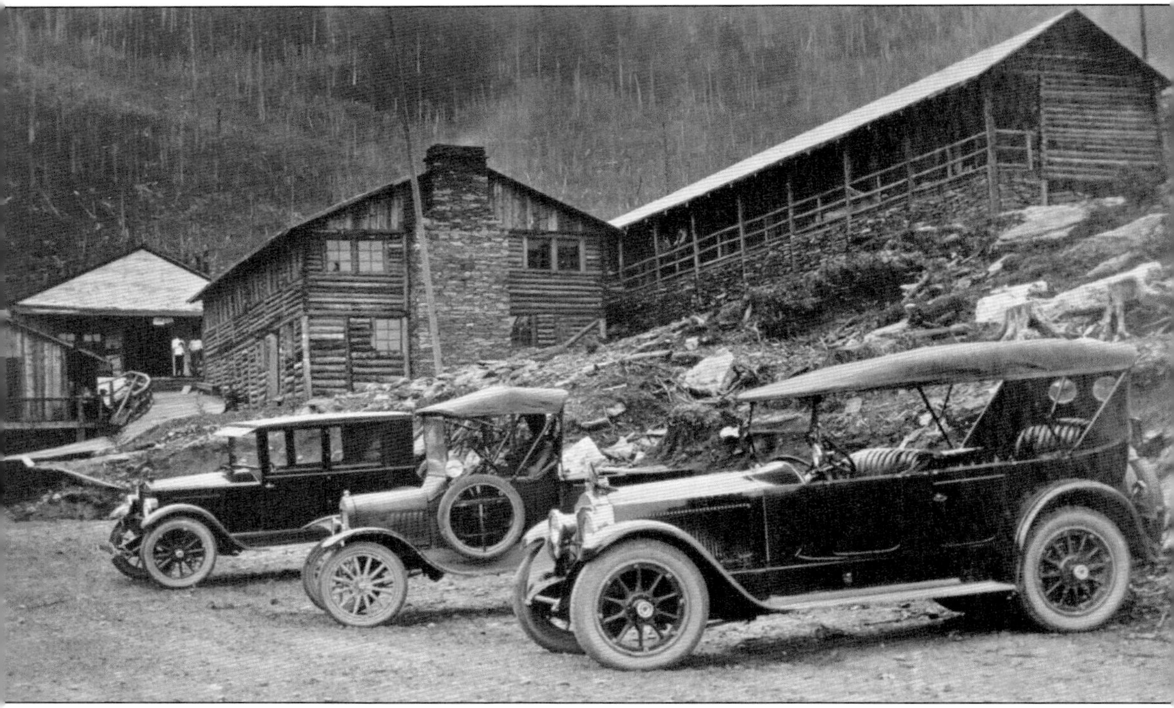

The hard work of local men and women created the area's state parks, roads, and buildings to be enjoyed by all. Civilian Conservation Corps Camp Alice, located near Mount Mitchell in the South Toe community, provided a site where many "Greatest Generation" men served in the CCC, including Warren Burdett McAlister and the Phillips sons. Nationwide, the CCC planted three billion trees and constructed 800 parks. (Courtesy of Regina Wilson.)

Six

Feed, Seed, and All We Need

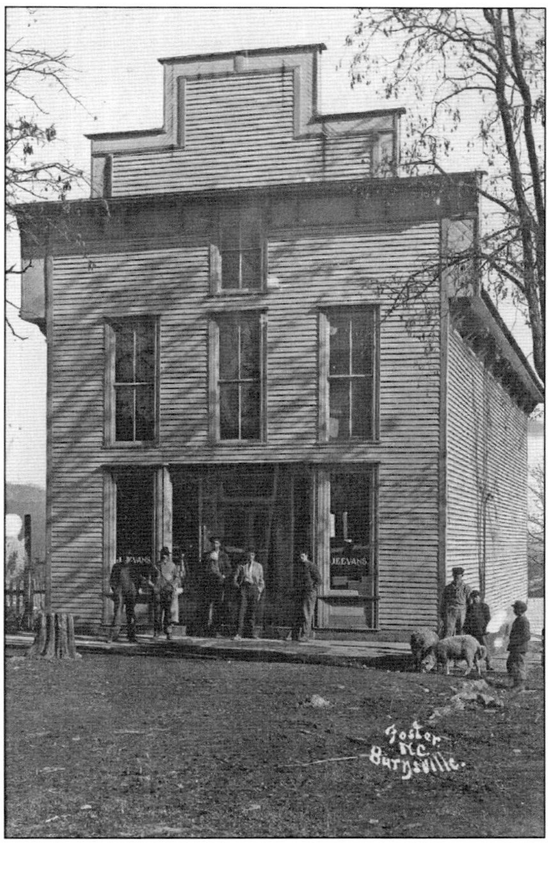

Evans' Store, owned and operated by J.E. Evans since 1910, stood on the Town Square. Troy McCurry managed it as a variety store. Pictured from left to right in front of the store are Lawrence Evans, nephew of John; Mack Elliot, who married an Evans; and two of his sons. (Courtesy of Nancy Randolph Silvers.)

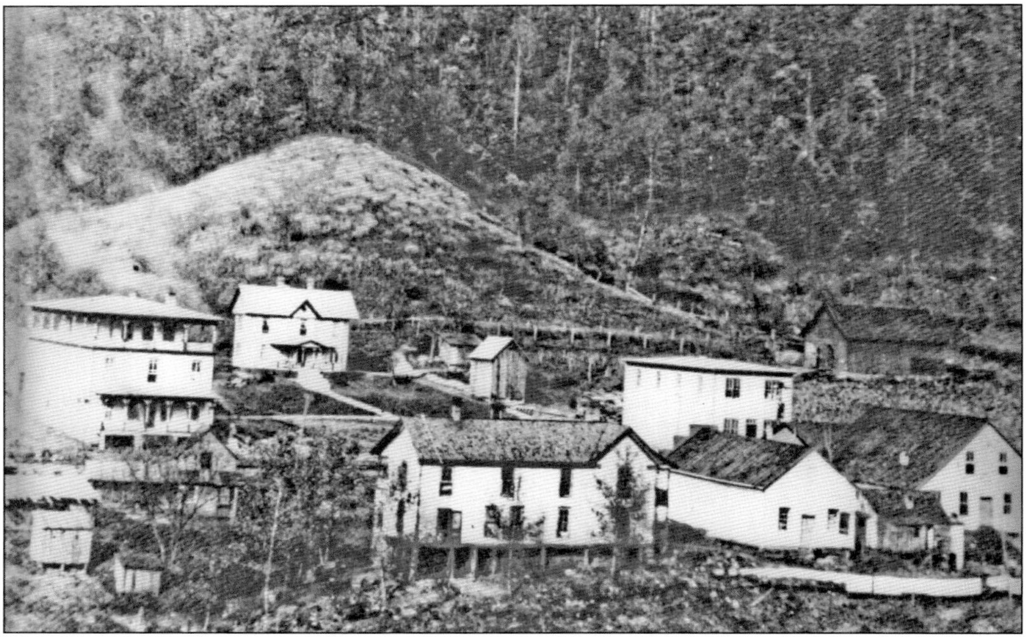

Huntdale once was a bustling community. Bob Griffith's store and post office are shown in the top left of this image, next to his hotel and home. A dwelling house graces the lower left, next to a railroad house where the crew stayed at layovers. At the lower right are a mill for grinding corn and a warehouse. (Courtesy of James Byrd and Wayne and Phyllis McKinney.)

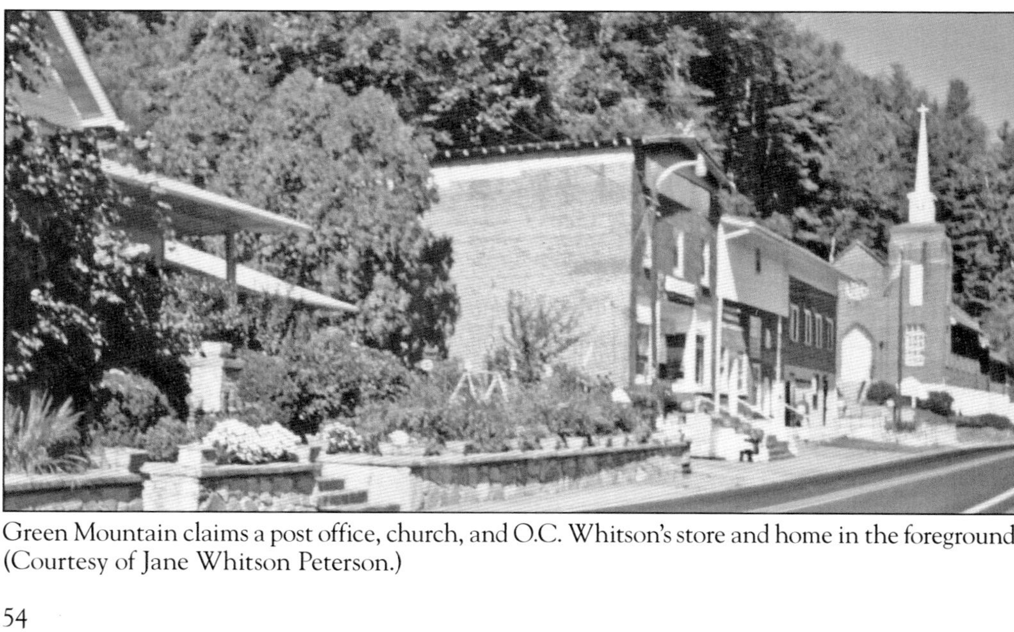

Green Mountain claims a post office, church, and O.C. Whitson's store and home in the foreground. (Courtesy of Jane Whitson Peterson.)

In 1987, Parzady and O.C. Whitson rest for a moment in front of their store, a longtime landmark and family legacy in Green Mountain Township. (Courtesy of Jane Whitson Peterson.)

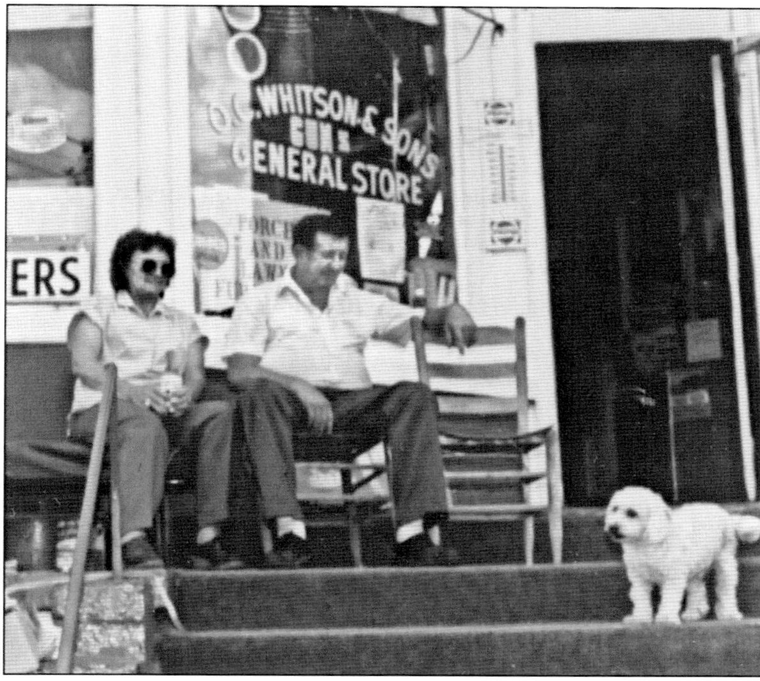

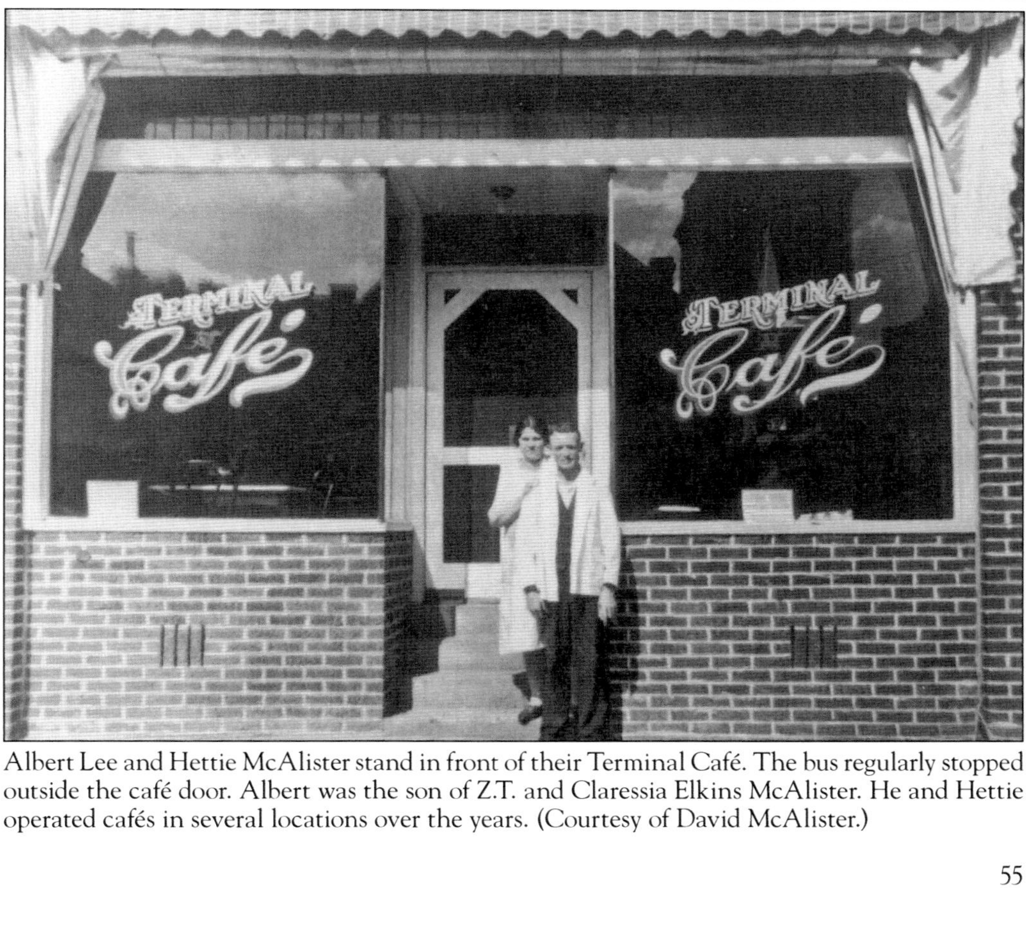

Albert Lee and Hettie McAlister stand in front of their Terminal Café. The bus regularly stopped outside the café door. Albert was the son of Z.T. and Claressia Elkins McAlister. He and Hettie operated cafés in several locations over the years. (Courtesy of David McAlister.)

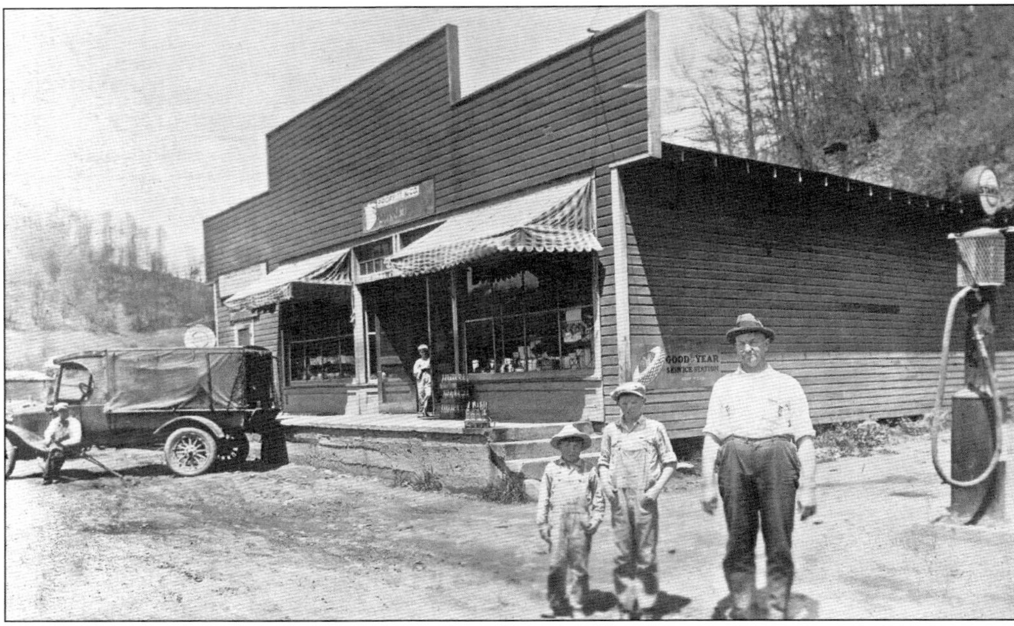

The Proffitts' store on Bald Creek burned to the ground on September 14, 1948. Ralph is seen here in the foreground with sons James (left) and Glenn Proffitt. The brick Proffitt's store, owned by Glenn Proffitt and operated by James Proffitt and family, became a gathering place. Sarah Ellen remembered helping her aunt Kittie sort and bag loose candy at Christmastime. The Bald Creek School requested these treat bags for all the schoolchildren at the holiday season every year. (Courtesy of Sarah Woody Proffitt.)

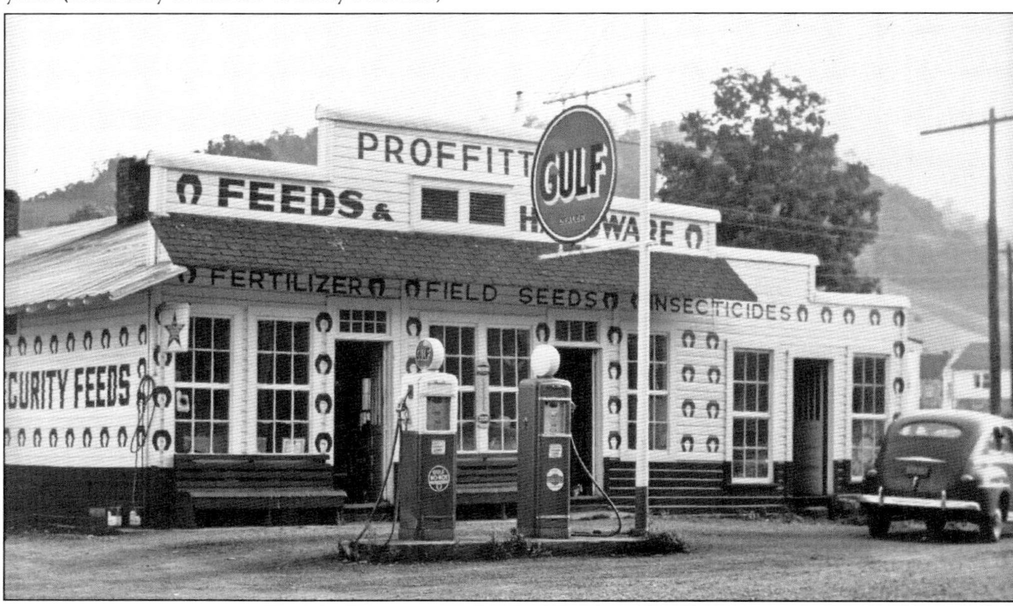

Glenn Proffitt's family owned and operated two stores in the Bald Creek community until the highway expansion took the properties. The store housed feed and other general merchandise. Son James, daughter Bill, and son-in-law Yates Bailey worked in the store during the later years. (Courtesy of Sarah Woody Proffitt.)

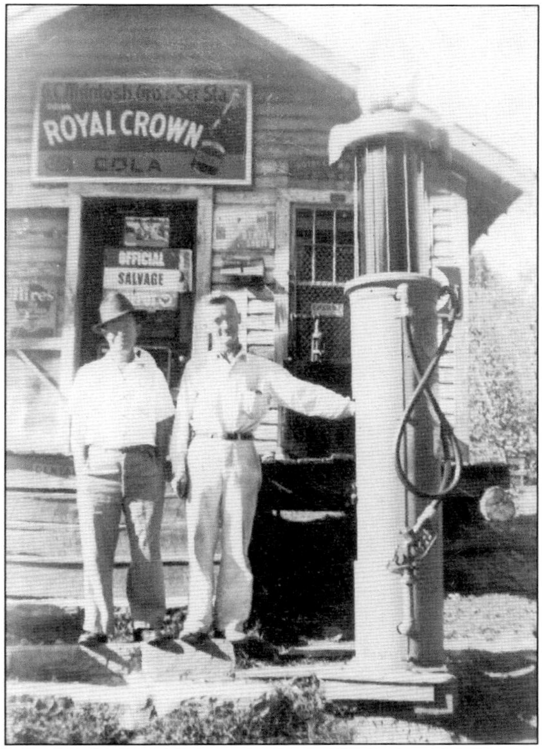

Vergie Johnson (left) and Grover McIntosh (right) stand in front of their brand new gravity-fed gasoline pump in front of their grocery, salvage, and service station. (Courtesy of Carol and Joe Renfro.)

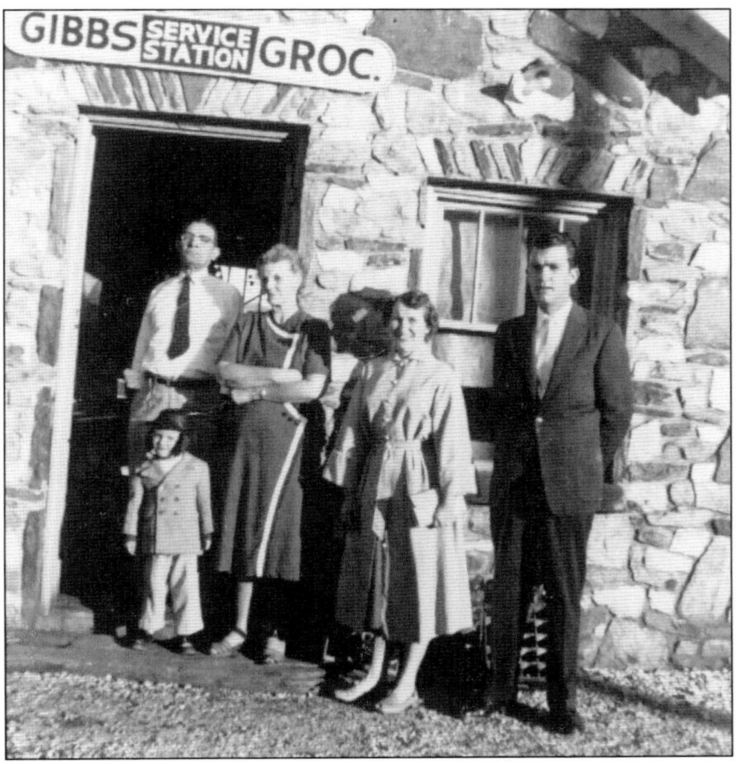

The jukebox played nickels and Mildred stood on a tobacco box to see over the counter when she first started working at Gibbs's Grocery. On opening day, gas coat 18¢ a gallon. The grocery's gone now, but the front rock wall still stands in Celo. Here, from left to right, are Edd Gibbs behind Tony, who grew up to run Phil's Tire Shop in town; Lula Gibbs; Mildred Gibbs Harris; and Phil Harris. (Courtesy of Mildred Gibbs Harris.)

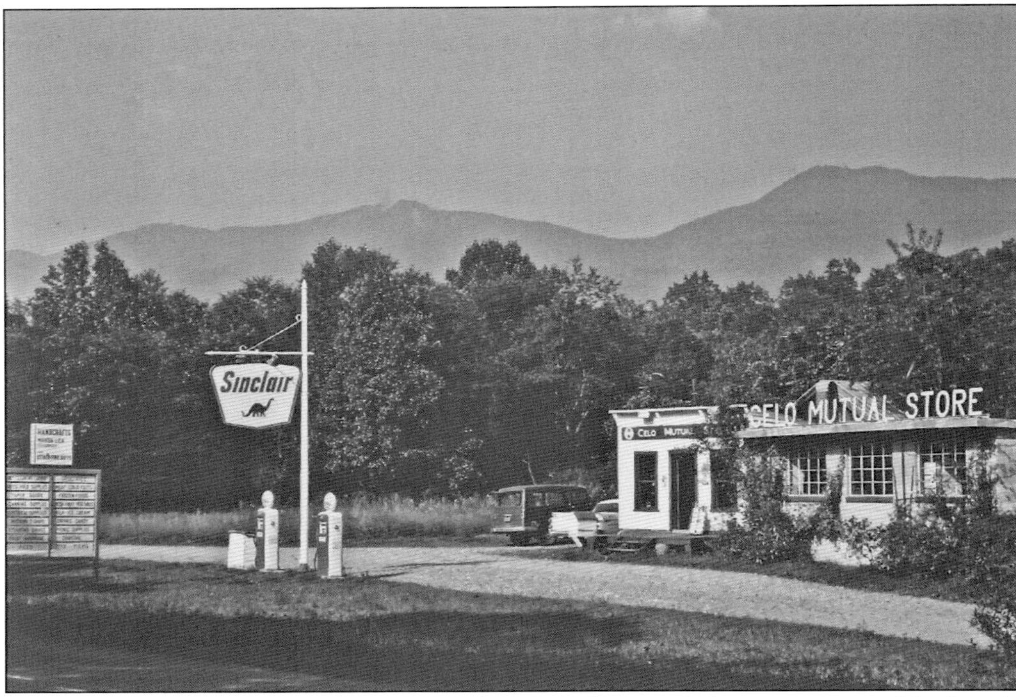

The Celo Mutual Store on Highway 80 South, near Celo, provided groceries, animal feed, tools, hardware, and handicrafts. Peter Schwintzer, a senior officer in German Air Force Intelligence in World War II, managed the store. His family moved to Celo after the war at the encouragement of his brother-in-law, the longtime Celo Health Center doctor Elpenor Ohle. Peter's store later transformed into the current Toe River Crafts Store and Celo Food Co-op. (Courtesy of Joseph Sasek family archives.)

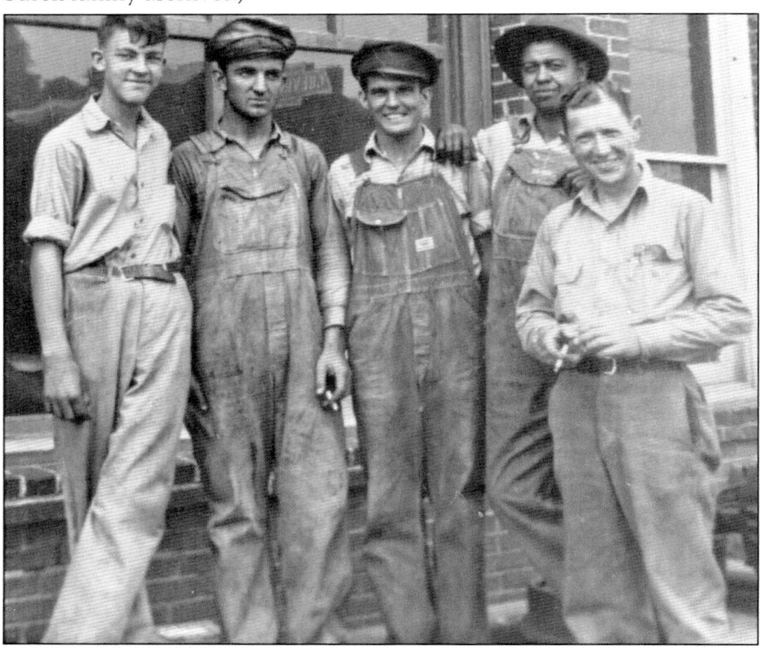

Ivan Westall sold the tire store to Phil Harris, and here stand the store's first employees in 1944. Seen from left to right are Phil Harris, Sam Burleson, Lawrence Robinson, Ted Jackson, and Ivan Westall. (Courtesy of Mildred Gibbs Harris.)

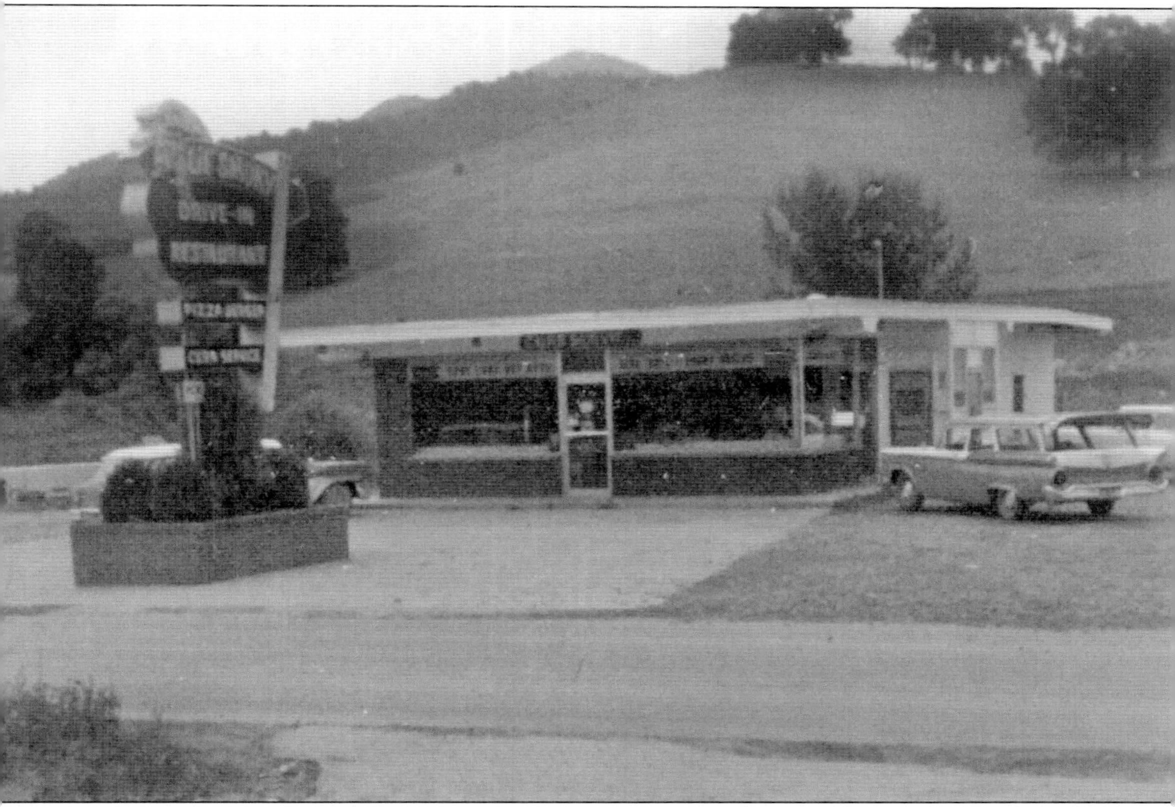

Pictured here about 1958, Lee and Myrtle Slagle opened the Li'l Smokey Drive-In, which catered to new trends including curb service (something unique in its heyday), and later, they built and operated the Amber Jack Restaurant. (Courtesy of Vickie Slagle Fortune.)

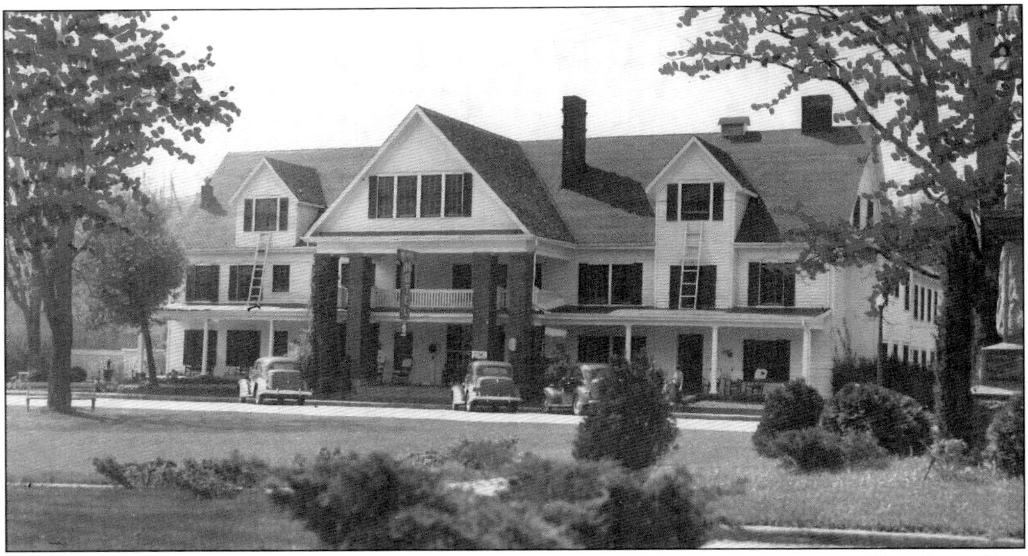

The NuWray Inn opened at a stagecoach stop when Yancey became a county in 1833 and is still in operation today. Will Roland's skill as a chef helped make the NuWray Inn successful. He married Hattie Flack Roland, who lived to be 107 years old and once worked for Pres. Franklin Roosevelt in Warm Springs, Georgia. They had five sons: Charles, Merle, Ralph, Frank, and Leroy. This photograph was made by Edwards Printing Company; at that time, they were the best printers in Burnsville. (Courtesy of Yancey History Association.)

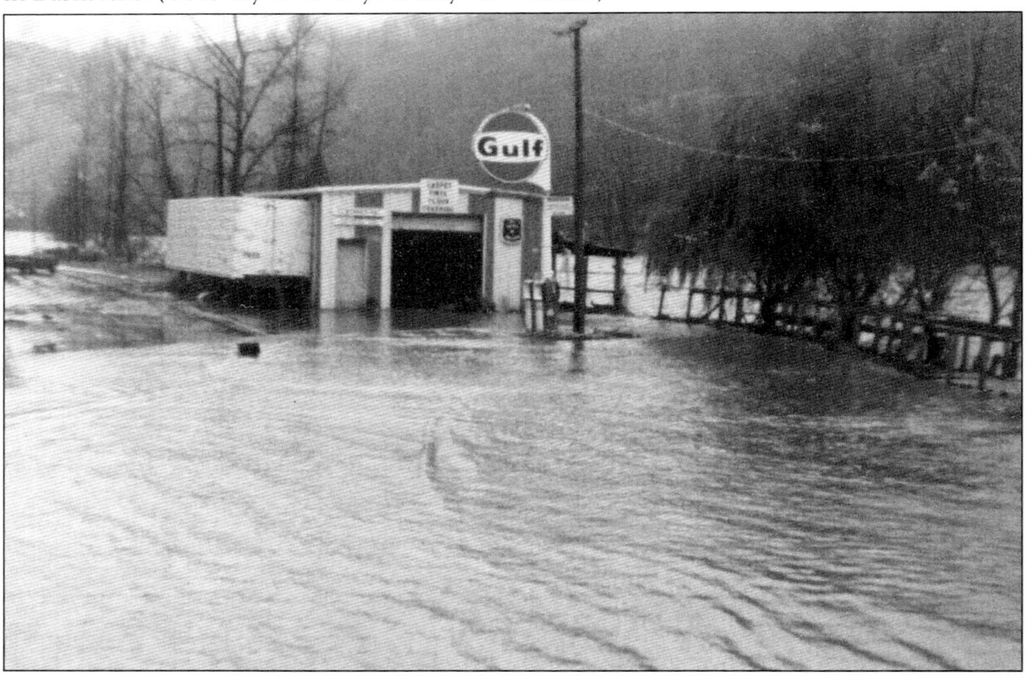

Green Mountain Township business owners worked hard to clean up after the big flood that hit on November 6, 1977, but some could not survive the devastation. The Yancey Railroad was abandoned after the bridge piers were damaged, and the Cane River Dam never recovered fully, either. (Courtesy of Jane Whitson Peterson.)

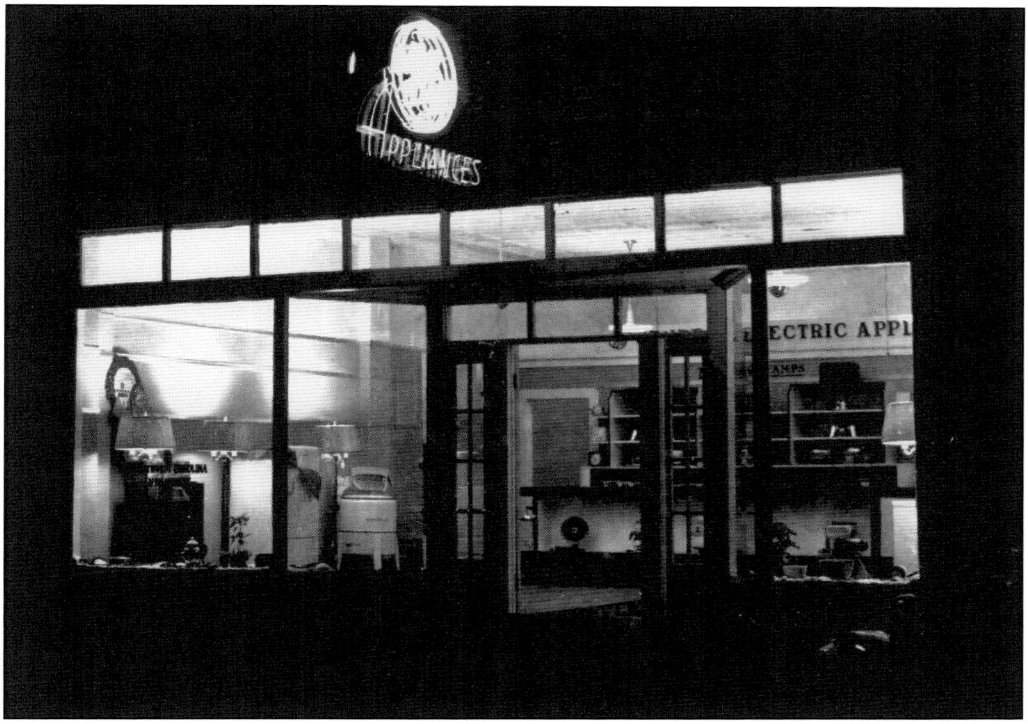

This appliance store sold all the electrically powered conveniences when they first reached Yancey County. (Courtesy of Sarah Woody Proffitt.)

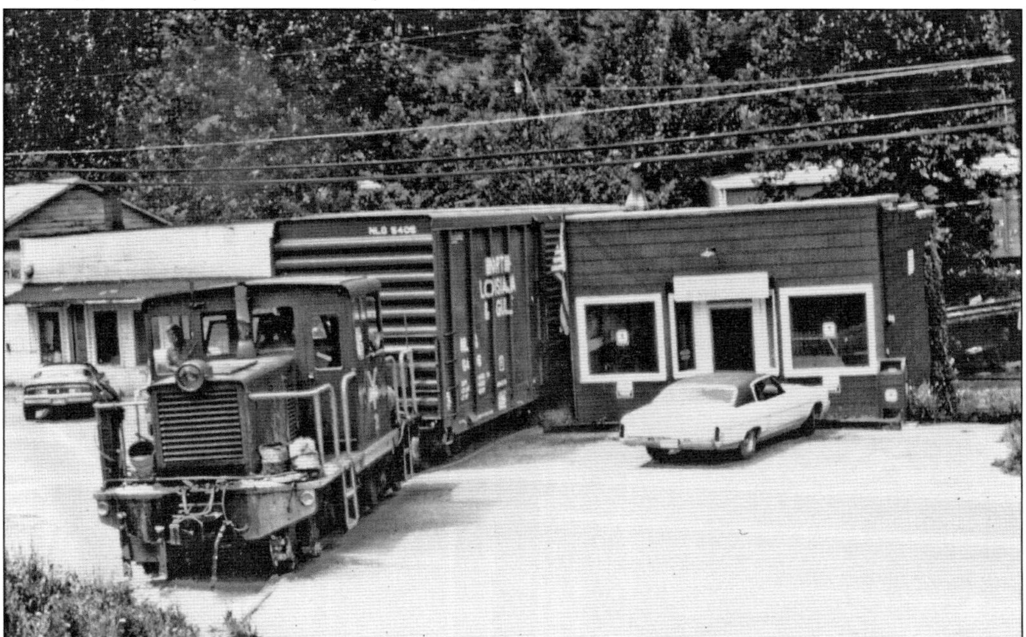

The Micaville Post Office once had a close neighbor—a tad too close for comfort. The train slipped between two buildings with nary a whisker to spare. (Courtesy of Yancey History Association.)

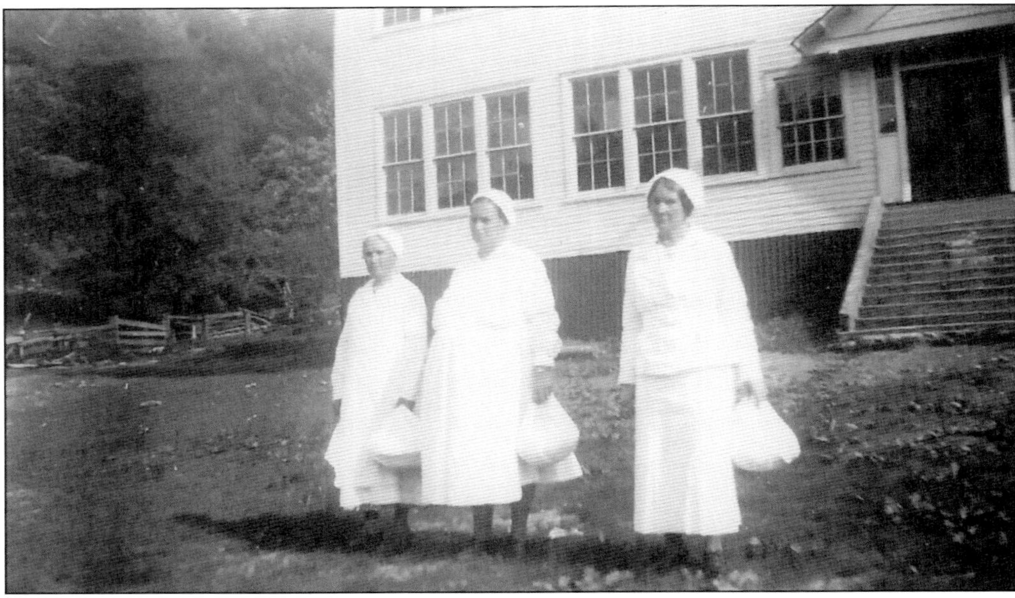

Three local midwives who were also sisters were, from left to right, Mary Jane Hensley, Winnie Hensley Lewis, and Mamy Arphenie Hensley Edwards; they were the children of Gilbert and Caroline Shelton Hensley. With the lack of doctors in the mountains, midwives commonly assisted with births throughout the county. The little sacks that they carried contained the instruments they used to deliver the babies, such as crochet hooks, forceps, twine, and smelling salts. (Courtesy of Thelma Carmack.)

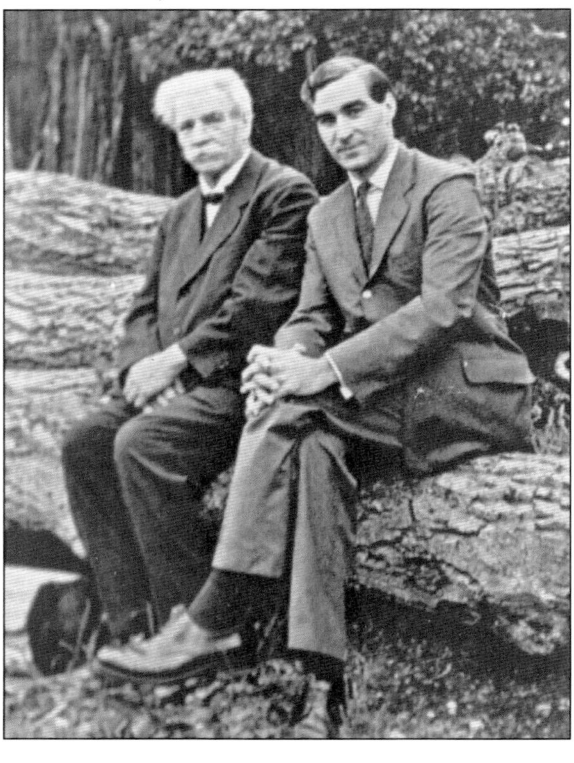

Dr. Fergus Pope (right), a much-loved area physician, also worked in Africa with Dr. Albert Schweitzer (left). Fergus and Ruth Pope settled in the Celo area, where Ruth started the first Montessori school in Yancey, initiated an annual classical music extravaganza, and led yoga classes. (Courtesy of Ruth Pope.)

Seven

Down the Dirt Road

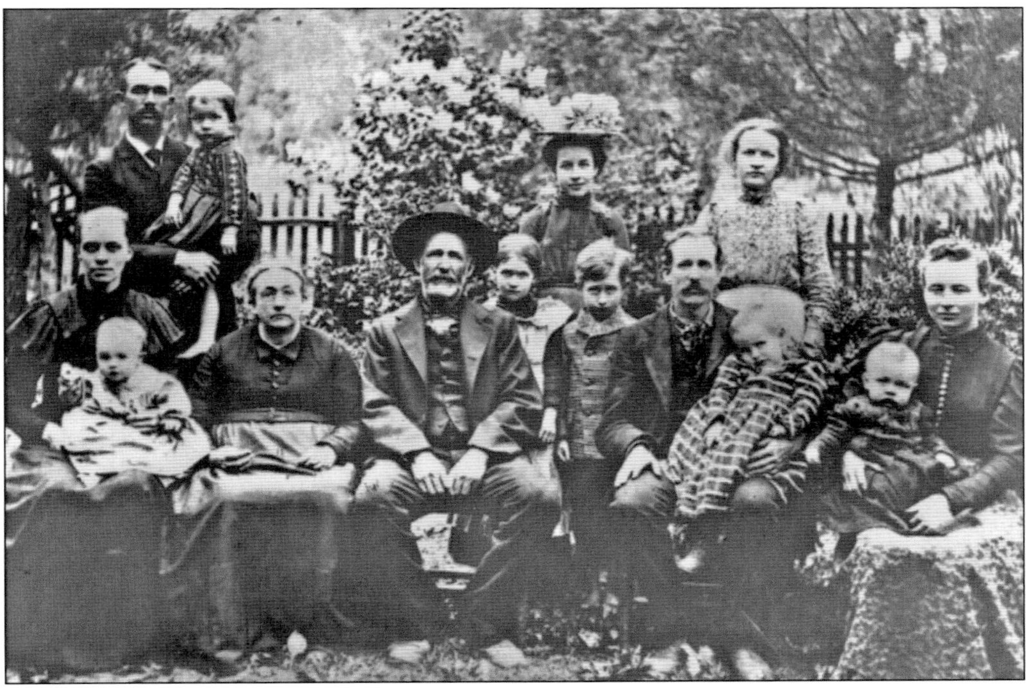

At the end of the 19th century, the Deytons of Green Mountain had this family portrait made. Pictured here from left to right are (first row) Texanna Woody Deyton holding baby, Ora, Pinkey Deyton, Basil "Bass" Deyton, and Etta Garland Deyton, his second wife, both holding babies; (second row) Rob Deyton, Etta's sisters, and, between Pinkey and Bass, Ettie and Charlie Deyton, the two children of Bass and first wife Mary Bailey Deyton. (Courtesy of Charlotte Anglin.)

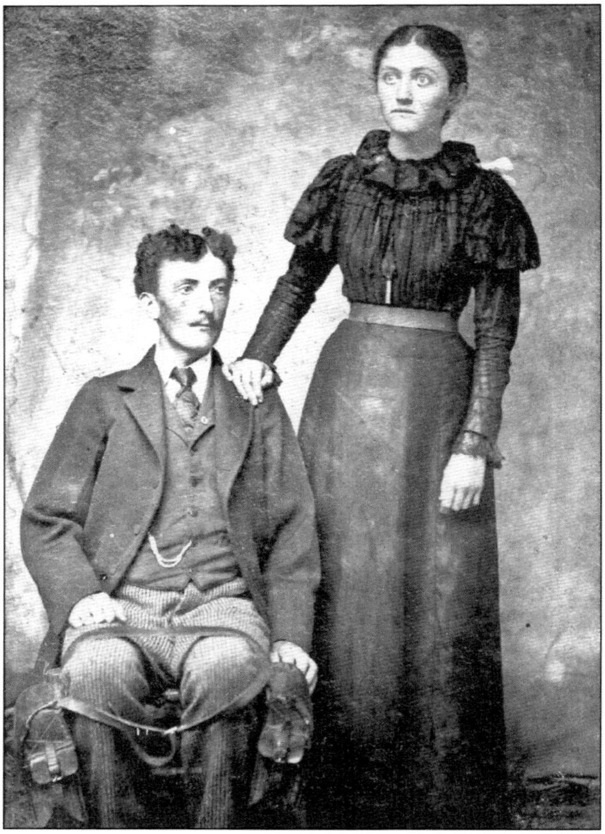

Miles O'Conner Gardner and wife Julia Banks posed for a wedding portrait at the end of the 19th century. Con, as he was called, later married Polly Honeycutt, daughter of Andy Honeycutt. The Gardners pioneered this land, and in this photograph, Con keeps his saddlebags securely on his knees. (Courtesy of Elaine McAlister Dellinger.)

Charlie Honeycutt held an annual reunion for many years. The son of Cora Honeycutt Bradford, he is pictured here with his wife, Hettie, (front and center) along with three of their daughters, Ester (middle left), Georgie, and Joanne (middle right), and several grandchildren in July 1990. Charlie was born in the Bald Mountain area; later in life, they moved to Johnson City, Tennessee. (Courtesy of Elaine McAlister Dellinger.)

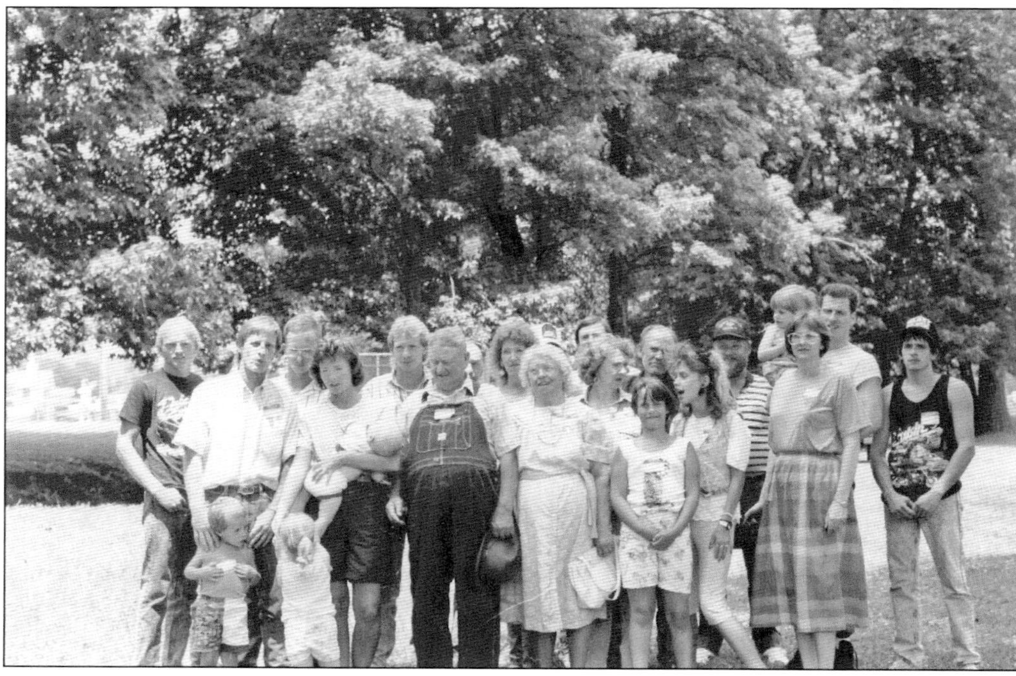

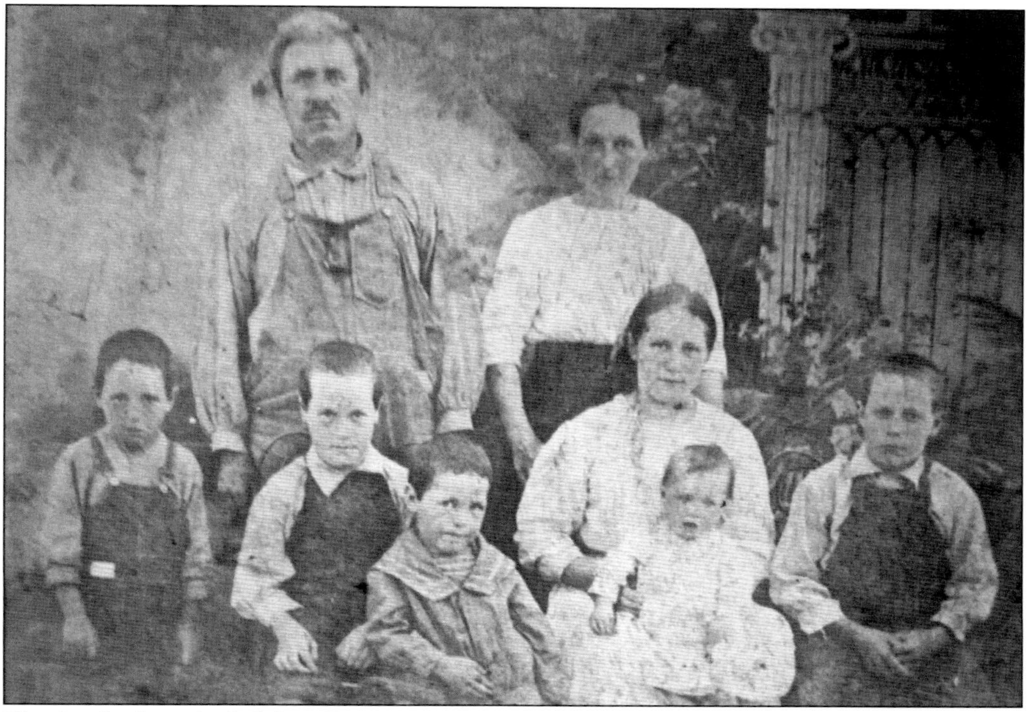

The family above hailed from Egypt Township. Andrew Johnson Shelton and Nancy Moriah Hensley took care of their own children and others, too. (Courtesy of Elaine McAlister Dellinger and others.)

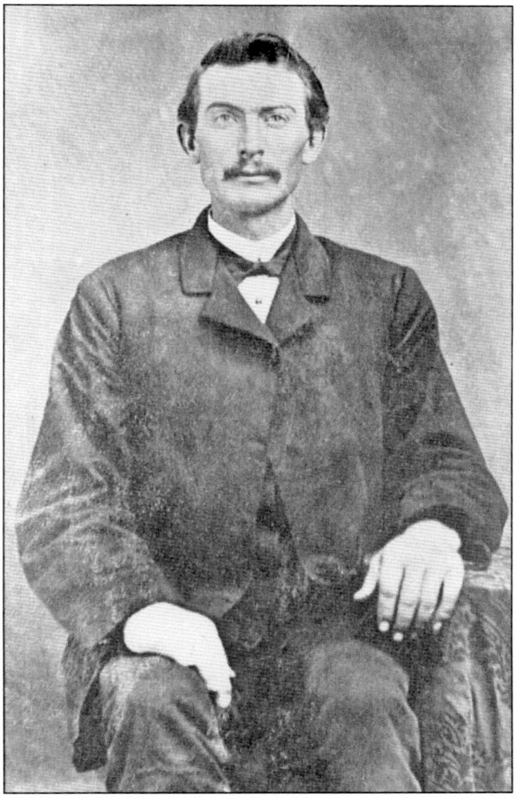

Washington Crumley Young, born in 1857, lived in Shoal Creek in the Windom Community. He married Harriet Young. (Courtesy of Barbara Ford.)

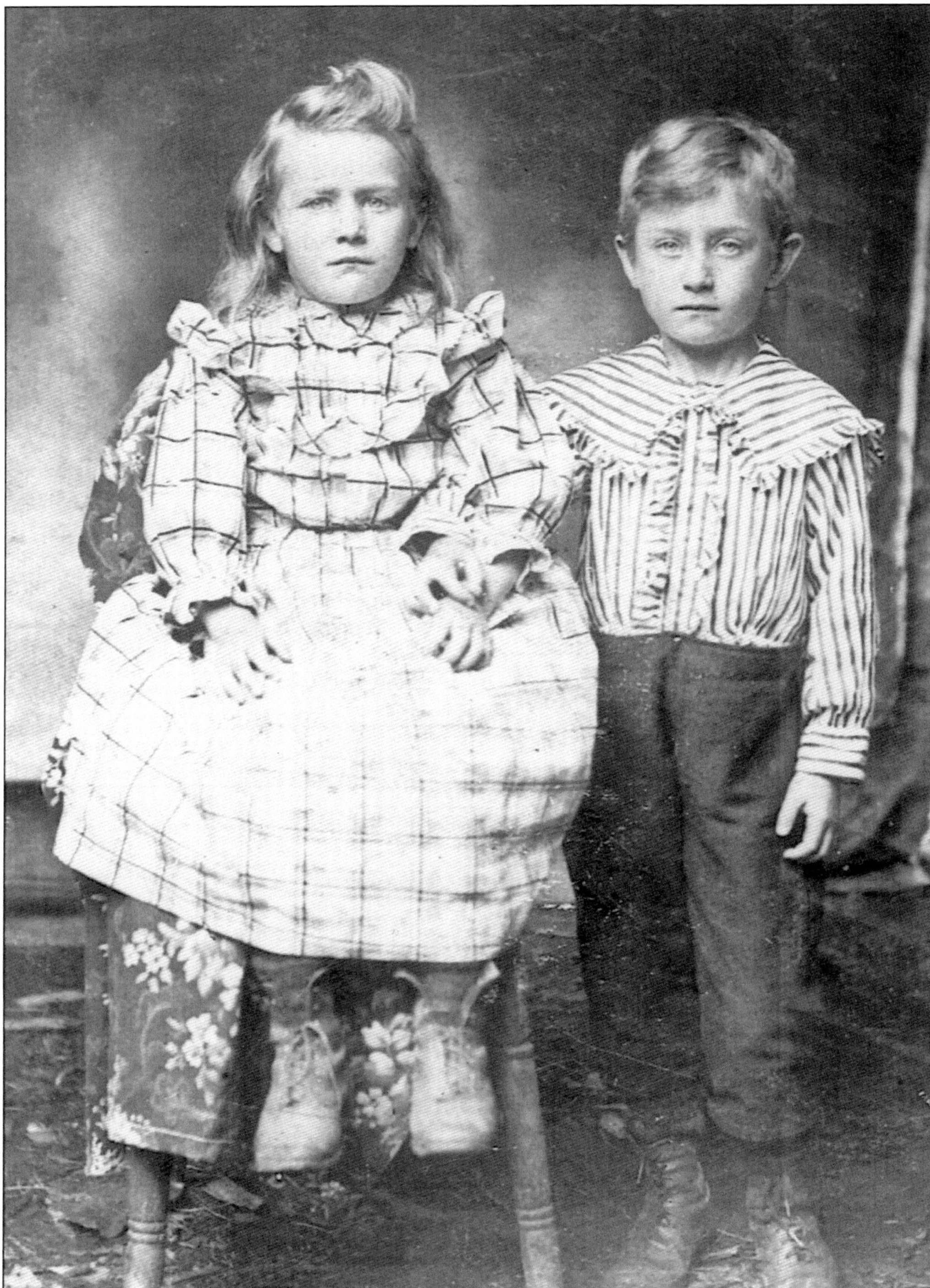

Etta and Charlie Deyton, children of Mary Bailey Deyton and Basil Deyton, lived in the Brush Creek area of Yancey and posed for this photograph in 1900. (Courtesy of Charlotte Anglin.)

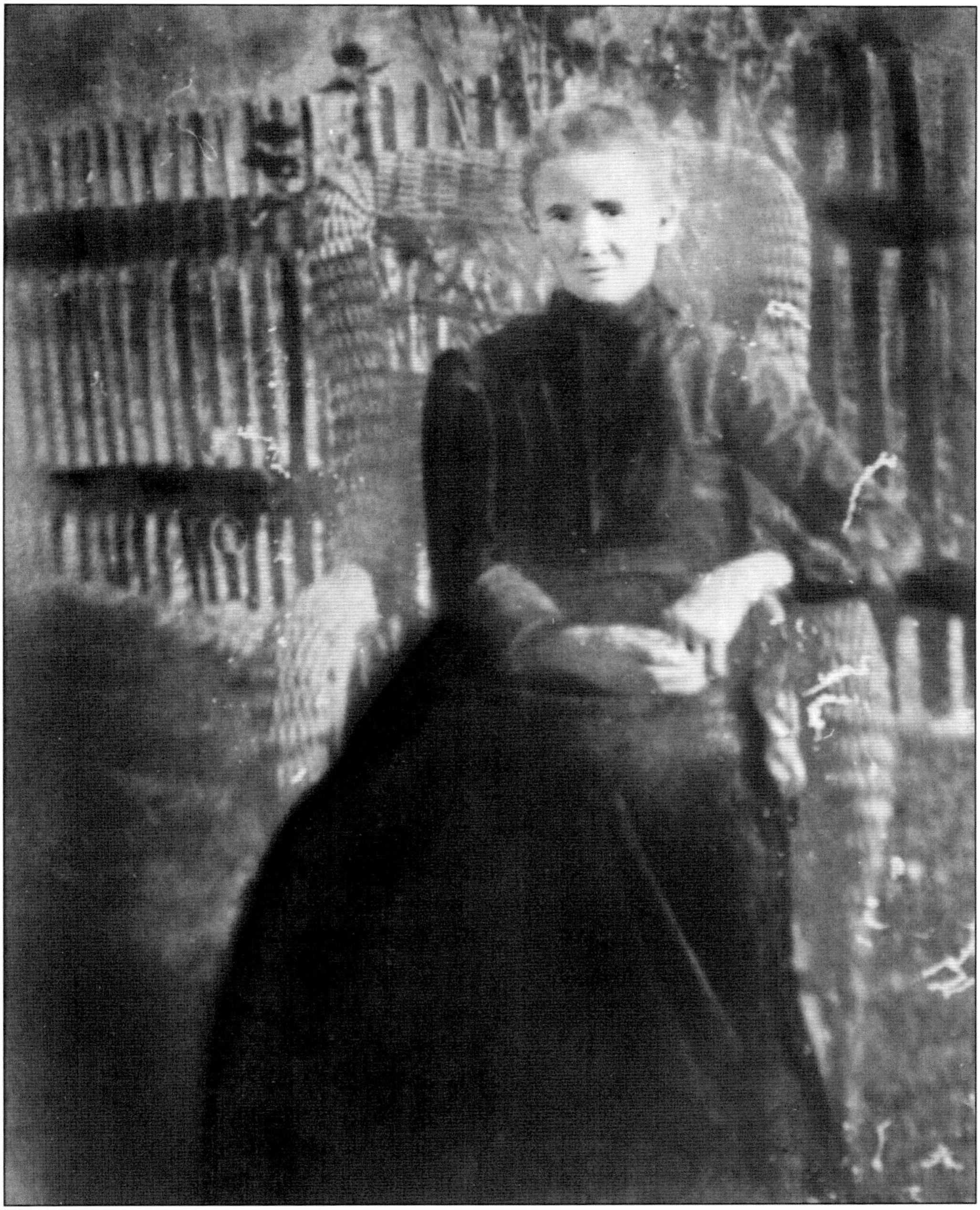

Lucretia "Crettie" Ray Dellinger was the wife of Logan Gamewell Dellinger, mother of Nathaniel Shelby Dellinger of Burnsville, and sister to Dr. Landon and Marion Ray. (Courtesy of Charles Lee Dellinger.)

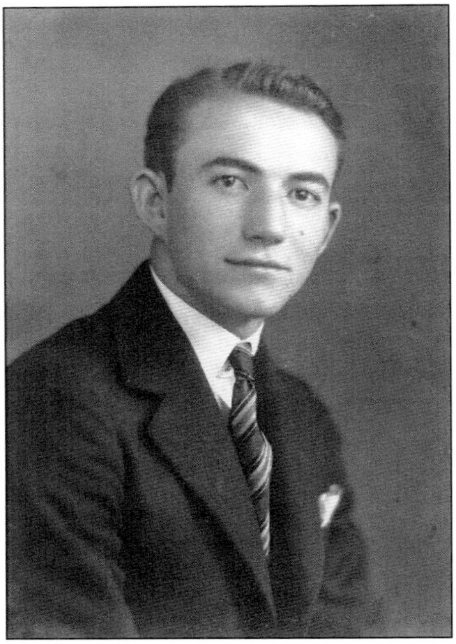

Roy Proffitt was the youngest son born to Albert Hooker Proffitt and Alice Wampler Proffitt of the Bald Creek community. Roy served as a teacher and was principal of the Bald Creek High School for several years. Later in his life, he moved to Charlotte, where he sold insurance. (Courtesy of Charles Lee Dellinger.)

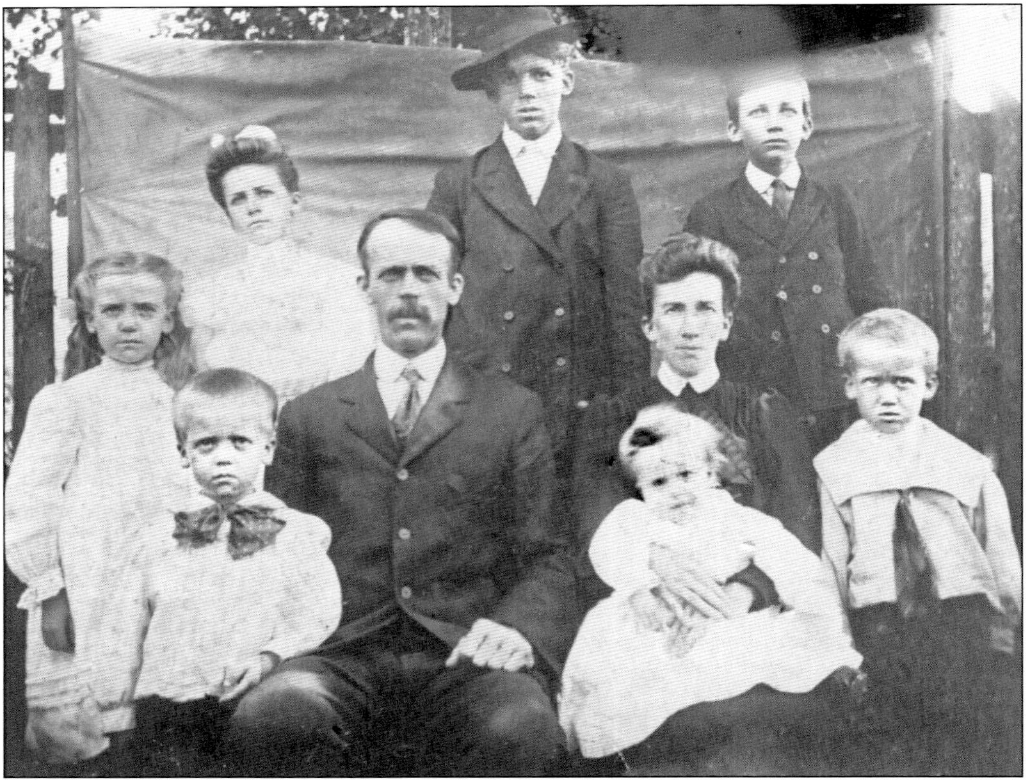

In this c. 1908 portrait of the Thomas Gamewell Dellinger family, seen from left to right are (first row) Joe Henry and Claude; (second row) Mamie, Thomas Gamewell, wife Margaret W., and Ebe; (third row) Dorothy, John, and Lyda. (Courtesy of Thomas P. Dellinger.)

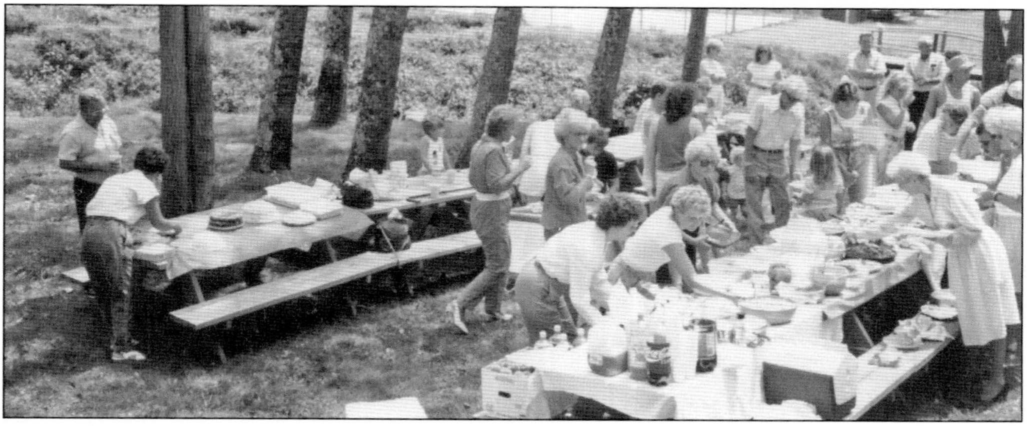

Descendants of Randolph and Elizabeth McAllister—more particularly, the children of John Wesley McAlister—meet in Burnsville, only a short walk from where Randolph and Elizabeth once lived. Many of the older generation has passed away since this photograph was taken in 1990. Among those pictured are Janie and Ralph McAlister, Babe and Virginia McAlister Ogle, Estoy Smith McAlister, Birdie McAlister, Barbara McAlister, Shirley Buchanan, June Jerome, Catherine and Bob Thomas, Edna McAlister, Charles and Elaine Dellinger, and many of the children and grandchildren. (Courtesy of Elaine McAlister Dellinger.)

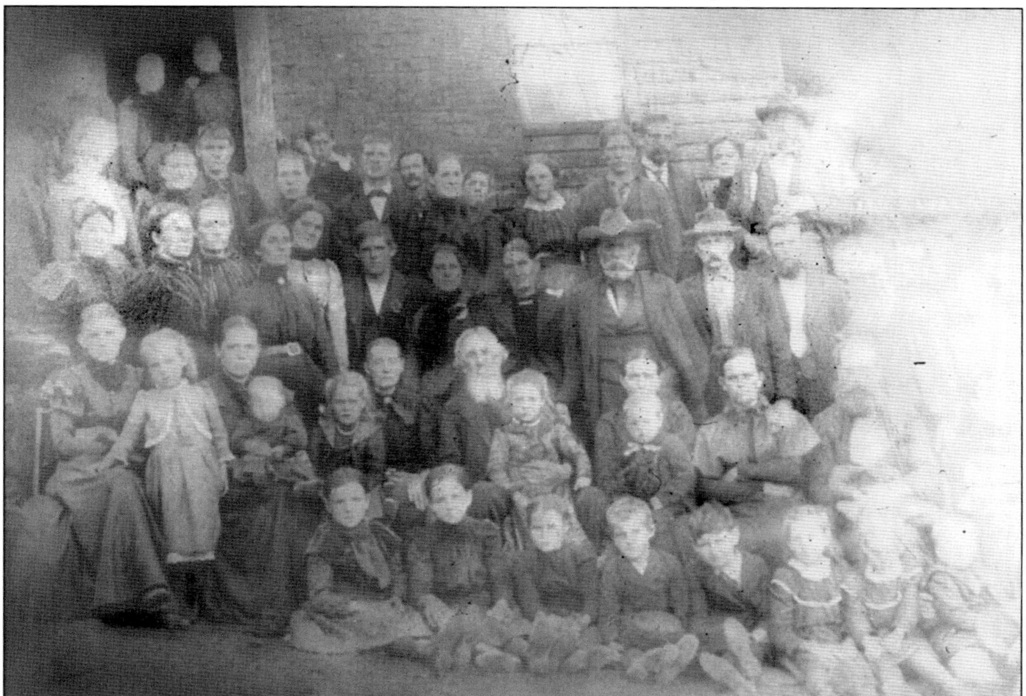

This 1899 family reunion brought together descendants of Logan Henry Dellinger, a slave owner. He served in the War Between the States under Brig. Gen. John Wesley McElroy in the 111th Division. His house servants lived in the basement of his home. One of them, fondly called "Aunt Channie," remained with the family even after the War Between the States. She later married William Wilson of the Whittington Farm. She died at age 98 and is buried in the Ray Cemetery off Prices Creek. (Courtesy of Charles Lee Dellinger.)

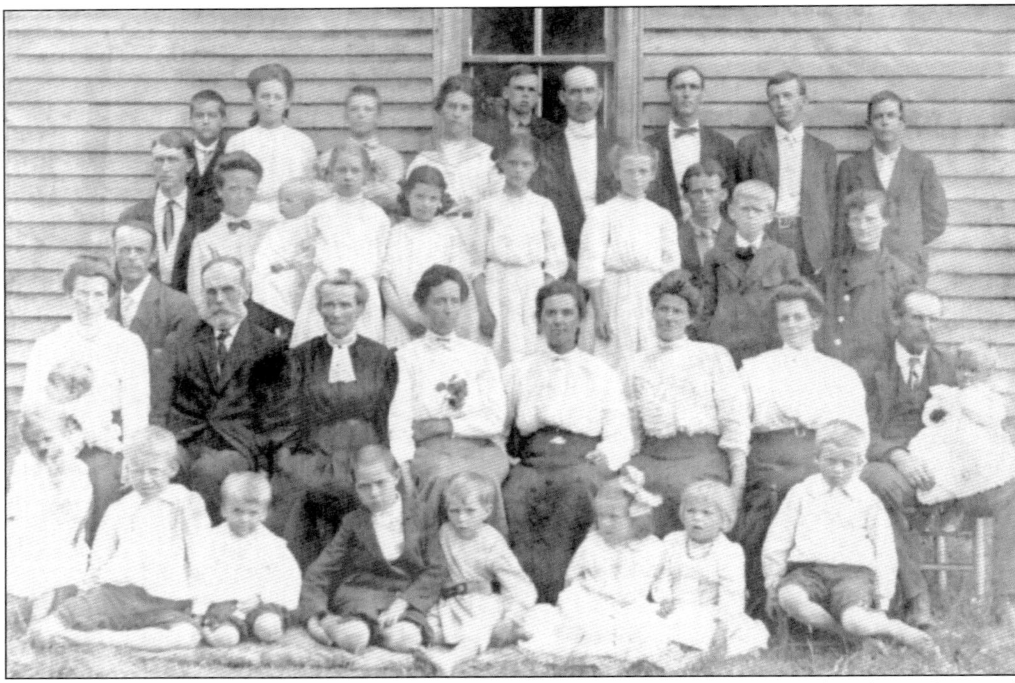

This 1911 photograph from the Pensacola area depicts the Dellinger and Ray family on Concord. Among those seen here are Solomon Dellinger, wife Mary Ann Ray, their son Thomas G. and his wife Margaret Wilson, and their daughters Margaret E., Sallie, and Joanna, posed with their children. (Courtesy of Thomas P. Dellinger.)

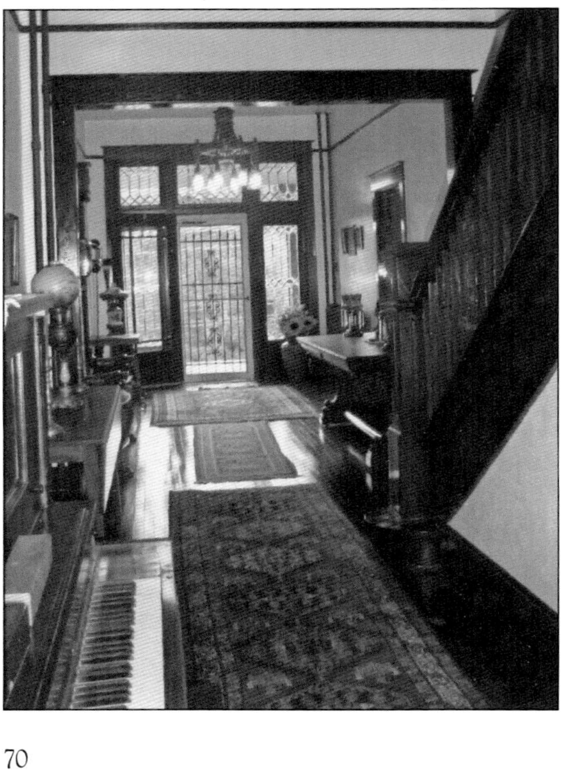

The Maples began as the home of John Watson, husband to Willie Dell. When he died in 1920, she began taking in boarders. When Willie Dell's brother-in-law started a boys' camp near the land, campers' parents stayed at the Maples. A nine-hole golf course graced the area. The house became the SEE Celo Painting School in 1948. It was sold to John Mays in 1960 and became Yancey County Child Development Center, the second CDC in North Carolina. Now the house has returned to its roots as a private home owned by Sam and Dixie Styles. (Courtesy of Dixie Styles.)

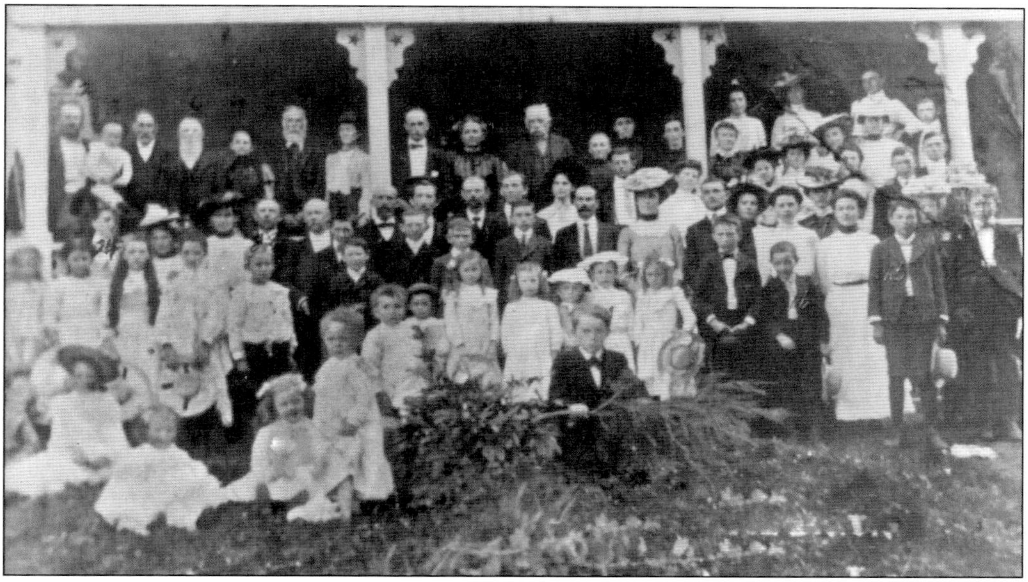

This Henry Ray reunion occurred in 1900. Many of Henry's descendants still remain in the Possum Trot community and beyond. (Courtesy of Virginia York.)

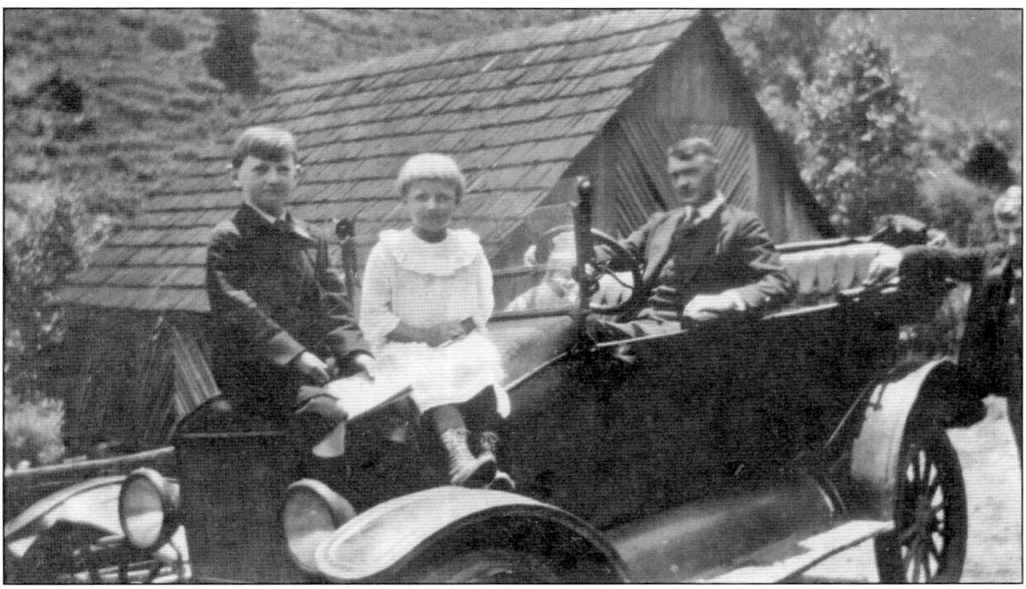

Monroe McIntosh was a Yancey County educator and family man. After Sunday school, he sometimes took the kids for a spin in his 1920 Ford, the family's first car. Seen here from left to right are Ward McIntosh, Doris Edwards, and Monroe McIntosh. (Courtesy of Carol and Joe Renfro.)

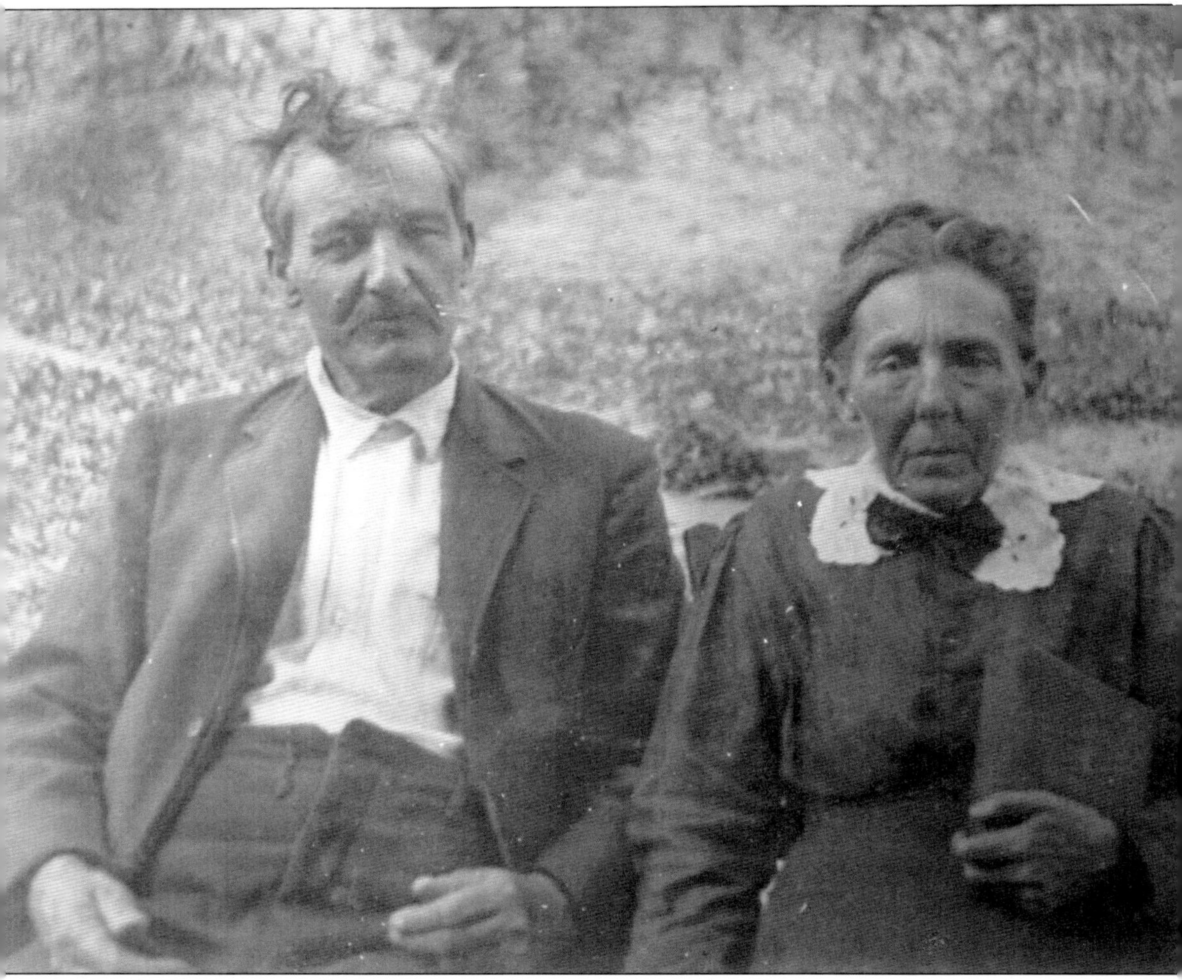

John and Rachel Allen McFalls lived on Pine Swamp when they were raising their family. They are buried at the Cane River Baptist Church cemetery with her parents, along with some of her children and their children's children. John's father had some connection with the Red String Society, believed to be part of the Underground Railroad in the Buck Creek area during the War Between the States. Rachel had three children (Mary Ann, Stonewall Jackson, and Andrew Jackson) by Andrew Jackson Brown prior to her marriage to John. (Courtesy of Elaine McAlister Dellinger.)

This bride and groom in horse and buggy are celebrating their wedding day. (Courtesy of Carol and Joe Renfro.)

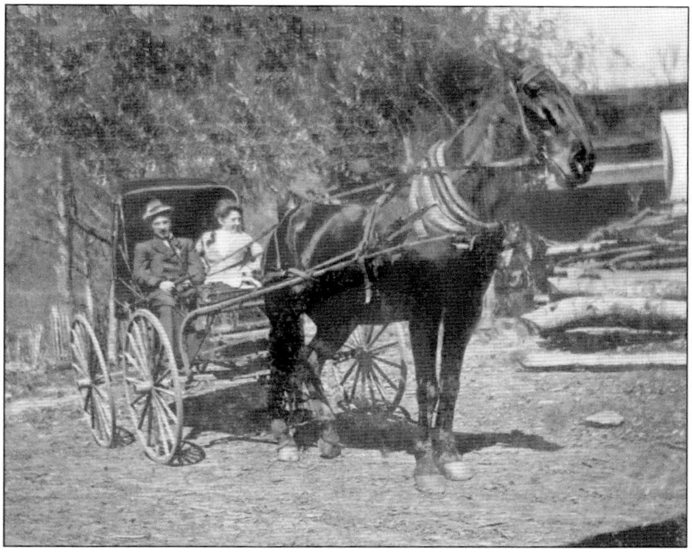

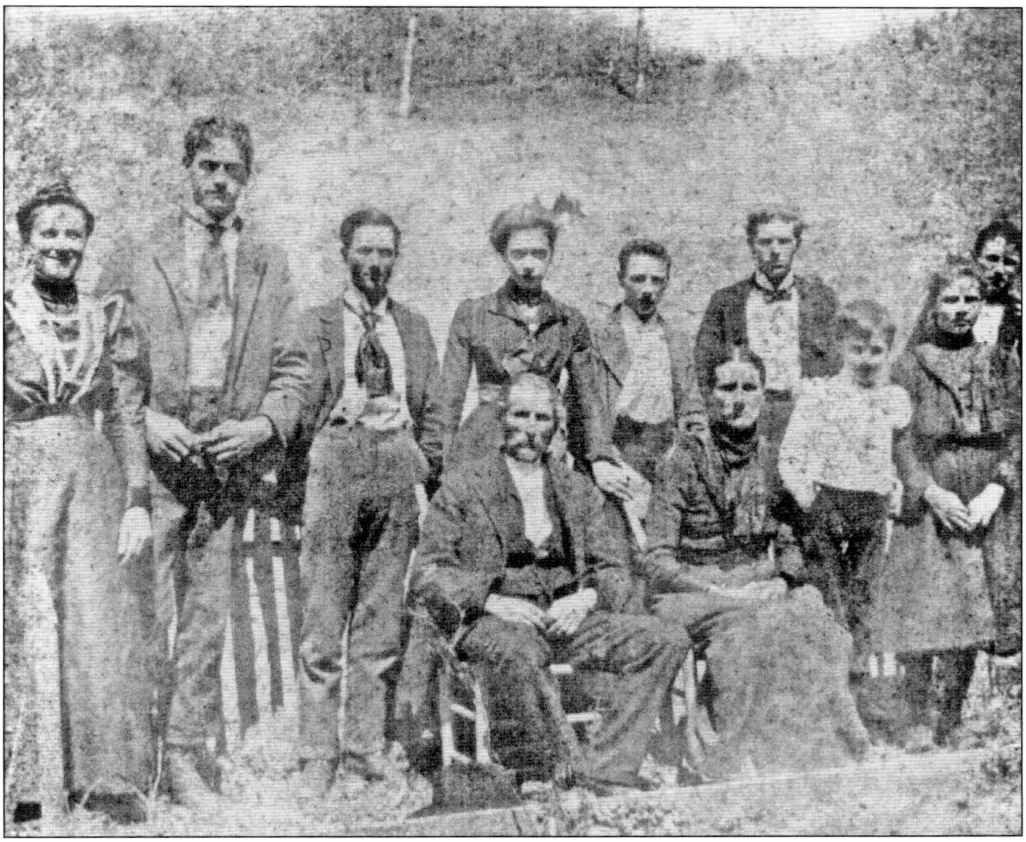

The Ervin Hensley family hailed from Bee Log. Ervin served as a Confederate soldier in Company C, 58th Rangers Infantry, North Carolina Troops. His discharge shows a "distinguished service" record for having been a substitute for his father Wallace C. Hensley, who had become ill and forced to return home to Bee Log. (Courtesy of Mike Shelton.)

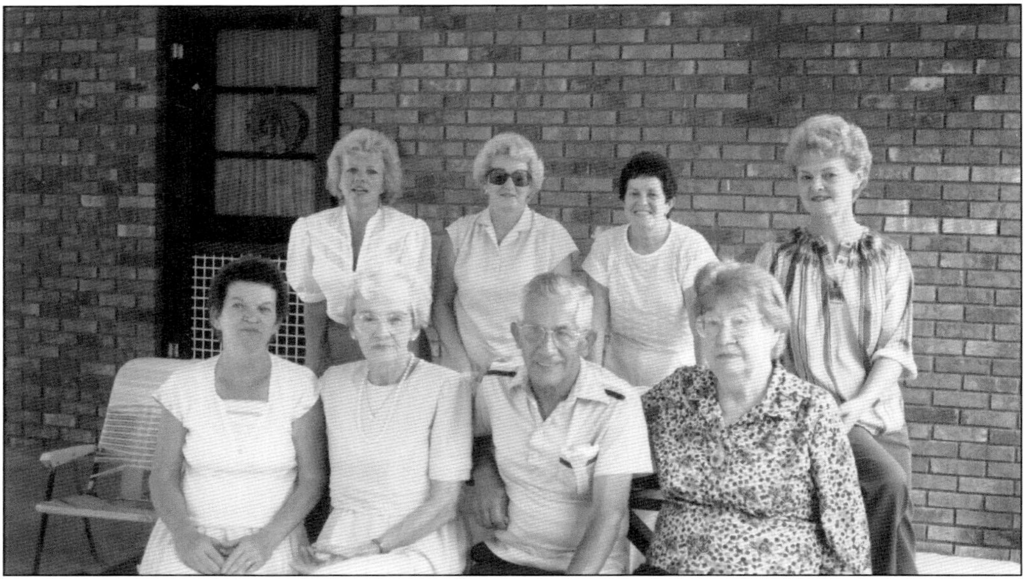

This 1989 photograph shows McAlister family members at the home of Margaret McAlister Crisp and her husband, Lewis. Seen here from left to right are (first row) Margaret West, wife of Howard; Estoy McAlister, wife of Fred McAlister; Howard West, brother to the McAlisters; and Birdie McAlister, wife of Burdett McAlister; (second row) sisters Catherine McAlister Thomas, Virginia Ogle, Edna McAlister, and Margaret Crisp. (Courtesy of Elaine McAlister Dellinger.)

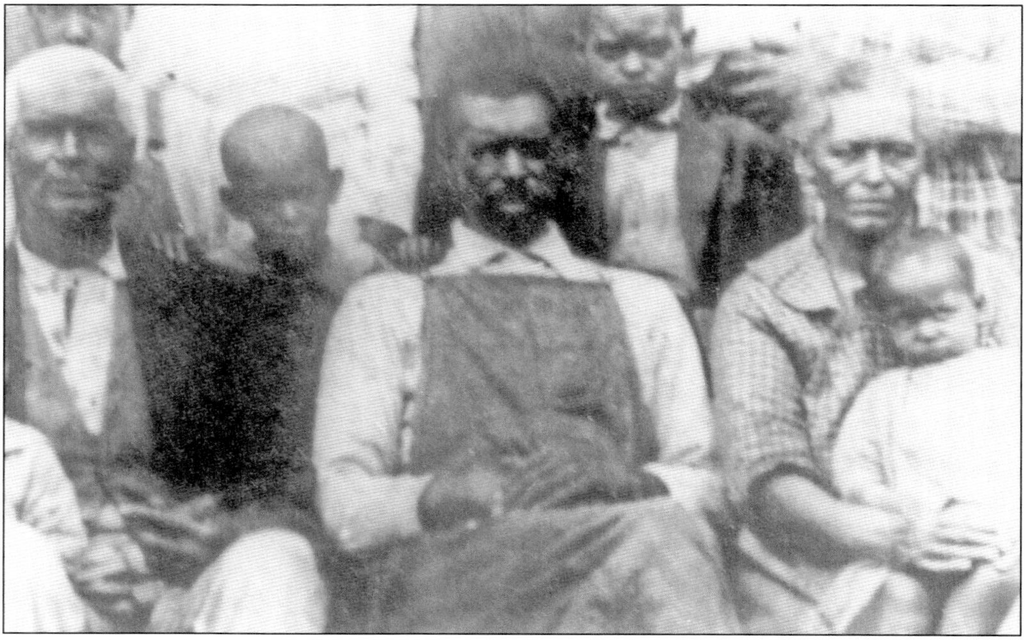

Rev. Grady Riddle is pictured here with his family when he was a young man. Born in January 1908, he became an ordained African Methodist Episcopal (AME) minister and died in March 2003. He had pastored Griffith Chapel AME Zion Church in Burnsville. He is buried in the Horton Hill Cemetery with his parents, Edward and Hattie Young Riddle, who also appear to be pictured here with him. (Courtesy of Elaine Gales.)

The best way to access the unique community of Lost Cove was to go to Mitchell County at Poplar and come by railroad track for two to two and a half miles until the traveler found a trail leading up from the old Wiley Tipton or Lost Cove Station mail drop, then head up the mountain the last half-mile to three-quarters of a mile by foot into the cove. Pictured here are some of the Miller family of the cove. (Courtesy of Grant Ward.)

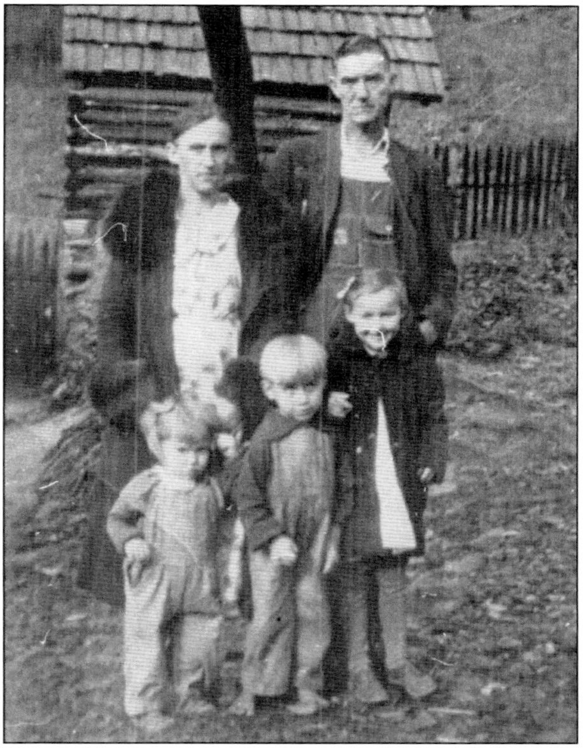

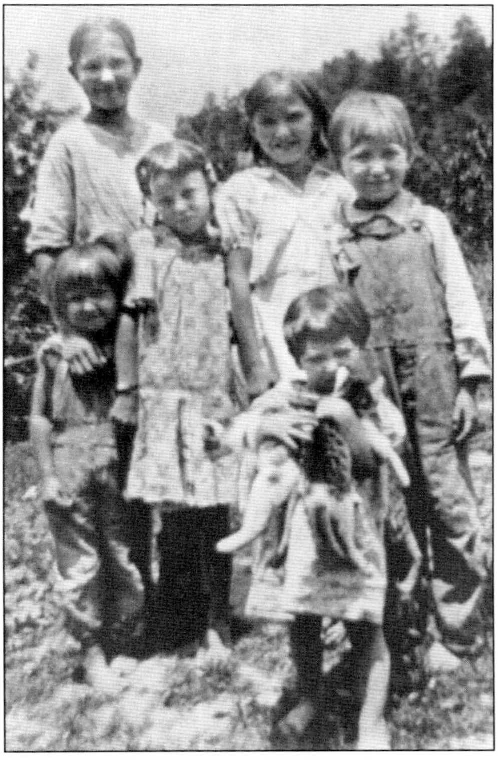

Lost Cove residents included four main families who lived and raised their families in the cove: the Millers, Tiptons, Baileys, and Bryants. They often worked part of the year in Erwin or Unaka Springs and returned to the cove the remainder of the time. Pictured here are some of the Miller children from the cove during the 1940s. (Courtesy of Grant Ward.)

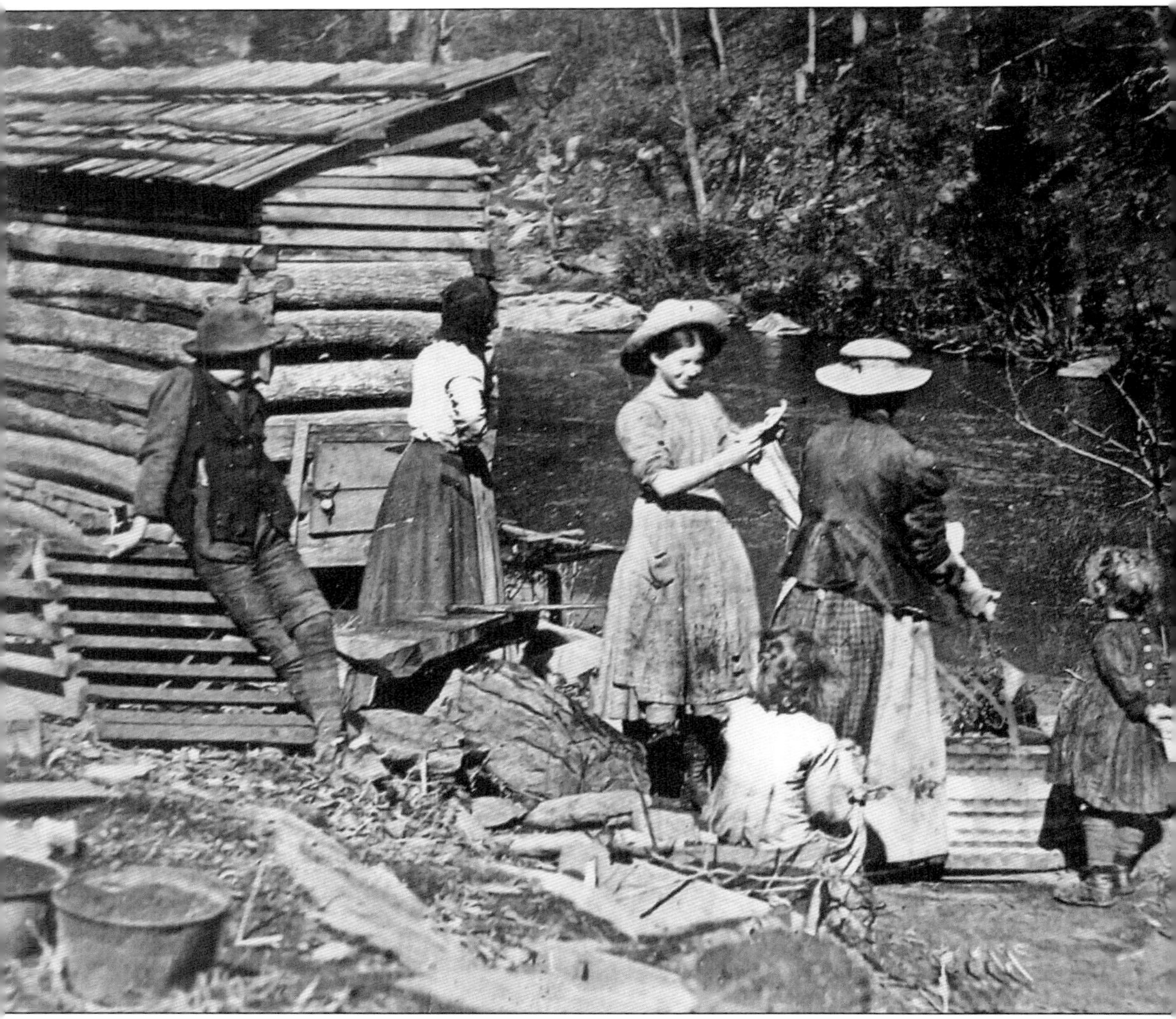

Pictured here around 1910 is the Howard family, washing clothes in Bald Creek near the Bee Log community. From left to right are Avery Howard, Sarah Howard, Nora Howard, Nancy Brown, Velda Brown, and Stella Howard. (Courtesy of Dorothy McMahan.)

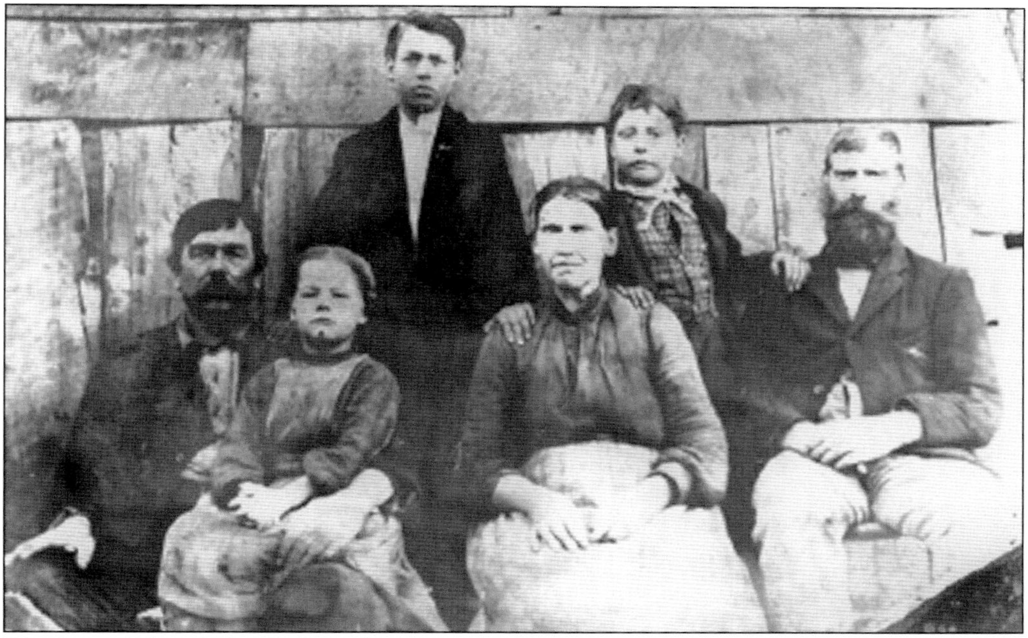

The Jasper Edwards family from the Bee Log community is pictured here. At the far left in the first row is Jasper (1850–1912), the son of "Sheep-Eating Jim" Edwards. To the right of him is his granddaughter Lethia (born 1903). To the right of Lethia is Jasper's wife, Mary Jane Lewis Edwards (1852–1917), the daughter of Robert Lewis and Martha Willis. On the far right of the first row is Chedo Lumuel Edwards (1871–1960). In the second row, from left to right are Noah (1896–1933) and Alonzo "Lonnie" (1900–1989). (Courtesy of Mike Shelton.)

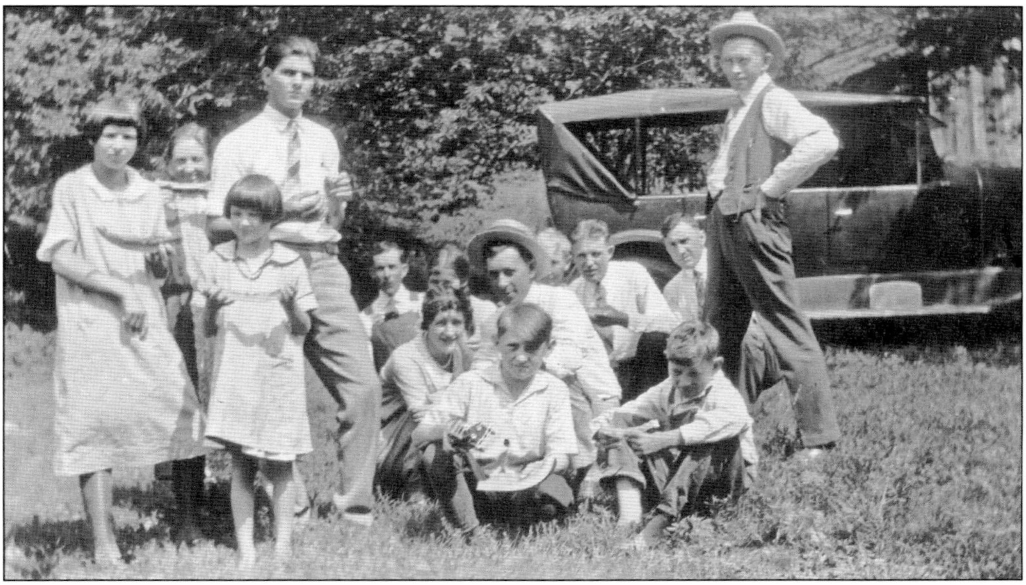

The Renfro family loved their REO. Shown here are Ruby Renfro, Kittee Hensley McIntosh, Charles Renfro, Elizabeth Renfro, Ward McIntosh, Lloyd Hogal, Willard, Carl (standing, in vest), Don (curled up, front) J.W. Renfro, Margaret Willa "Bill" Renfro, Margie, and Zelze. (Courtesy of Carol and Joe Renfro.)

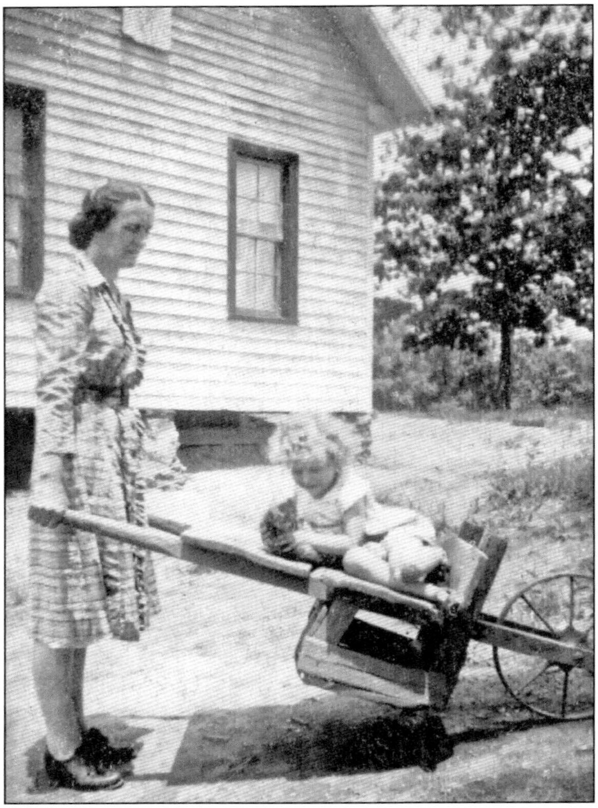

Lucille Hughes gives a ride to her young friend, Bonnie Bedford or Gladys Ponder, in a homemade wheelbarrow. (Courtesy of Robin Owen.)

Nathaniel Shelby and Martha Hutchins Dellinger farmed near Burnsville on Dellinger Hill. They owned all the land on the hill; back then, it ran from near where the West Burnsville Church of God now stands to the road leading to the new health department and medical center. His father Logan Gamewell and grandfather Logan Henry owned even more adjoining land. Notice Shelby's leggings, popularized in the early 1800s. (Courtesy of Charles Lee Dellinger.)

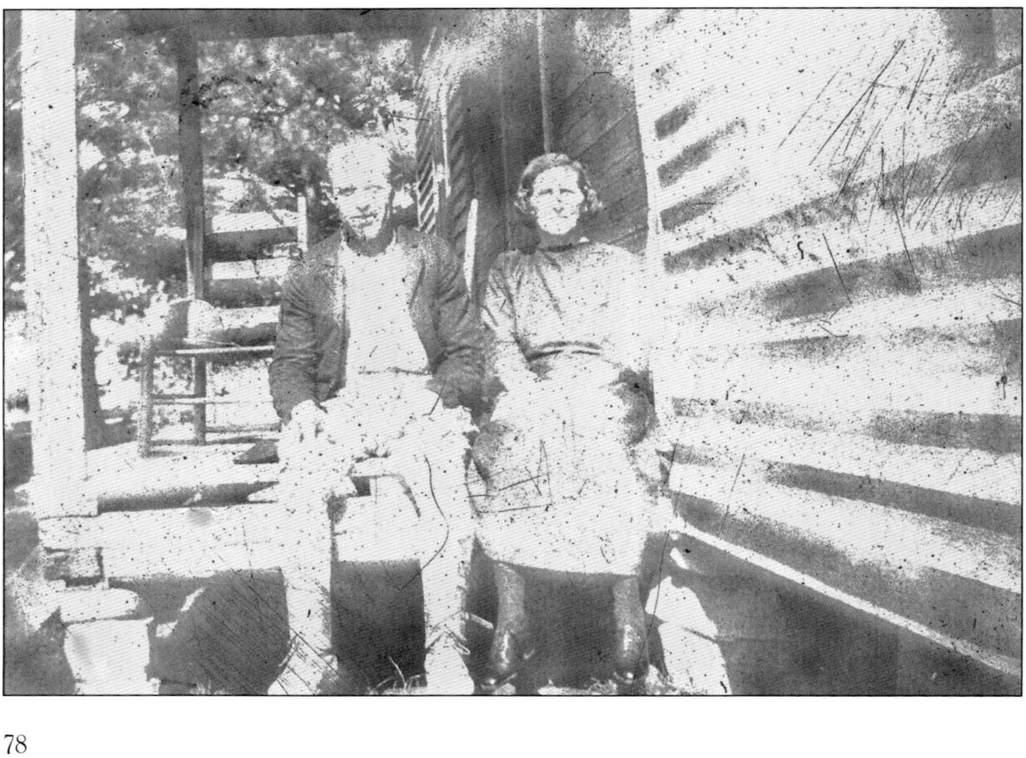

Silas Willard McIntosh resided in Bee Log in 1900. He lived to be 93 years old. (Courtesy of Carol and Joe Renfro.)

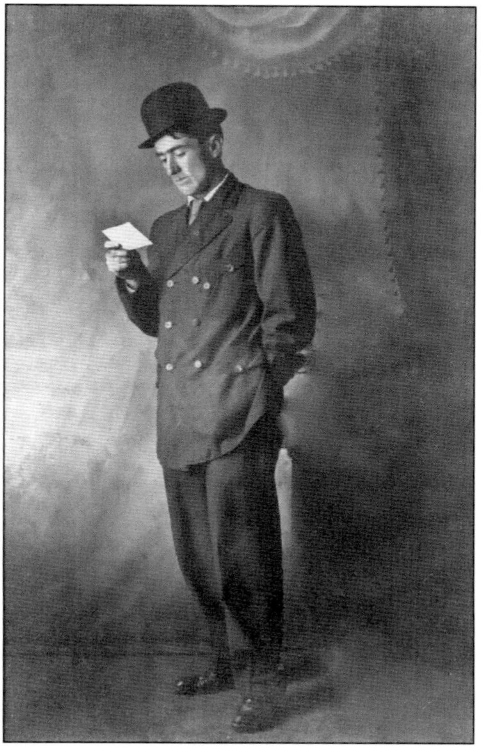

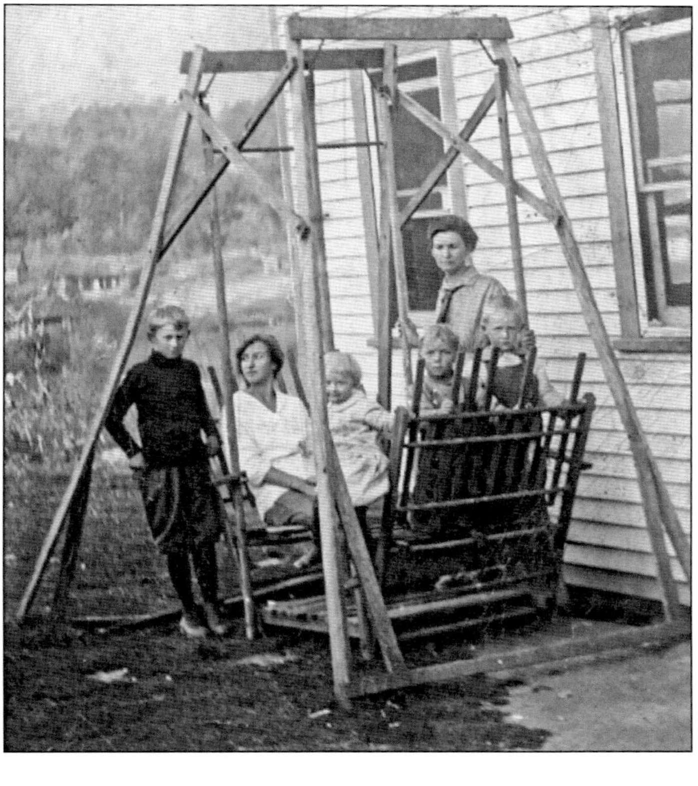

The porch swing provided some serene moments. Seen here from left to right are Lee Evans, unidentified, Elizabeth Evans, Selvey Ramsey, Sol Evans, and Pruella Evans (standing). (Courtesy of Nancy Randolph Silvers.)

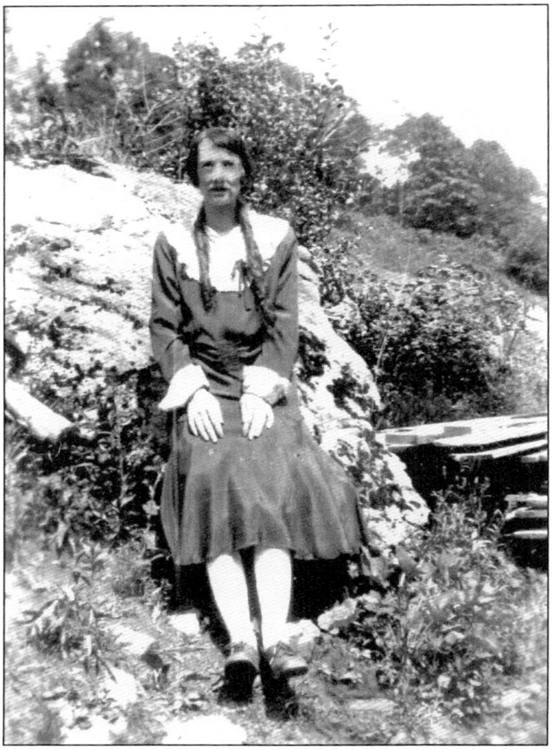

Ethel Honeycutt, the daughter of Irene Ledford, lived in the Bald Creek area. (Courtesy of Elaine McAlister Dellinger.)

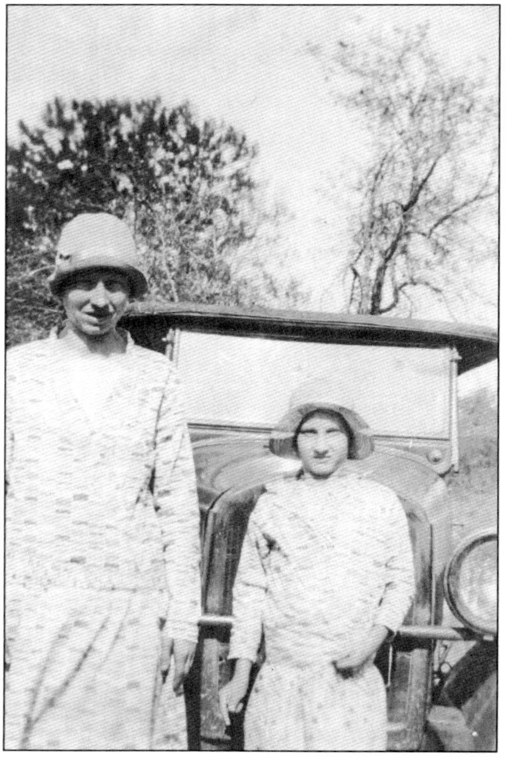

Shown here are Aleathia "Leathie" Honeycutt (left) and baby sister Lillian "Lillie" standing in front of their brother Hayden's 1920s car. Leathie never married and died in 1930. Lillie married Lonnie B. Woody. They lived on Hardscrabble Road. (Courtesy of Elaine McAlister Dellinger.)

Warren Burdett and Birda Elizabeth "Birdie" Honeycutt McAlister had this picture taken at Birdie's sister Ida Robertson's house in Lickskillet in the spring of 1940, a few months before they married. Warren served in World War II, and Birdie was a devoted housewife and mother of two girls, Elaine and Shirley. They were married 43 years until his death in 1983. (Courtesy of Elaine McAlister Dellinger.)

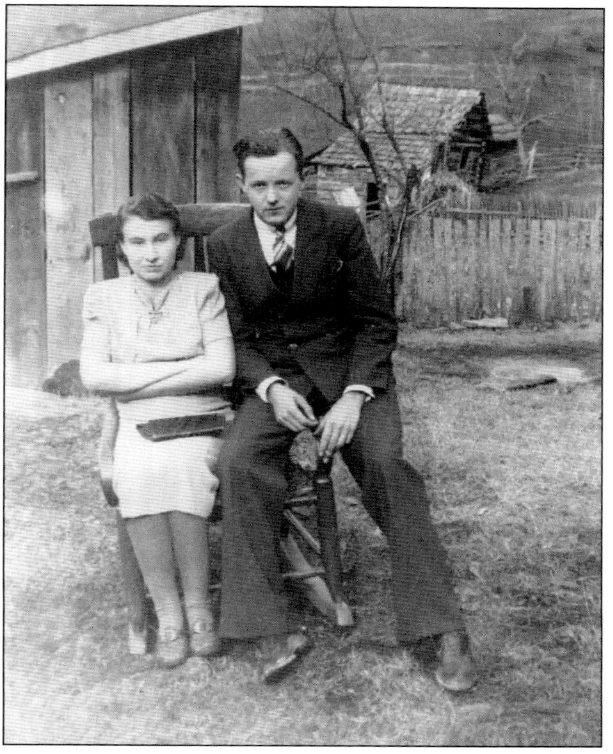

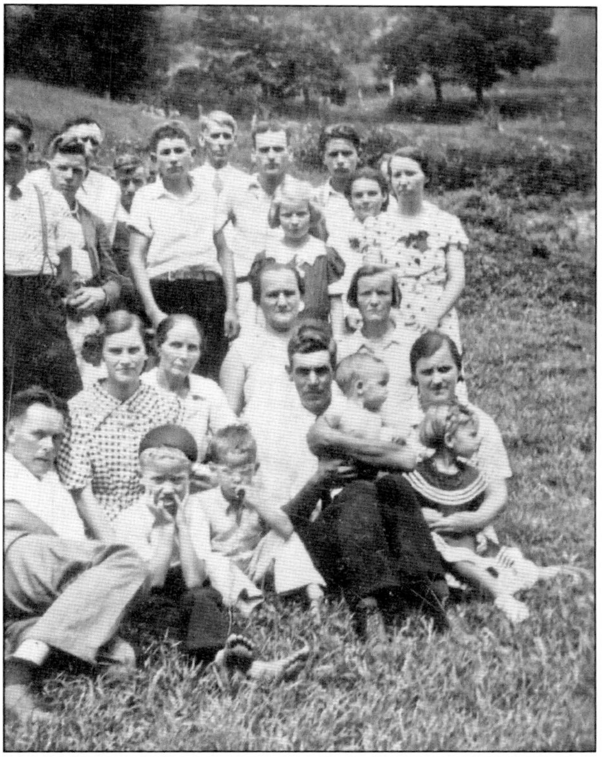

The Hilemon family lived in Higgins. In 1936, they gathered at Bill Wheeler's home. Pictured here from left to right are (first row) Banister Hensley, George "Buck" Randolph, Dexter Randolph, Andy Tipton holding J.T. Randolph, and Madge Wheeler Randolph holding Lillian Randolph; (second row) Pansy Wheeler, Bertha Hilemon, Linda Hilemon Wheeler, and Rose Hilemon Tipton; (third row) Mabel Hilemon and Zula W. Wheeler; (fourth row) Jim Wheeler, Will Wheeler, Tom Wheeler, Lawrence Tipton, and Florence Tipton; (fifth row) four unidentified. (Courtesy of Carolyn Wheeler Byrant.)

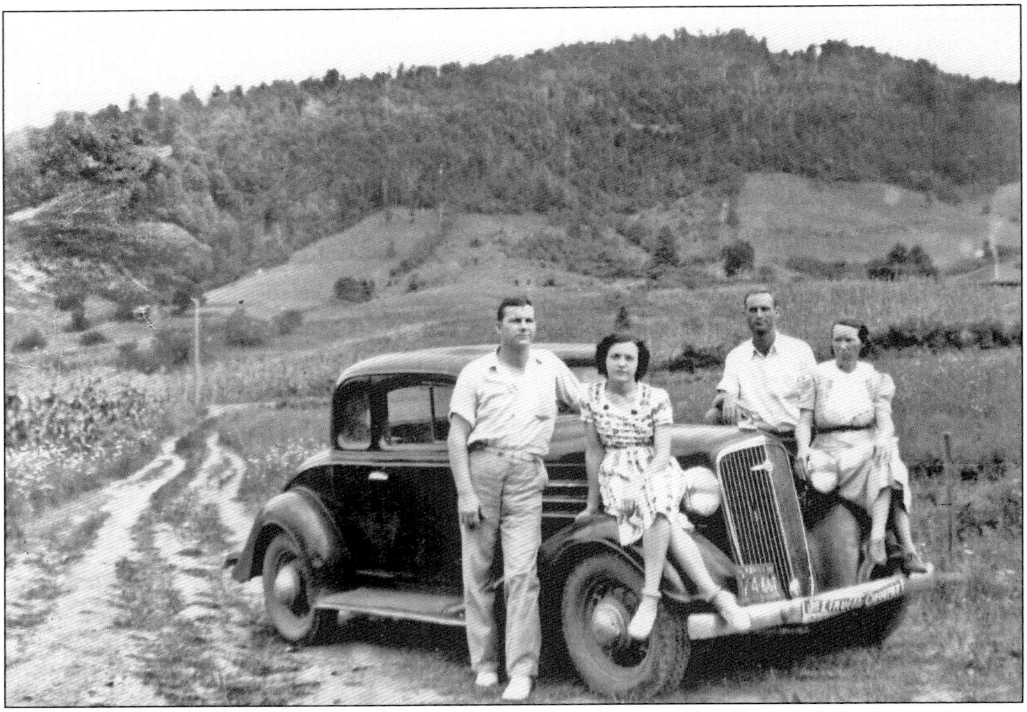

George and Zula Womack Wheeler (the couple at right) owned a dairy farm in Yancey, and Zula wrote gospel songs and poems. They met in a hospital where Zula worked as a nurse. George was foreman at a prison, and a prisoner turned a barrel of oil on him and tried to escape. Zula nursed George back to health, and they stayed together ever afterwards. Here, they relax after a ride with her brother Worth Womack and his wife, Mamie. (Courtesy of Carolyn Wheeler Byrant.)

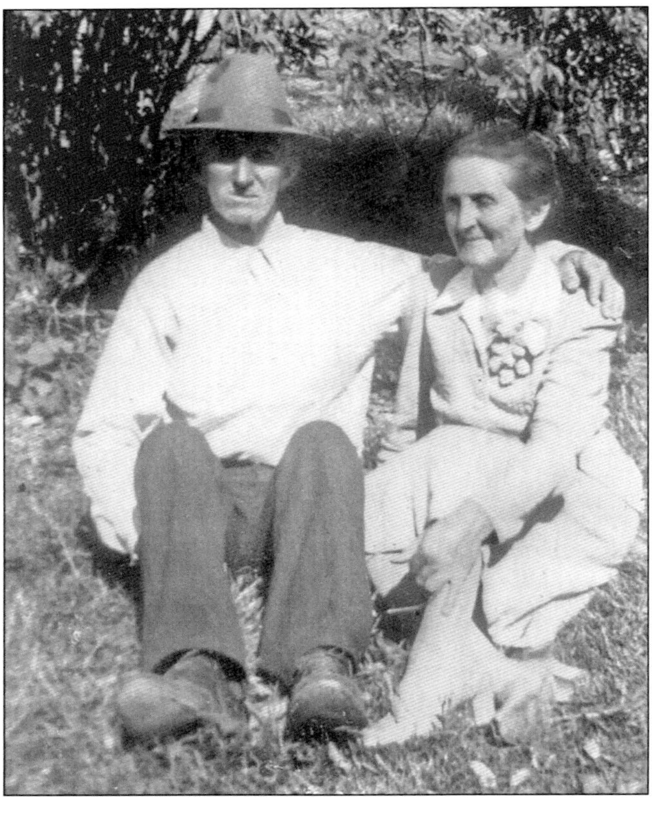

William M. Hughes and Addie Banner Brinkley, born in 1884, resided in the Shoal Creek community. (Courtesy of Robin Owen.)

Isaac M. and Sallie King Randolph lived on Angel Branch Road in the Swiss community. They had the following children: Lourene, Inez, Madge, Ben, Roy, Sam and Billy. Two of their children, Jeter and Bobby, died at young ages. (Courtesy of Nancy Randolph Silvers.)

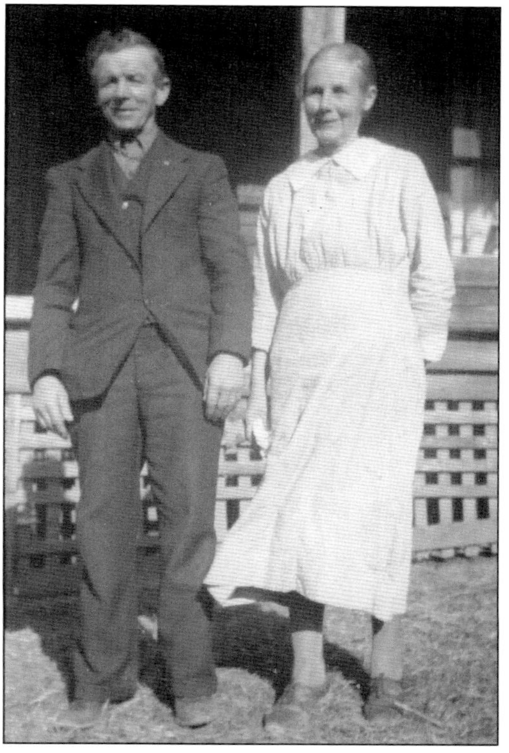

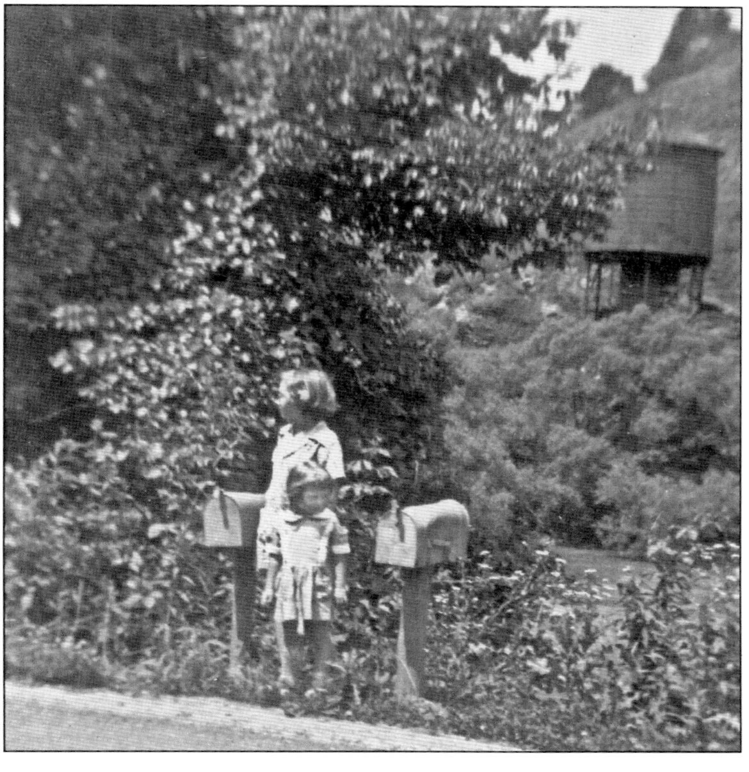

In years past, the highlight of many a child was to watch for the "mail boy" to arrive. Betty Lou (left) and Linda Peterson were no different. The mail could bring anything—catalogues, letters from afar, cards—and in the days before cell phones and email, the mail meant the link to everything beyond Yancey County. (Courtesy of Betty Lou Young and Linda Peterson Cox.)

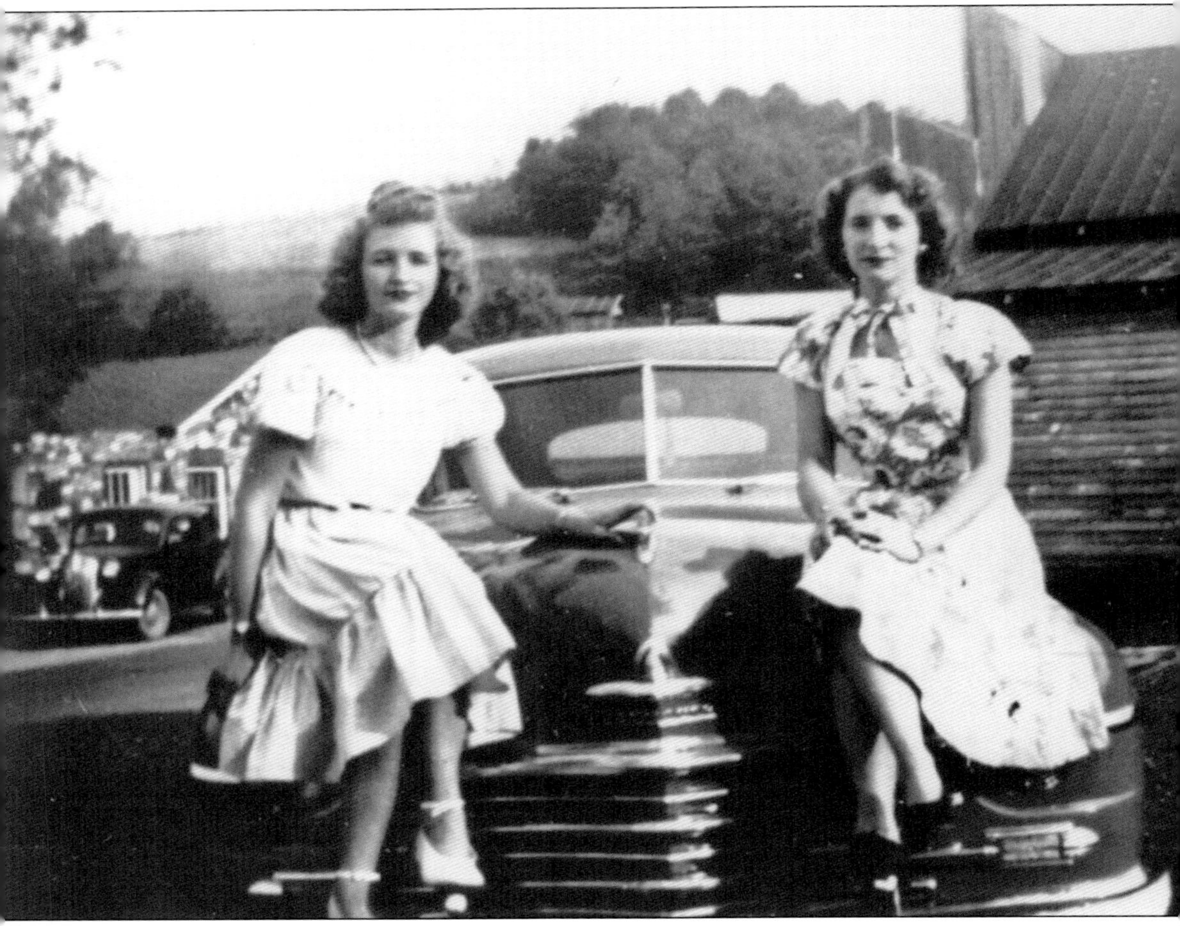

Marie Gibbs (left) and Mildred Gibbs sit on top of Mildred's first car, a 1947 Plymouth that cost $1,430 new. (Courtesy of Mildred Gibbs Harris.)

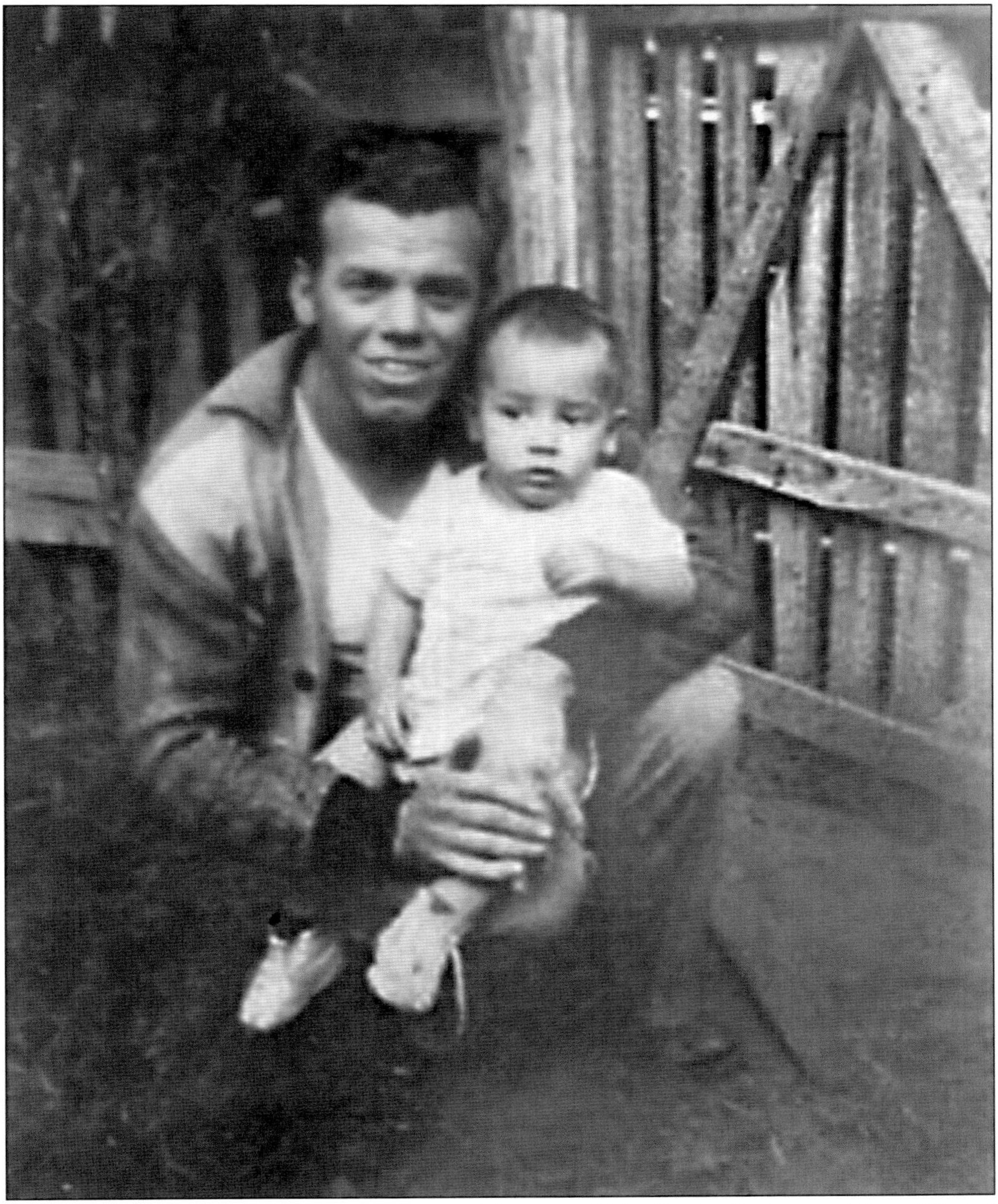

Paris Dillard Shelton Sr., born in Bee Log and the son of Riley Erwin Shelton and Dora "Dorie" Edwards Shelton, also of Bee Log, holds his nephew, Edward "Eddie" Shelton, the son of Henry Rush Shelton and Burleigh Shelton. (Courtesy of Mike Shelton.)

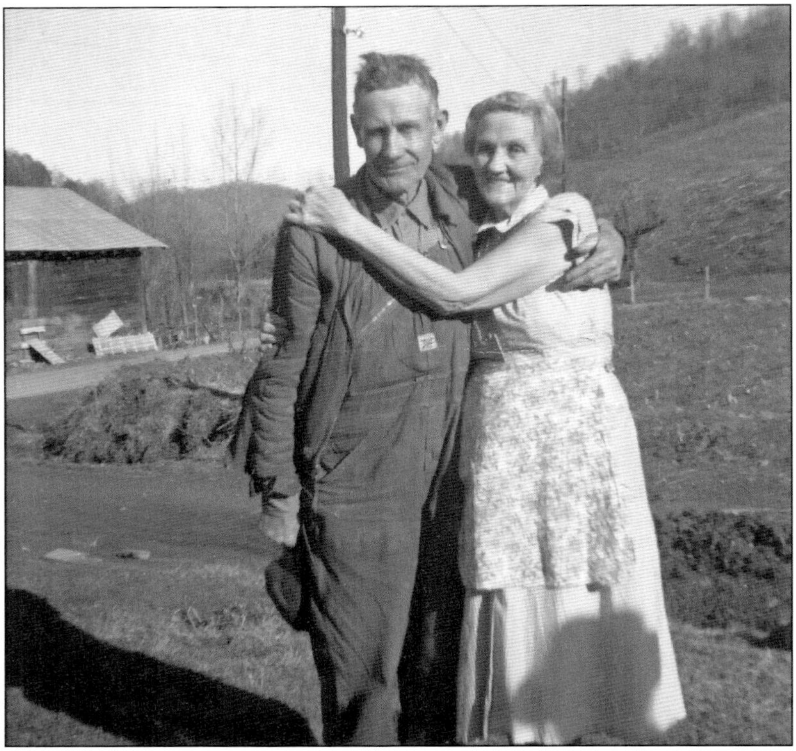

John Lafayette Penland and Bessie Metcalf Penland loved each other all their lives and worked hard on their land at Horton Creek. They had three sons. (Courtesy of Tim Penland.)

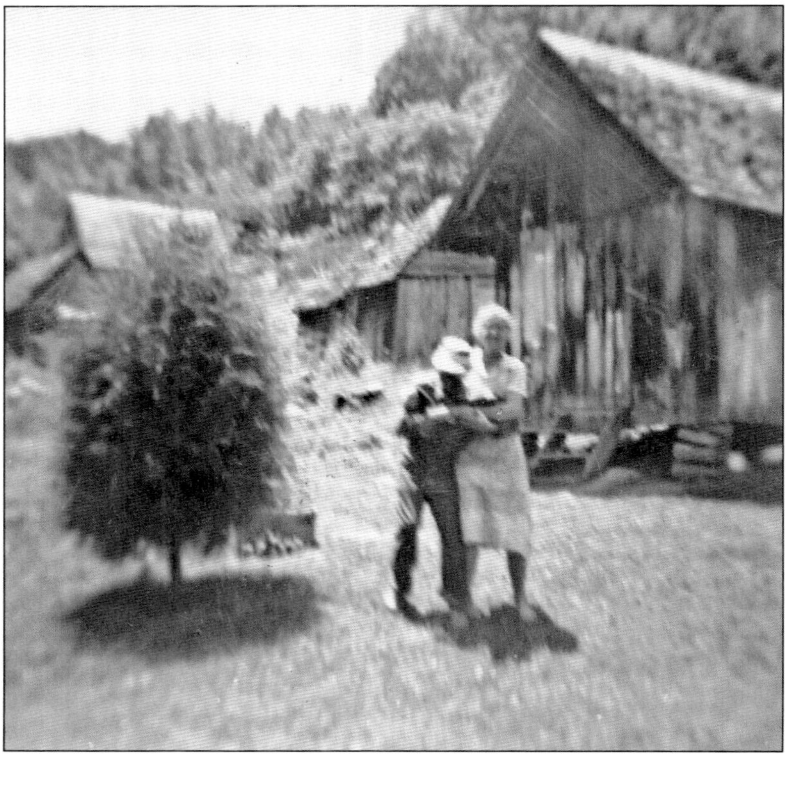

Charlie and Bertha Byrd lived in Green Mountain. They were caught in a playful moment in this 1957 photograph. The corn shed, the barn, the wood house, and the smokehouse are gone now. The yard had a washtub full of flowers; if something wore out for one use, it could be used for another. (Courtesy of James Byrd.)

Ona Woody and Charlie Hopson were wed in 1946, only months after his discharge in from the US Air Force (1943–1945). S.Sgt. Charlie Hopson served in the 568th Squadron as a B-17 Flying Fortress nosegunner with 33 missions over Germany and occupied territory. He came through the war unscathed except for a small shrapnel wound on his leg. He served his nation well. (Courtesy of Ona Hopson and Amy Hopson McCurry.)

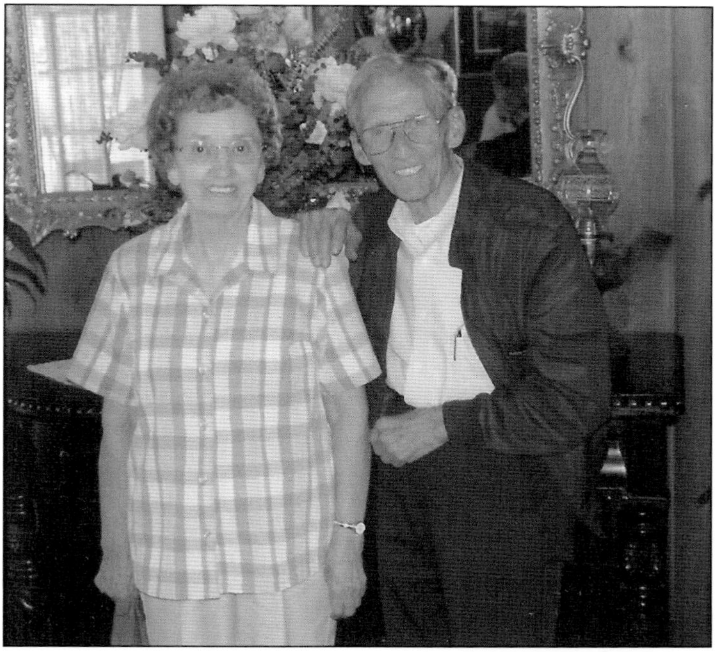

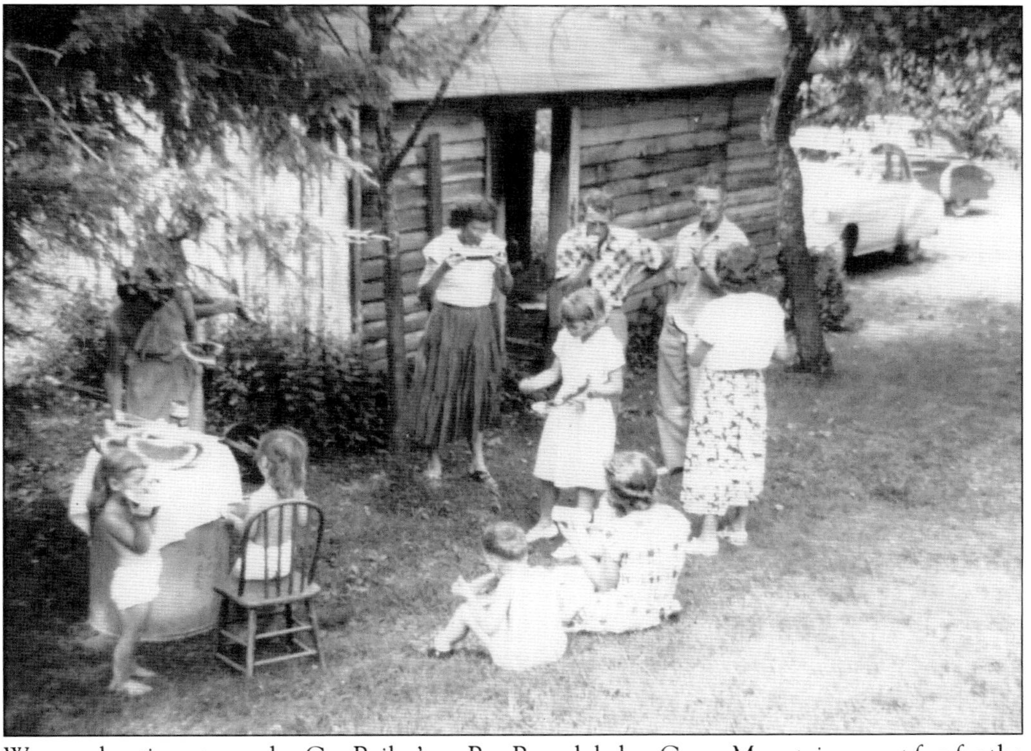

Watermelon time at grandpa Gus Bailey's on Bee Branch below Green Mountain meant fun for the whole family. Seen here from left to right are Linda Peterson, Judy Garland, unidentified, Bobby Schwager, Ruth Bailey Moody, Betty Lou Peterson, Kate Peterson, Gus Bailey, Park Peterson, and Mary Garland. (Courtesy of Betty Lou Young and Linda Cox.)

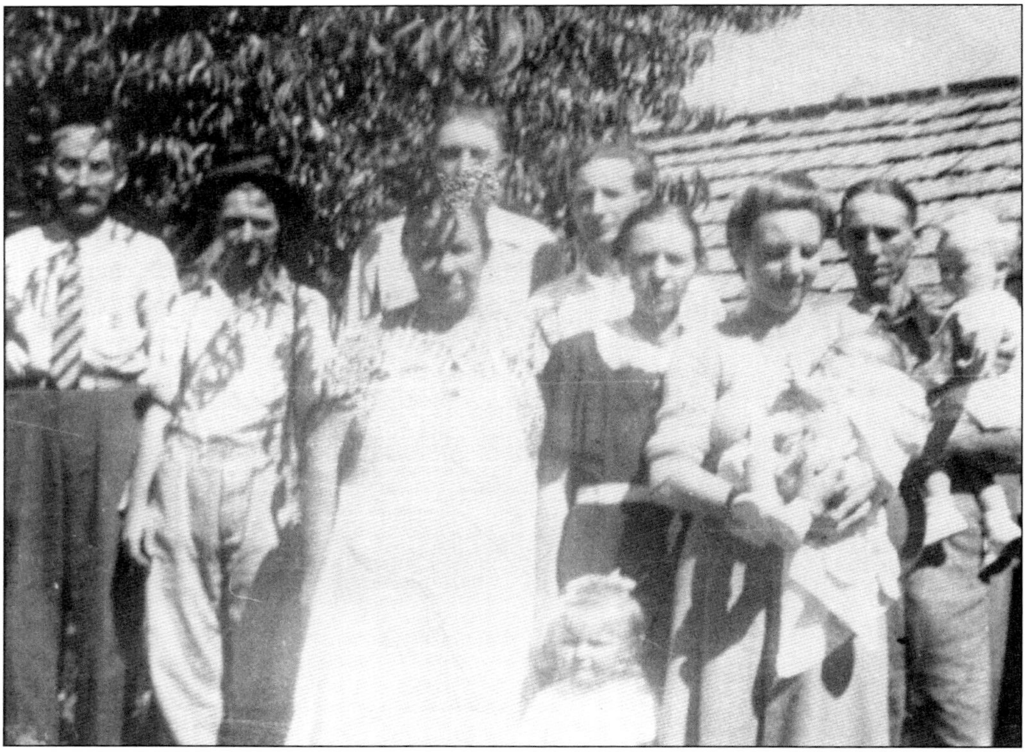

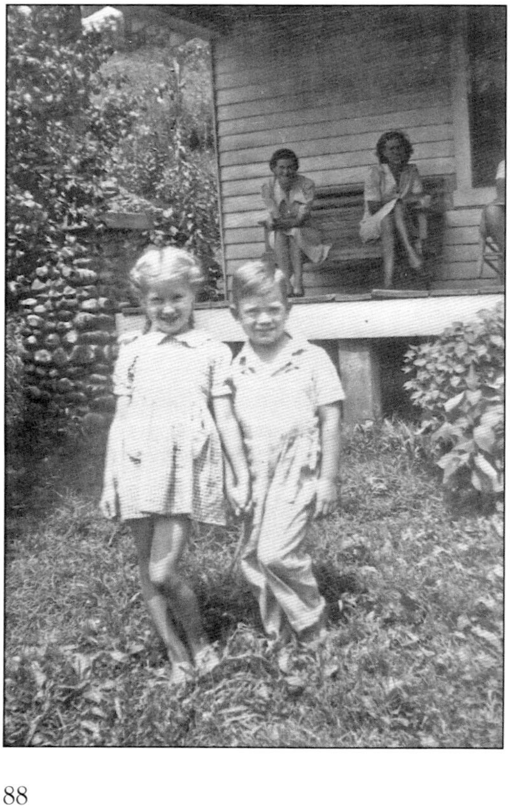

Lost Cove families have all moved out, and many of them have passed away, leaving only fragmented stories of their life and times in the cove. Pictured here are some of the faces one would have seen there. From left to right are Jace Miller, Sam Miller, Swin, Martha, Everett, Carrie, June, Carol, Ellen, Chester, and Russell Lyn. Lost Cove lay on the border between North Carolina and Tennessee. The depot once called Caro-Tenn was later known as Lost Cove. (Courtesy of Grant Ward.)

Cousins often become best friends, like Earl Webb and his cousin Annette Garland, seen here in the 1940s near Green Mountain. (Courtesy of Earl Webb.)

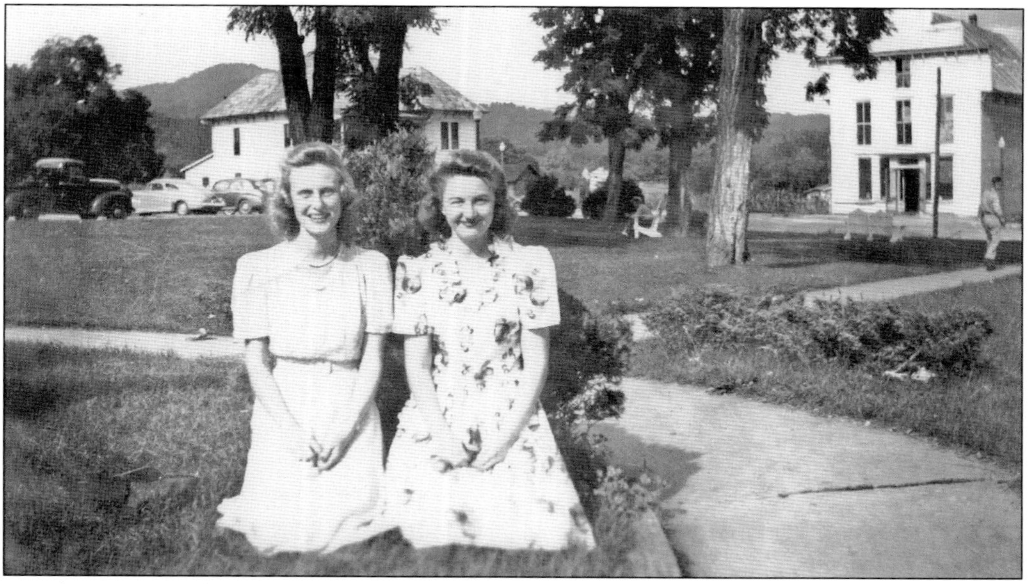

Martha Evans and Doris McIntosh relax at Burnsville Town Square in the 1940s. That town derived its name from Capt. Otway Burns, a noted sea captain and politician who supported education and the formation of new rural counties in North Carolina. (Courtesy of Nancy Randolph Silvers.)

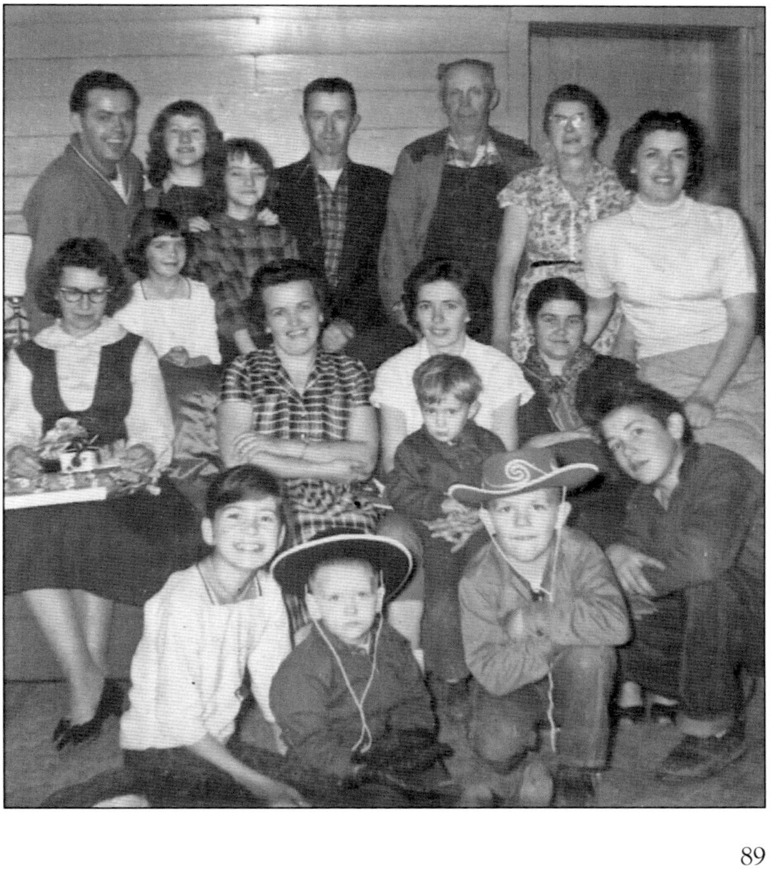

Yancey families often gather at the holidays, as the Anglins do here in 1960, sharing Christmas at Grandpa's. Seen from left to right are (first row) Faye Baker, Russell Shepherd, Randy Baker, Larry Shepherd, and Jimmy Anglin; (second row) Pearl Anglin, Willaree Baker, Irene Allen, Ivory Baker, and Grace Anglin; (third row) Bruce Anglin, Genella Anglin, Nina Allen, Cecil Anglin, grandpa Charlie Anglin, grandma Birdie Anglin, and Jerline Shepherd. (Courtesy of Roy Lee Anglin.)

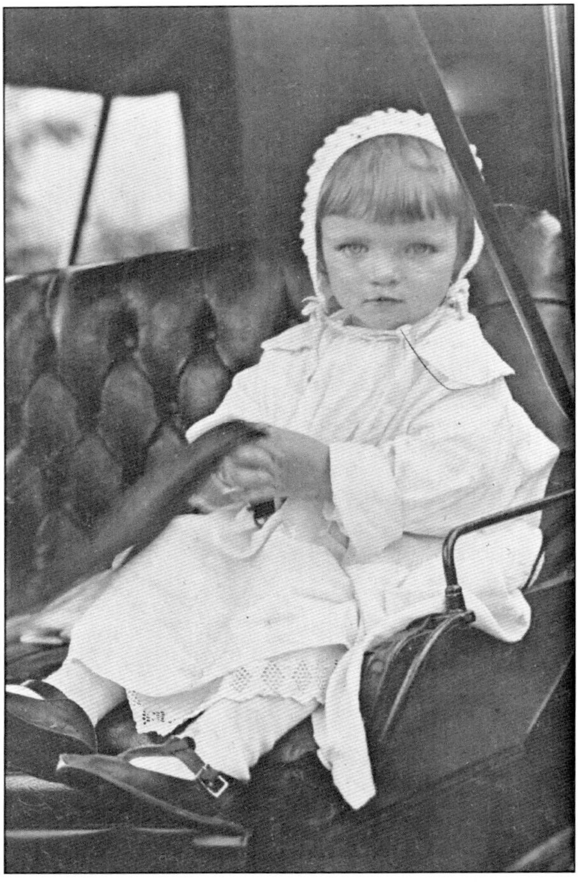

This sweet-faced child, James Proffitt of Bald Creek, grew up to be a well-known business owner in Yancey County. (Courtesy of Sarah Woody Proffitt.)

James and Sarah Proffitt wed at Burnsville Baptist Church on July 5, 1940. Little did the young boy in the beautiful gown pictured at left know that he would spend 58 years with the love of his life. Seen here from left to right are Olive Briggs, Bill Jester, Mary Glenn Proffitt, Max Proffitt, Helen Jester, Sarah Woody Proffitt, James Proffitt, Fleet Proffitt, Ralph Proffitt, Theresa Zimmerman, Yates Bailey, and Nan Worthington. (Courtesy of Sarah Woody Proffitt.)

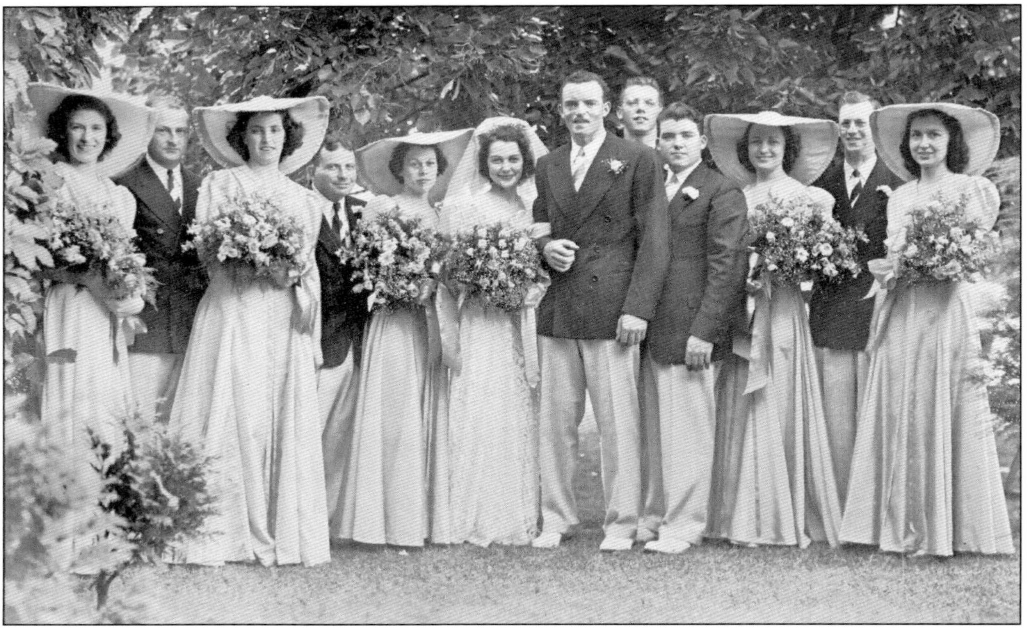

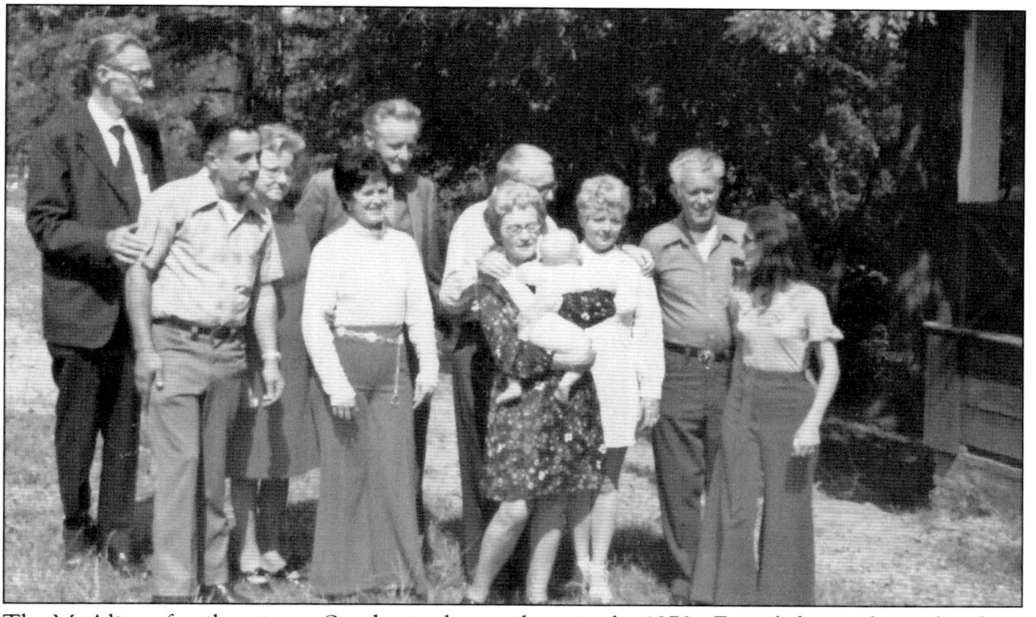

The McAlister family enjoys a Sunday in the sunshine in the 1970s. From left to right are brothers and sisters Frank, Howard, Edith, Edna, Burdett, and Fred McAlister, Estoy Smith McAlister holding a grandbaby, Catherine McAlister, Clyde Metcalf, and Dorothy McAlister. (Courtesy of Elaine McAlister Dellinger.)

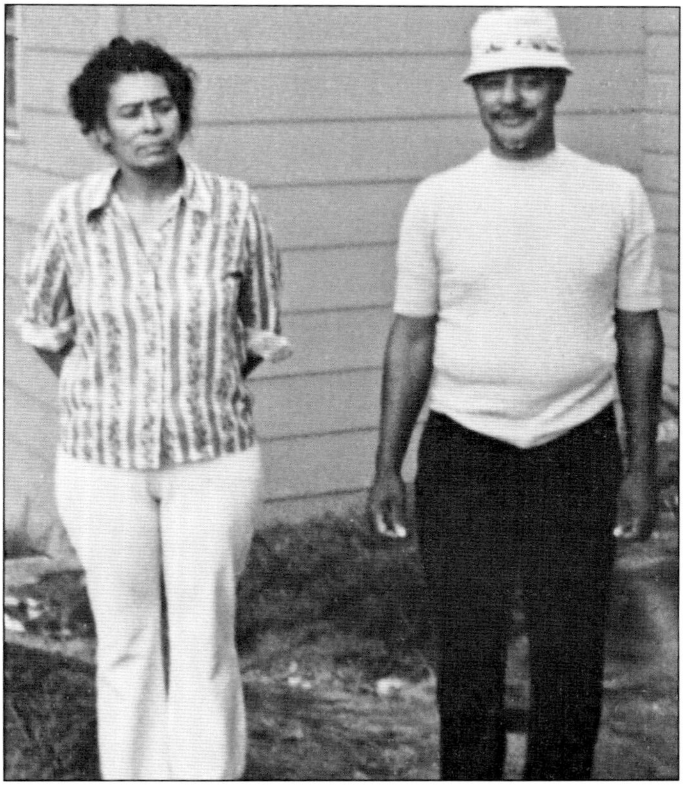

Charlotte Young and Columbus Barnett were married for 20 years. Columbus Barnett served on the ship named *Susan B. Anthony*, which was bombed in World War II. Their daughter, Shirley Barnett Whiteside, became the first to end segregation in Yancey schools, and their grandson, Bill Whiteside, became the first African American to serve on the Yancey School Board. (Courtesy of Shirley Barnett Whiteside.)

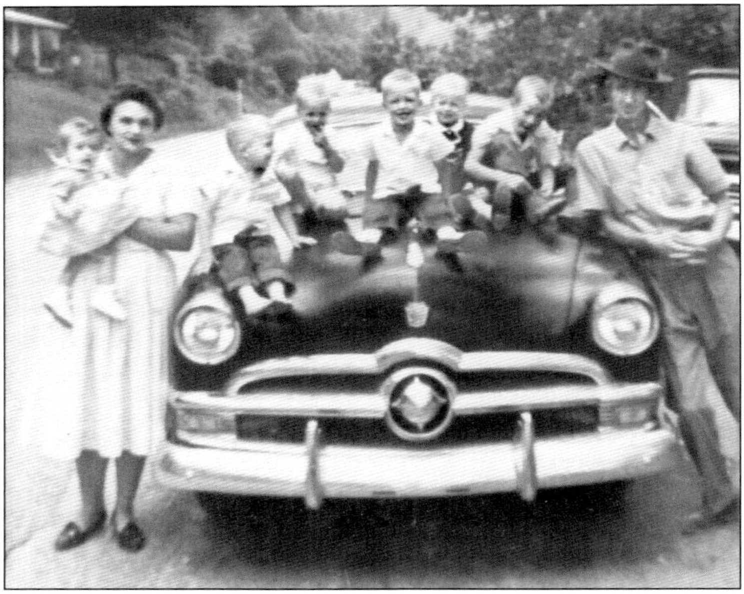

The Whitson family has continued the tradition of storekeeping at O.C. Whitson's store. Seen here from left to right are Parzady, Jean, Nick, Vincent, Vick, Joan, Ricky, and O.C. Jane Whitson, the youngest, was only a few months from being born. (Courtesy of Jane Whitson Peterson.)

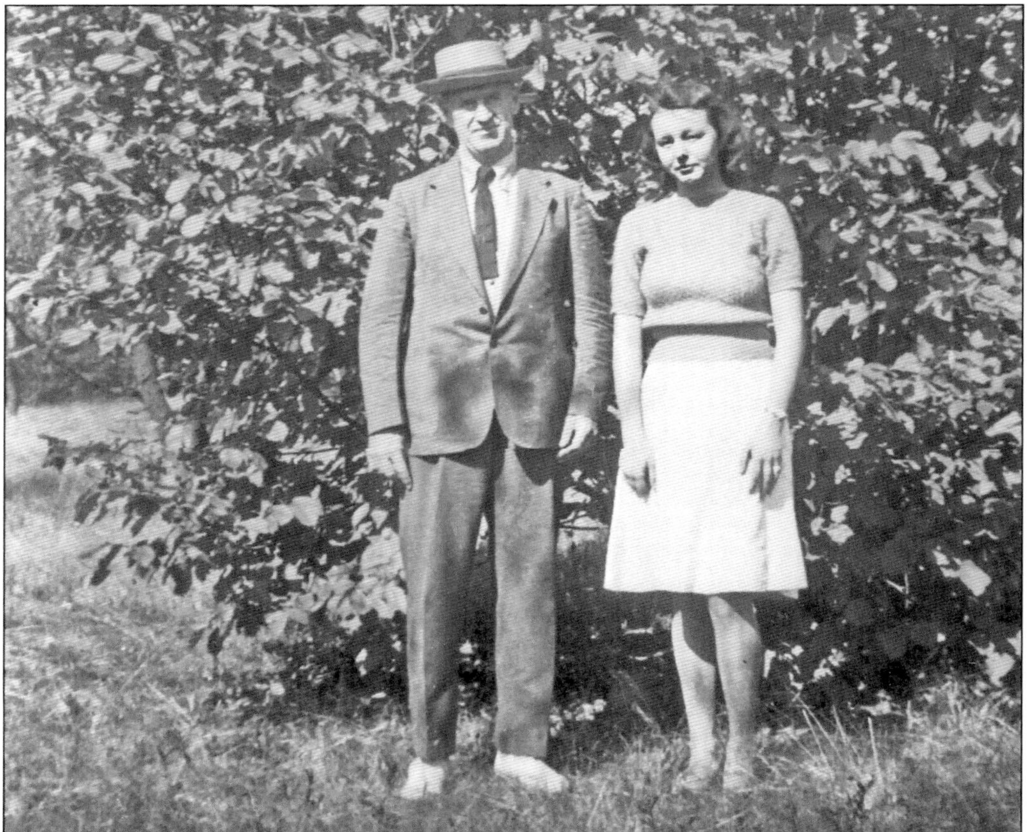

Carl McCandless, son of Henry McCandless, enjoys the sunshine with his wife, Pansy Louise McAlister McCandless, daughter of John and Lizzie McAlister. (Courtesy of June McCandless Jerome.)

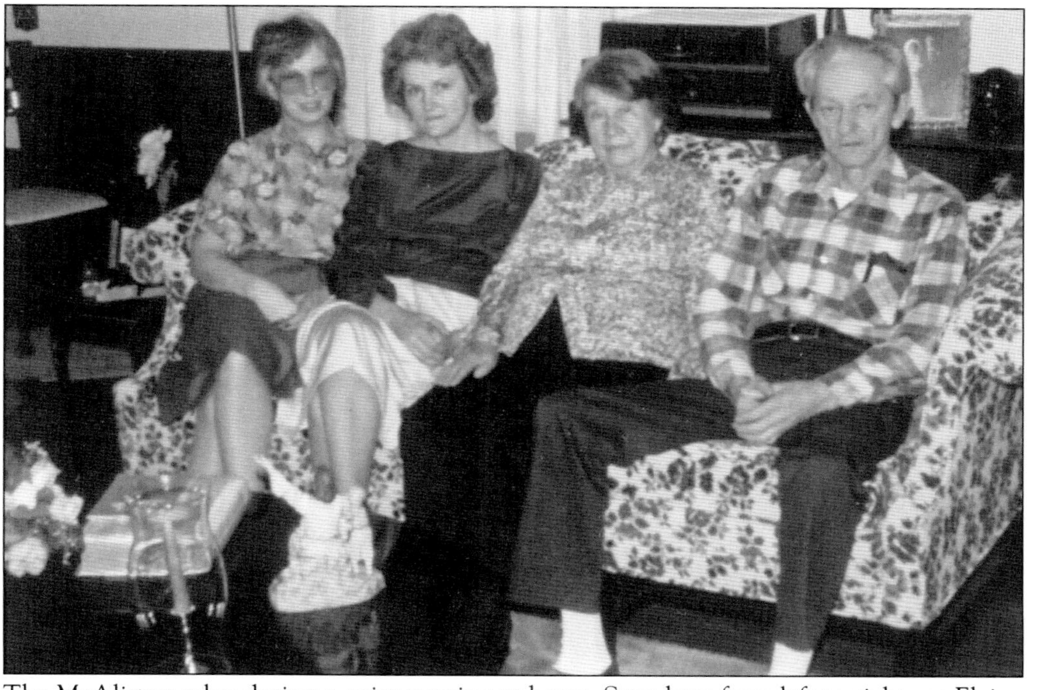

The McAlisters relax during a quiet evening at home. Seen here from left to right are Elaine McAlister Dellinger, Shirley Elizabeth Dellinger Buchanan, Birda Honeycutt McAlister, and Warren Burdett McAlister. (Courtesy of Elaine McAlister Dellinger.)

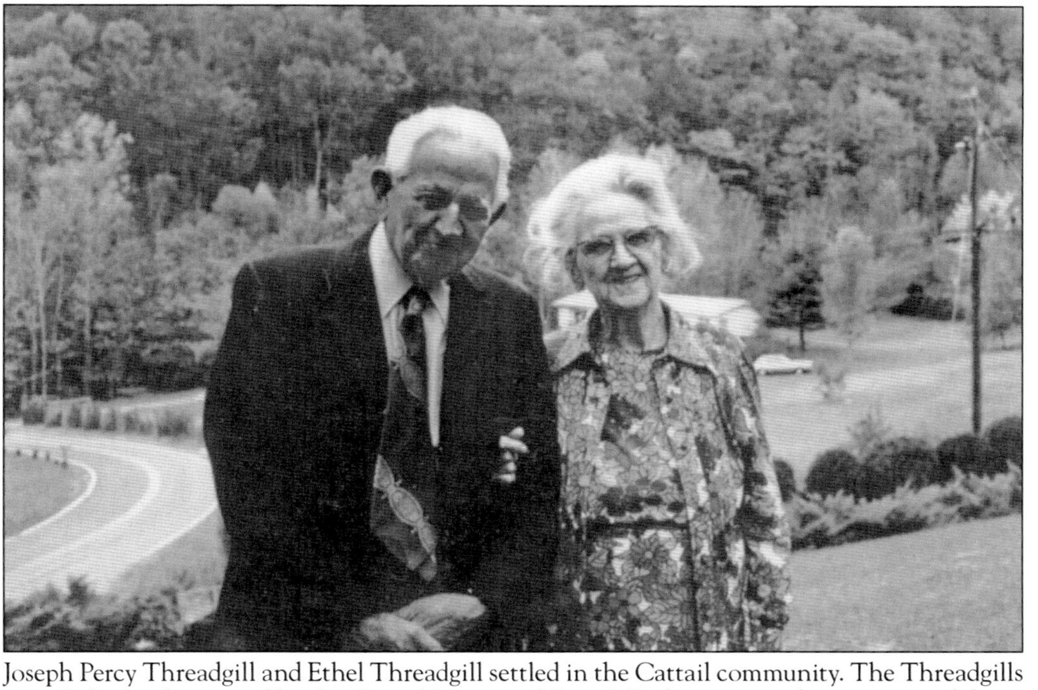

Joseph Percy Threadgill and Ethel Threadgill settled in the Cattail community. The Threadgills owned the land operated by the Cattail Mine, and Percy's Peak was named in memory of them. (Courtesy of Helen Threadgill Baden.)

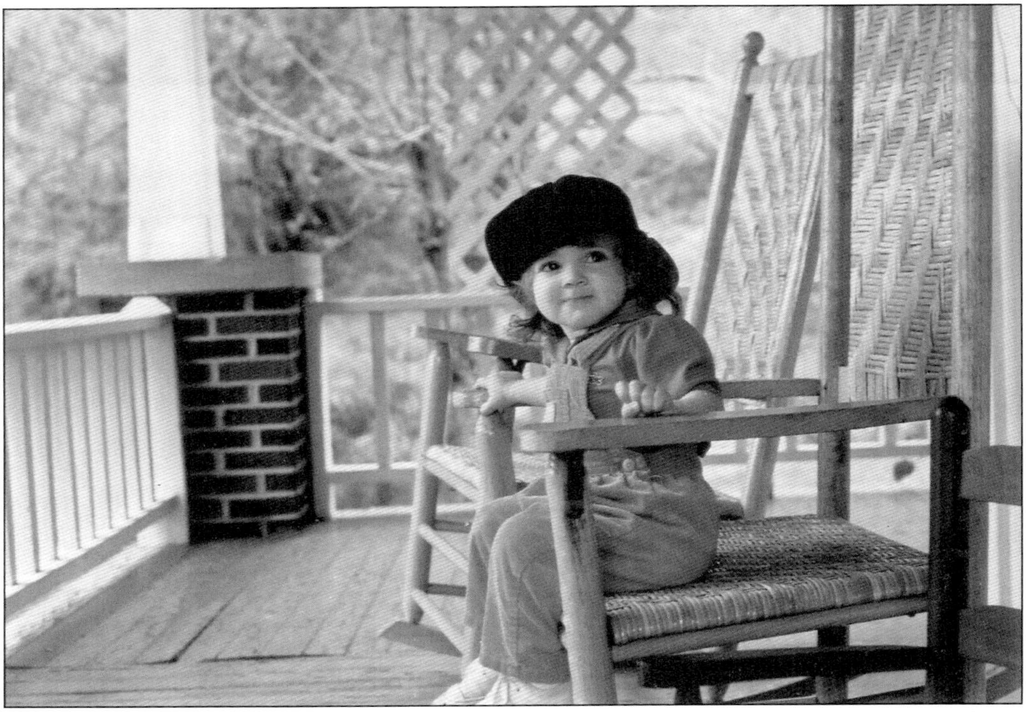

Claire Kaluzynski, daughter of Lynda Kinnane and Thomas Kaluzynski, rocks on the porch of her childhood home, which Henry Butner built just above the home place off Green Mountain Drive in Burnsville. Lawrence and wife Anna McCurry Butner and their children, Henry, Mary, Idyle, Carsa, and Lou Etta, enjoyed many years on this family farm. (Courtesy of Tom Kaluzynski and Linda Kinnane.)

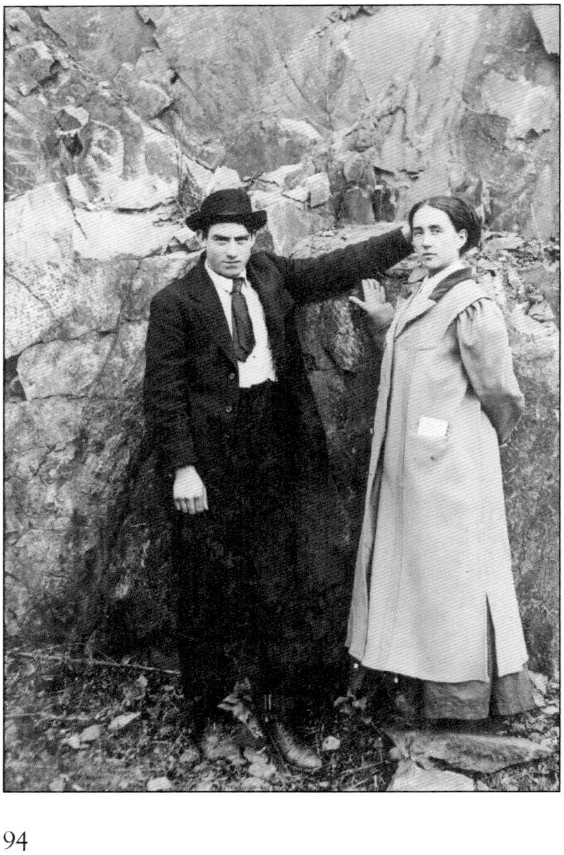

A Riddle man and Ethel Honeycutt stand together in Egypt Township, one of the earliest settlements in Yancey County. These rock formations resemble formations where archaeologically significant artifacts have been found dating as early as 3000 BC. (Courtesy of Elaine McAlister Dellinger.)

Eight

Natural Abundance

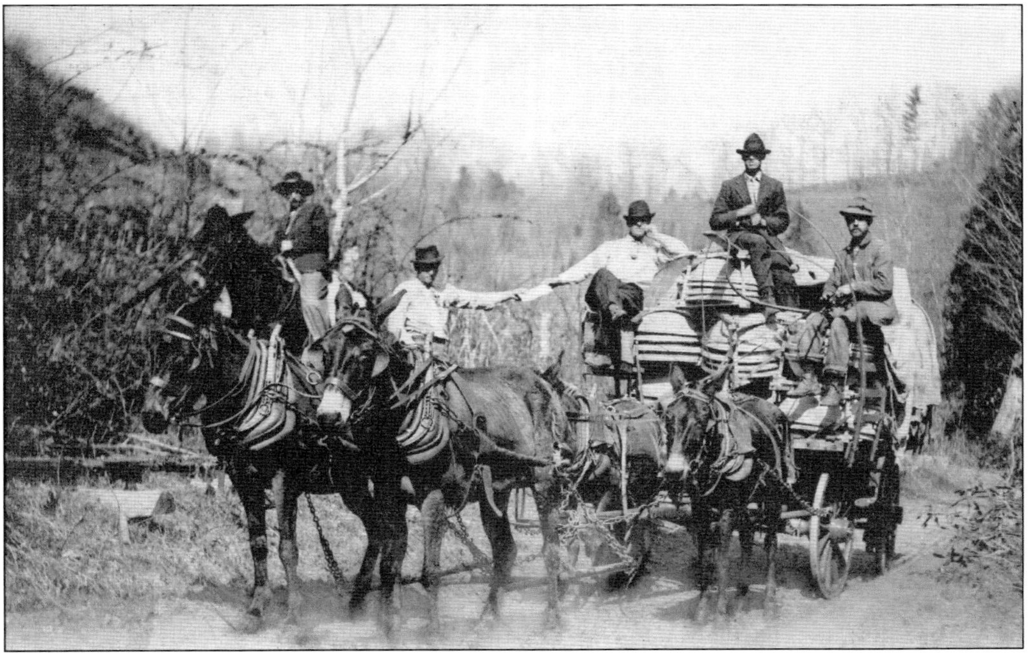

The deep forest in Yancey County offered abundant natural resources, and a bowl factory sprang up amidst the plenitude from 1907 to 1914. Seen here from left to right are Dave Duncan, Plen "Mail Man" Gurney, S. Willard McIntosh, Riley Shelton, and Andy Hensley. (Courtesy of Mike Shelton.)

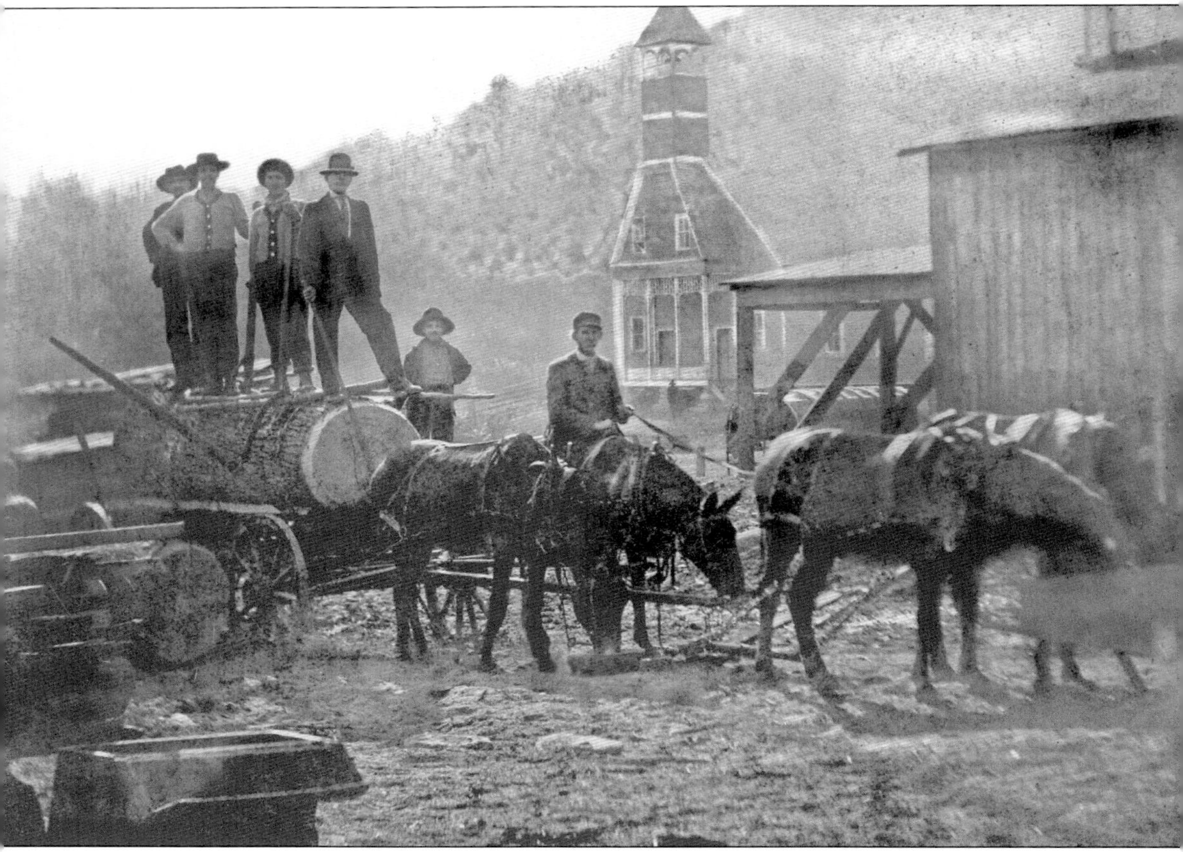

Workers at the bowl factory made $1.25 a day. Among those pictured here are Willard McIntosh, the local mail man, and others who are unidentified. (Courtesy of Carol and Joe Renfro.)

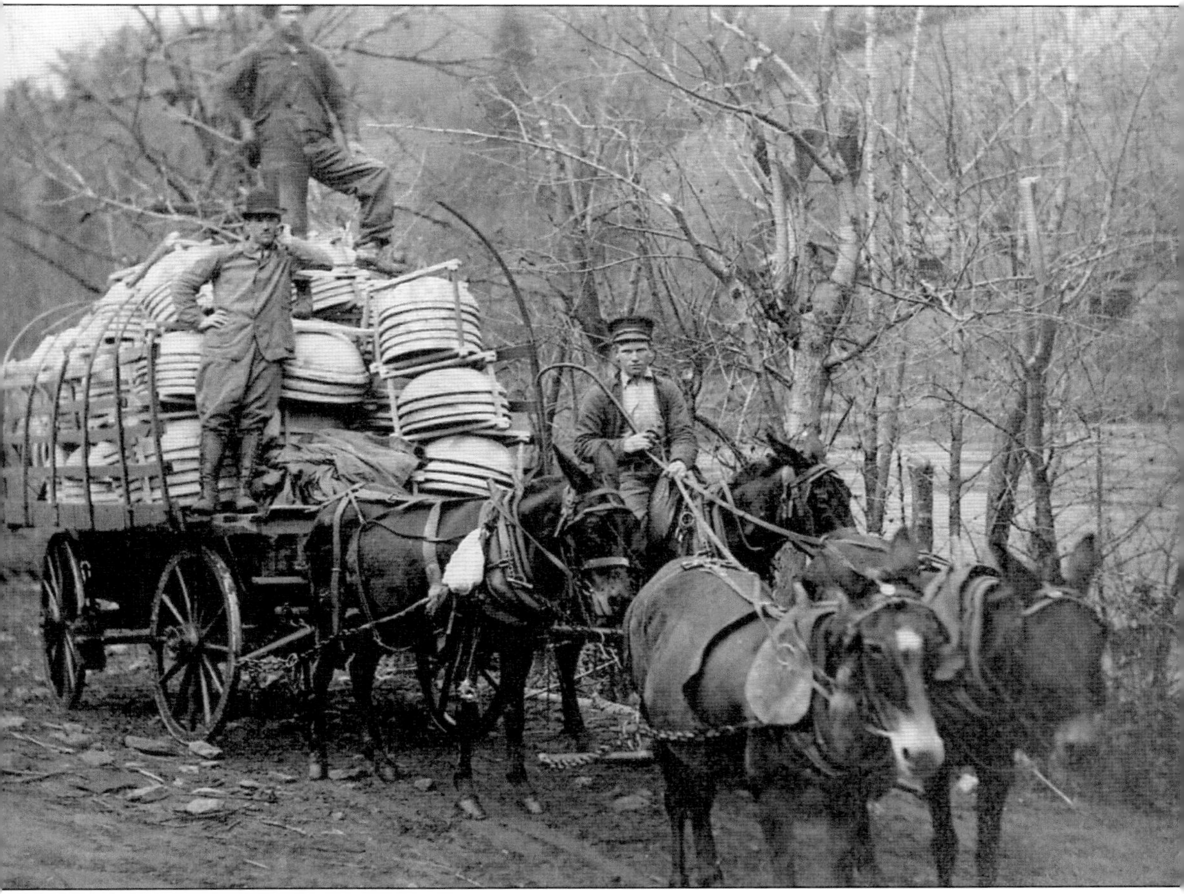

The wagonload of bowls manufactured in Bee Log went to the train at Huntdale to be shipped throughout the country. The Bald Mountain (Caney River) Railroad ran from Buck Town to Huntdale and went to the Clinchfield Line. In 1907, the Gunney Manufacturing Company paid $10 to lease land from Bacchus Hensley for five years. (Courtesy of Carol and Joe Renfro.)

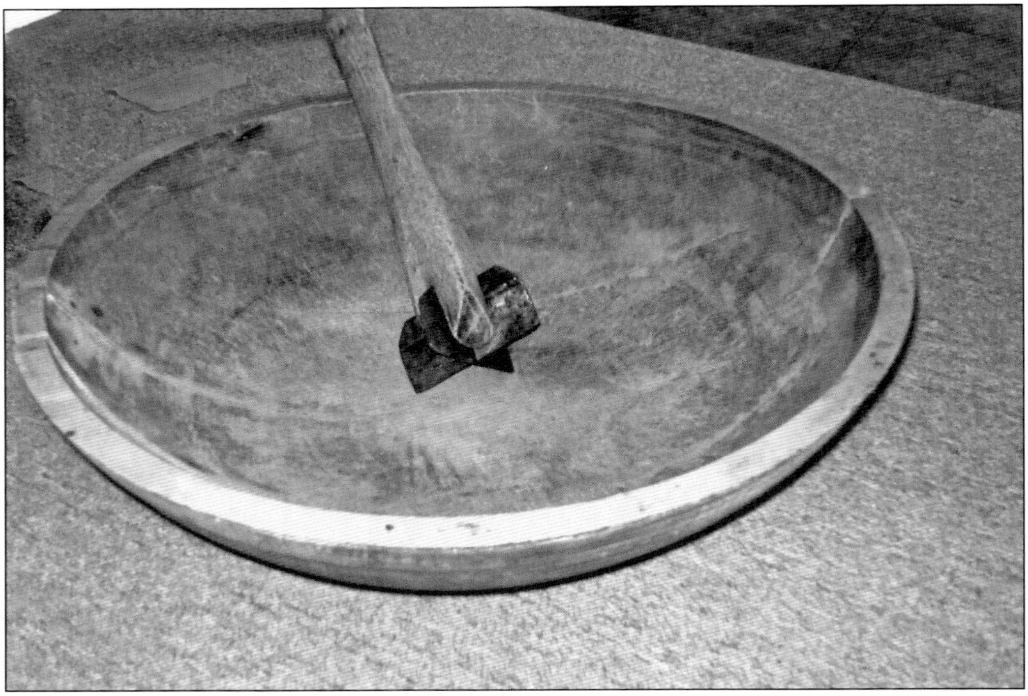

In 1909, the Yancey bowl factory at Bee Log was in its heyday. This bowl belonged to Dora Pate Hensley and was passed down to her daughter, Verlon Hensley Edwards, and on to her daughter, Judie Edwards Honeycutt. The bowls were made from yellow poplar and cucumber trees, soft wood that is easy to hollow. (Courtesy of Mike Shelton.)

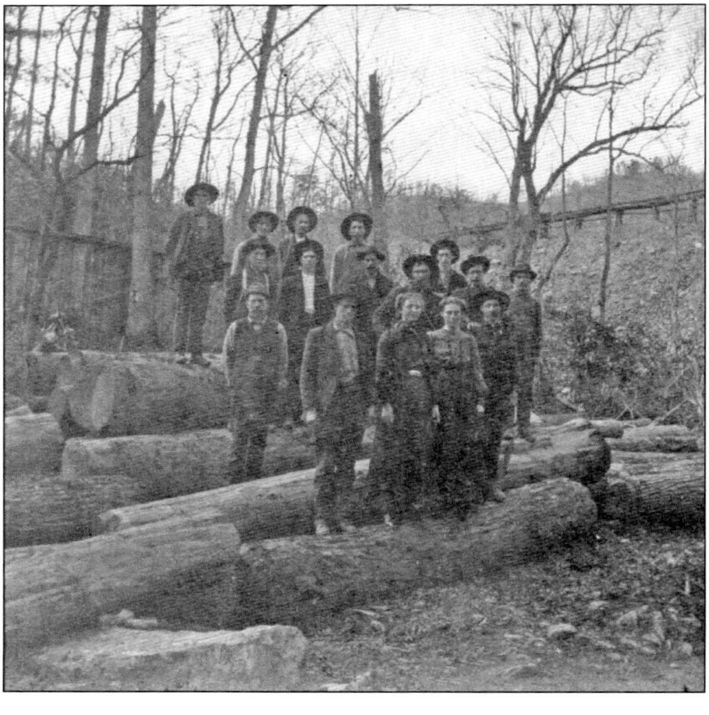

Many men, including the Jesse Phillips family, worked in a logging camp near Bee Log in the Egypt Township. Logging and lumbering became a primary industry in Yancey. Conservation efforts have emerged, but today, 18 companies still buy timber in the county. (Courtesy of Elaine McAlister Dellinger.)

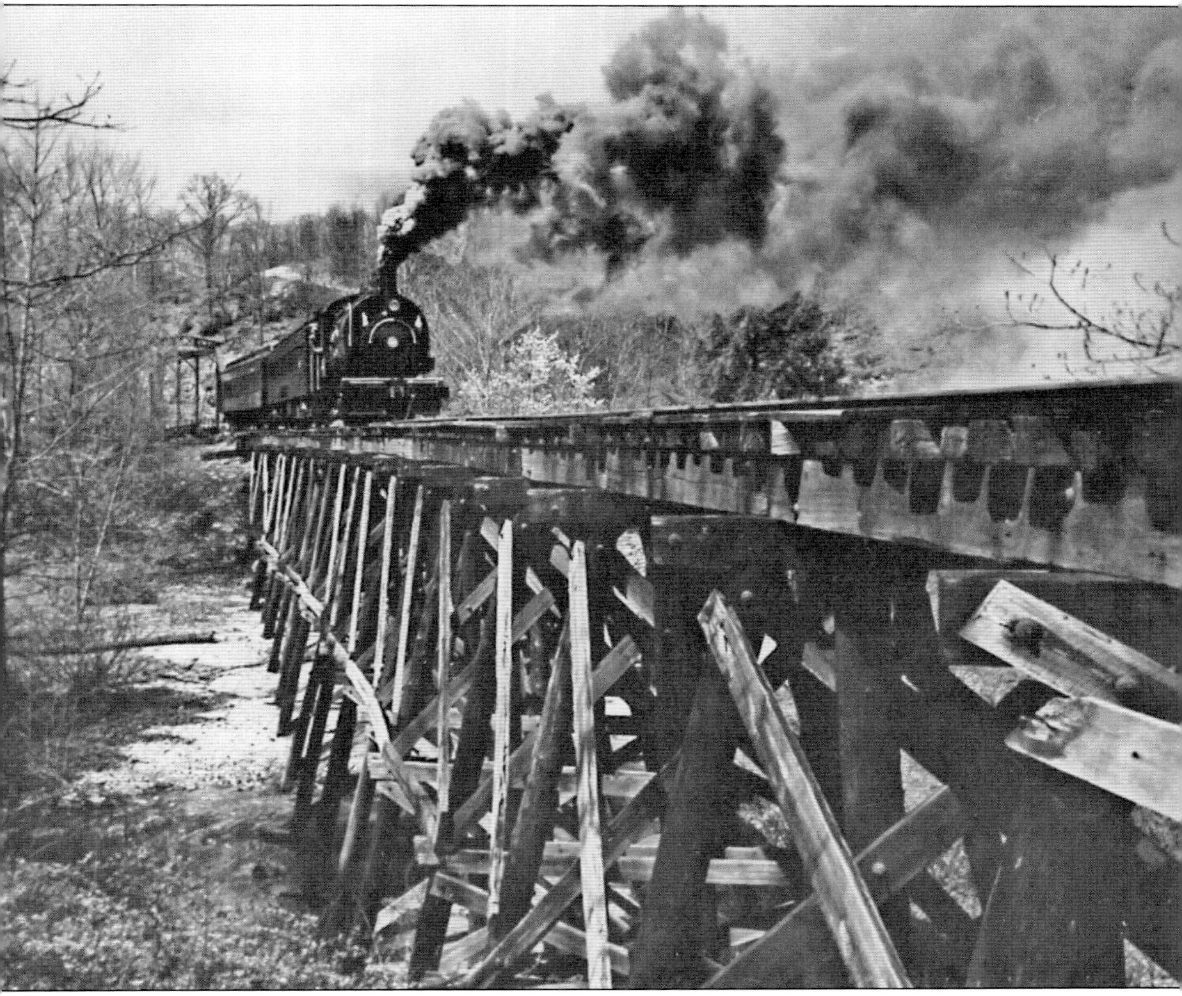

The Yancey Railroad was a short line that connected with the Clinchfield at Kona, North Carolina, and served the towns of Bacchus, Micaville (junction), Bowditch, Windom, and Burnsville. As early as 1913, Fred Perley and W.H. Crockett had made plans to operate a passenger train on the logging railroad for touring the Black Mountains. From the station at Mount Mitchell, it was 21 miles to Camp Alice (a three-hour travel time). The round-trip cost was $2.50. (Courtesy of Glenda Wilson.)

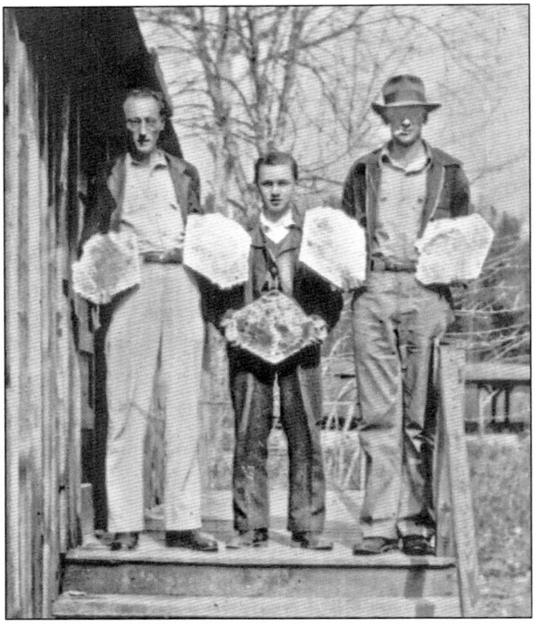

Mica glistens in silvery sheets that grow together to form books. The Cattail, Fanny Gouge, Green Mountain, Ray, and Balsam Mica Mines supplied sheets of muscovite used in making stove and furnace windows and electrical insulators. The mines began in the mid-1800s and became nationally significant during World War II, when European supplies became unavailable. The mines closed in the 1960s due to technology changes. These three men stand next to the Mica House, where the mineral pulled from the mines awaited transport. (Courtesy of Mildred Gibbs Harris.)

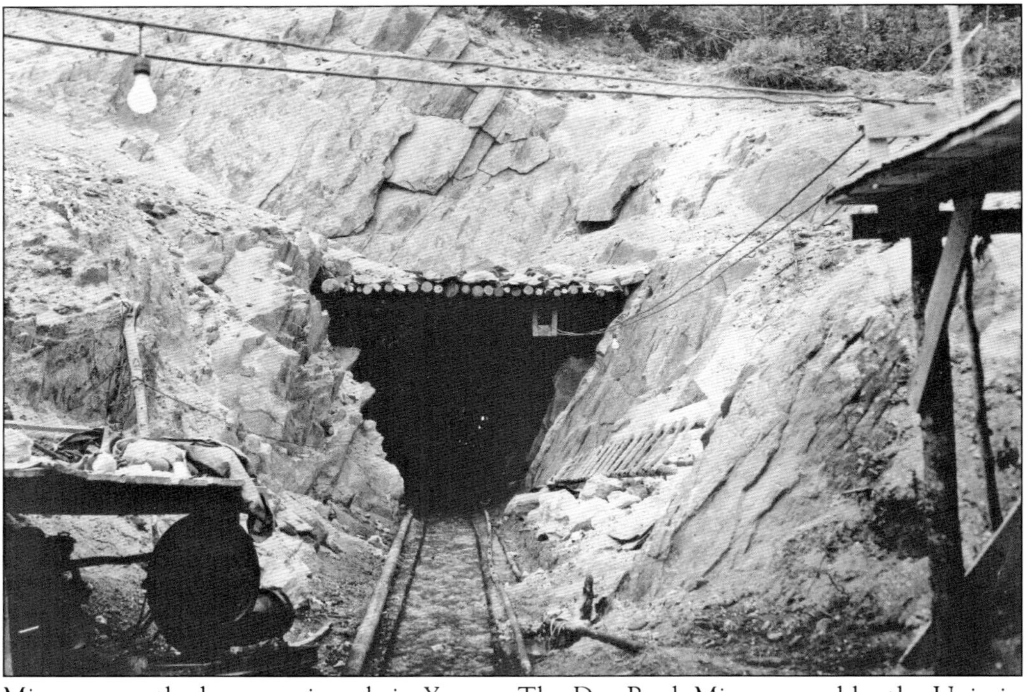

Miners unearthed many minerals in Yancey. The Day Book Mine, owned by the Unimin Corporation, is the only operating olivine mine in Yancey County. Corundum has been mined since before 1895 at the Hays Mine at Sampson Mountain near Bee Log. Soapstone is used locally for fireplace hearths, gravestones, bowls, and smoking pipes. Kyanite was mined at the Celo Kyanite Mine at the head of Allen Branch on the northern slopes of Bowlens Pyramid from 1931 to 1944. Kyanite, a lovely blue stone, is used in refractory ceramics, such as spark plugs. (Courtesy of Helen Threadgill Baden.)

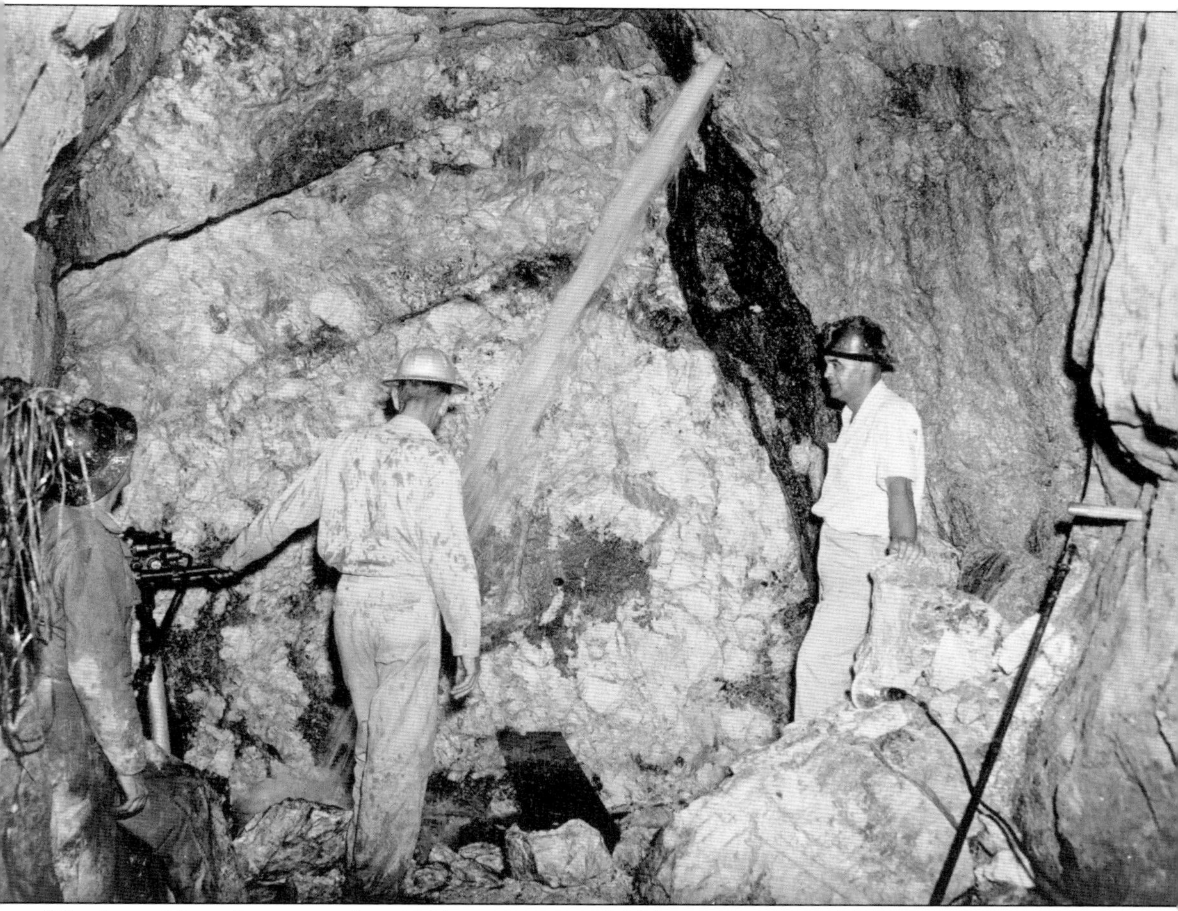

The Isom Mine first opened in 1874 as a mica and feldspar mine. One block mined in 1952 weighed 1,456 pounds. The mine had 475 feet of tunnel and employed 40 people. (Courtesy of Helen Threadgill Baden.)

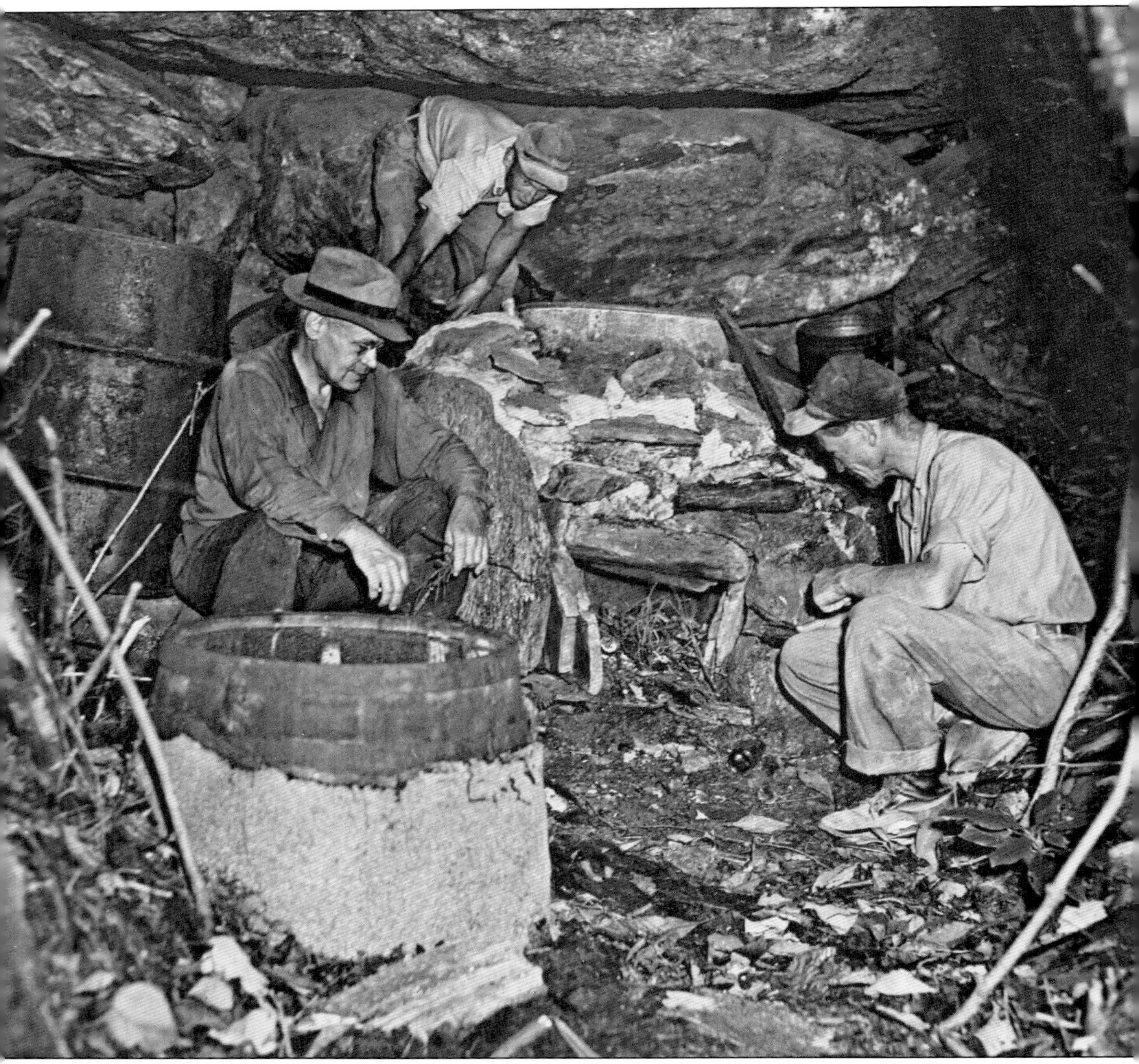

Edward Mack Jr. (seated at left) graduated from Princeton magna cum laude. He studied with Marie Curie at the Sorbonne and was a Guggenheim Fellow in Munich. He also worked on the atomic bomb. After traveling the world, Dr. Mack lived in Yancey County until the end of his life. Here he learns the finer points of making moonshine on Cattail Creek. Many moonshine stills dotted Yancey, which went dry at Prohibition and remained so until 2010. (Courtesy of Helen Threadgill Baden.)

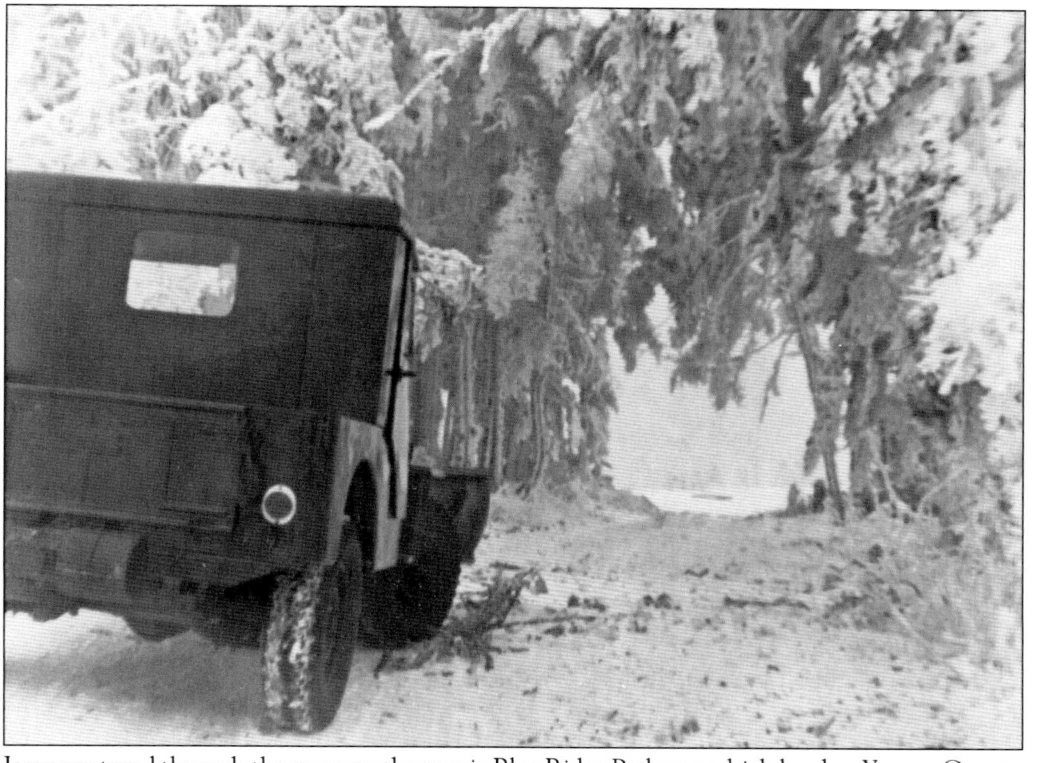

Jeeps ventured through the snow on the scenic Blue Ridge Parkway, which borders Yancey County from mile marker 339 at Crabtree Meadows to mile marker 360 at Balsam Gap. Highway 80 touches the parkway at mile marker 344. Travel included passage on both the Mount Mitchell and the Big Tom Wilson motor roads. The toll in 1926 was $1 for each adult. Some of these one-lane roads were so steep that schedules for ascent and descent were routine. By 1939, all roads were becoming toll free. (Courtesy of Regina Wilson.)

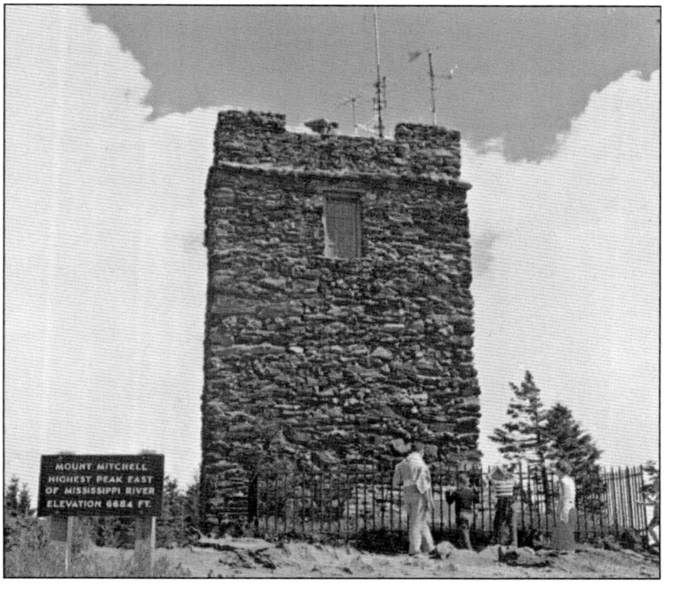

Two wooden towers preceded this stone tower on Mount Mitchell, at 6,684 feet the tallest mountain east of the Mississippi. Mount Mitchell State Park was formed in 1915 to preserve the forest and views for future generations. The mountain and park take their name from Dr. Elisha Mitchell, a professor at UNC-Chapel Hill who enjoyed measuring the mountains. He died falling down a waterfall as he tried to prove that Mount Mitchell was the tallest of the Black Mountains. It is. (Courtesy of Genevieve Harrison.)

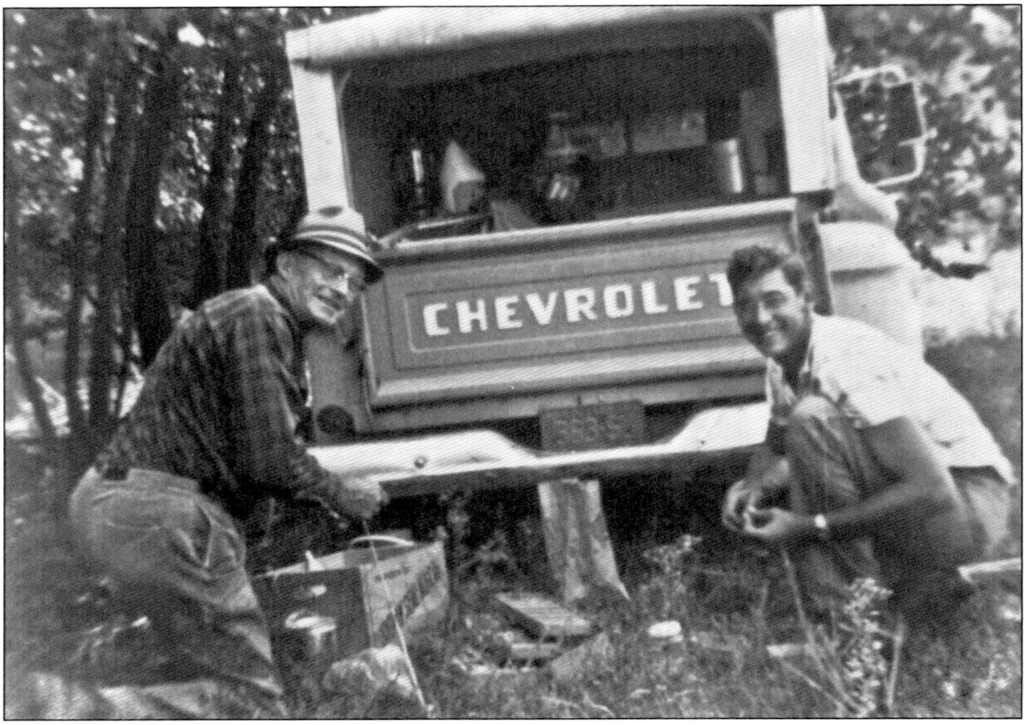

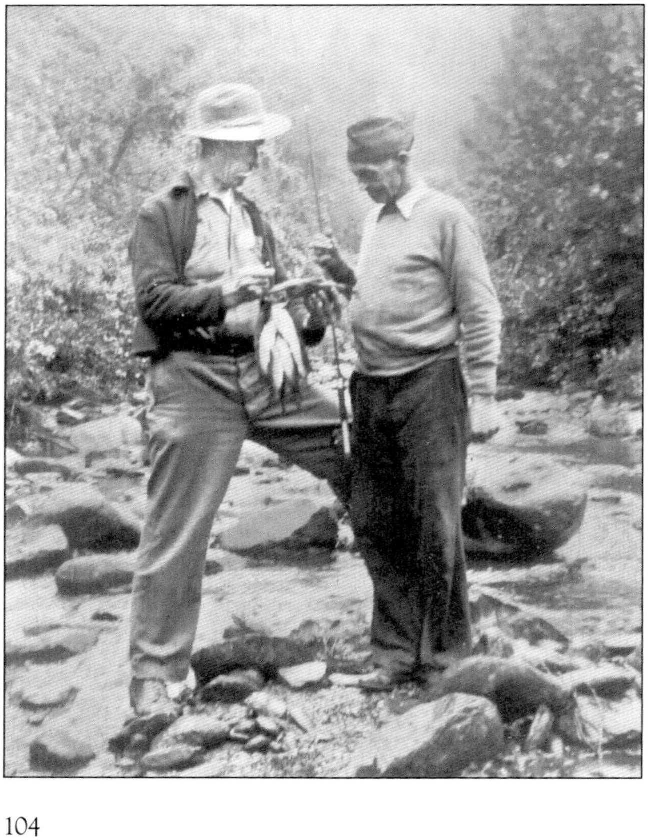

Nothing tops a fishing trip, like this one taken by Levi Deyton (left) and Lloyd Webb in 1952. The South Toe River and surrounding creeks had plenty of brook trout, brown trout, and rainbow trout. (Courtesy of Earl Webb.)

Lickskillet Creek, Lower Creek, Middle Creek, and Upper Creek have known some fine fishing, with wily wild trout, perch, bass, and sunfish. As the human population grew and fish population shrank, game wardens began to measure and count a day's catch. (Courtesy of Genevieve Harrison.)

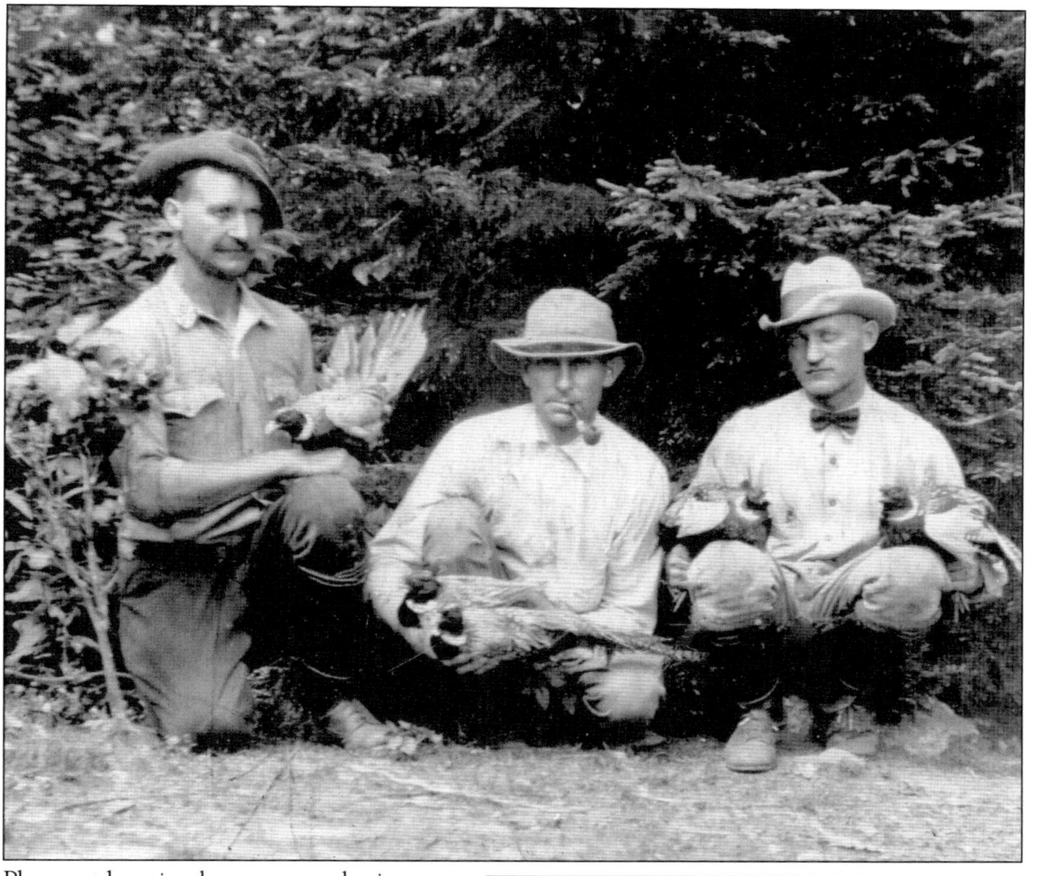

Pheasant hunting became popular in the South Toe area. Nelse Mease is in the middle here, with Chet McKinney at right. (Courtesy of Genevieve Harrison.)

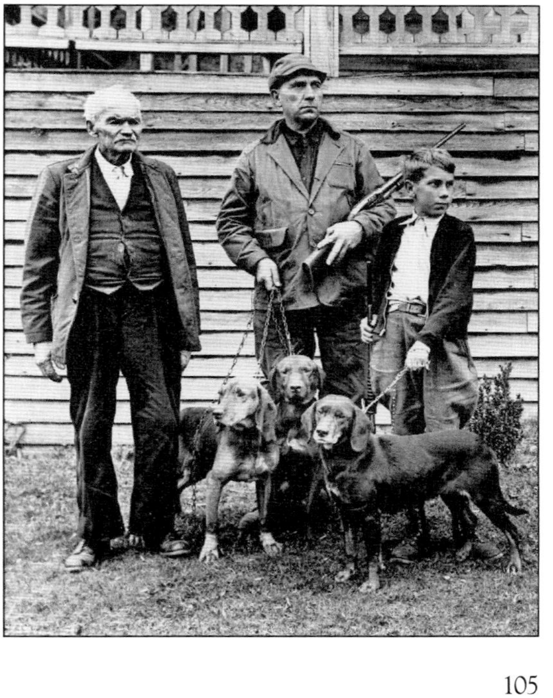

From left to right, Adolph, Ewart, and Dolph Wilson, sons of Big Tom Wilson, prepare to go bear hunting. The Wilsons were known as the best bear hunters anywhere. When Elisha Mitchell fell to his death, it was Tom Wilson who found his body at the foot of Mitchell Falls. (Courtesy of Helen Threadgill Baden.)

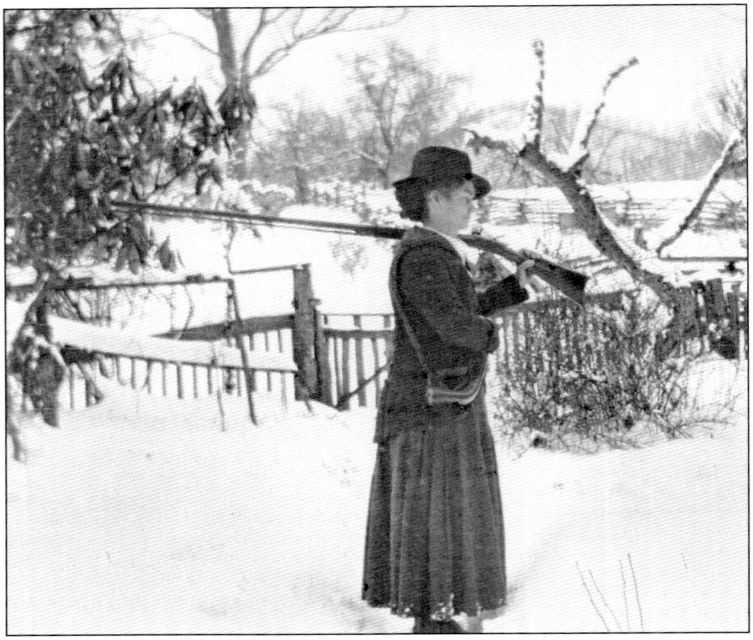

Women and men alike hunted for the family dinner. (Courtesy of Barbara Ford.)

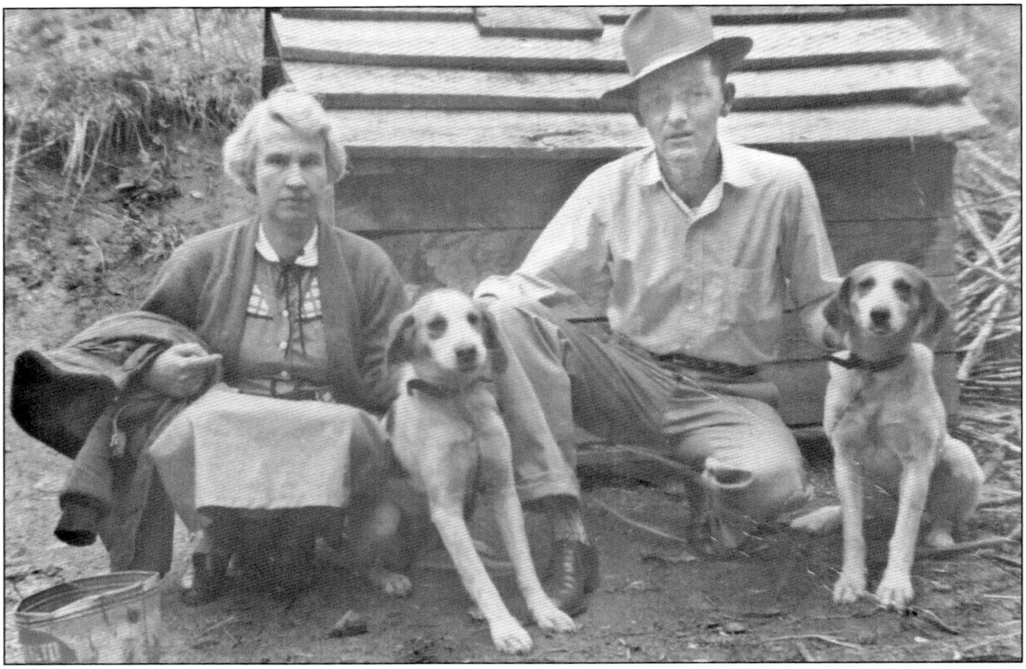

Fox hunting was a common men's Friday- and Saturday-night pastime from early on until the 1970s, when it began to fade in popularity. Warren Burdett McAlister was one of those fond of the sport. He is pictured here with wife Birda and his two prized hounds. He would spend many hours off in the night with neighbors Byrd McIntosh, George Angel, Lloyd Silvers, and his brother-in-law Hick Robertson, listening intently to the fox race as the fox and hounds traveled around the hills and valleys, each man sure his dog would be in the lead at some point during the night. (Courtesy of Elaine McAlister Dellinger.)

Nine

Love of Learning

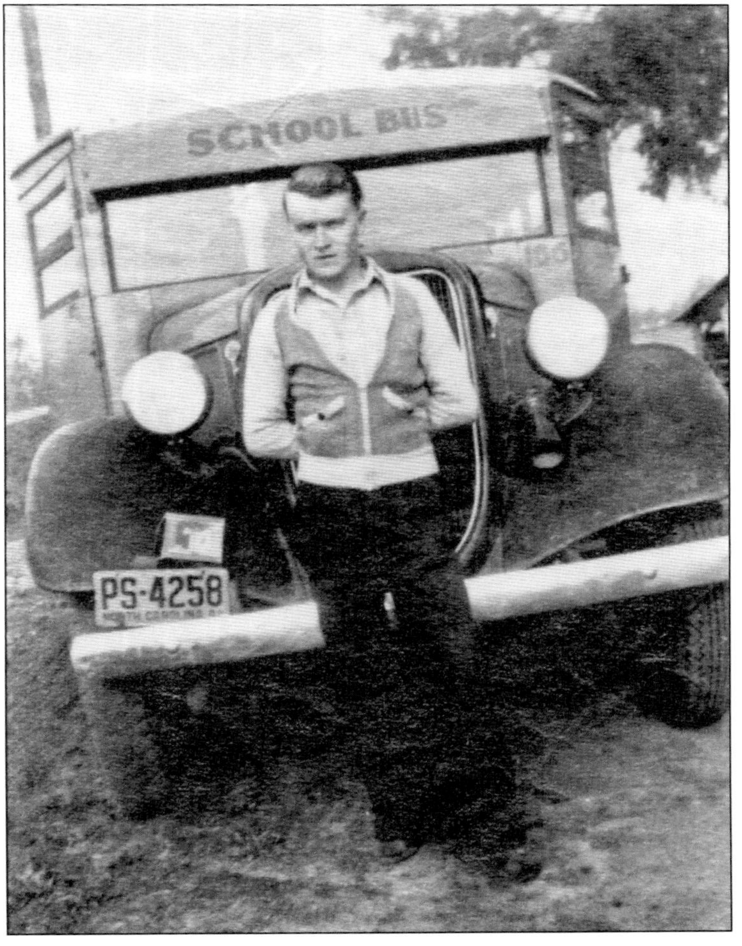

Henry Clay Radford was the son of William Baxter Radford and Elizabeth "Lizzie" Emmaline Hensley. (Courtesy of Mike Shelton.)

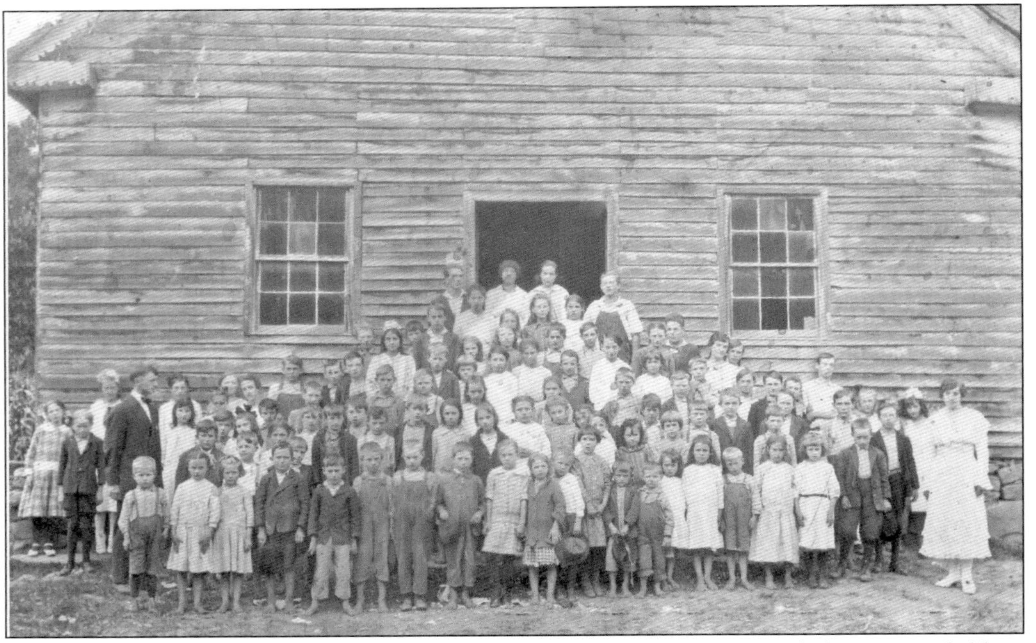

These students attended the one-room schoolhouse at Bee Log in 1917. Back then, most children did not wear shoes until the first frost. (Courtesy of Carol and Joe Renfro.)

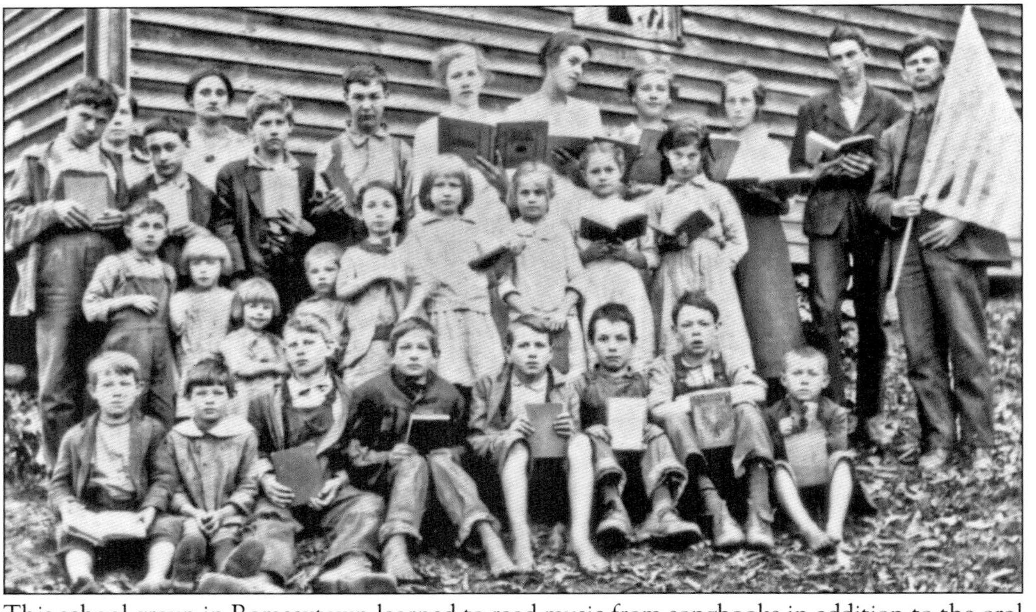

This school group in Ramseytown learned to read music from songbooks in addition to the oral tradition. Music was learned from ear to ear throughout the county, an important tradition. (Courtesy of Elaine McAlister Dellinger.)

Shirley Elizabeth McAlister (pictured here in the fourth or fifth grade) attended Bald Creek School. School photographs often provided an important family record of how children grew from year to year. Shirley married Marvin Buchanan and had two daughters, Tammy Diane Buchanan Austin and Vickie Lynn Buchanan Reeves. She died of ALS in 1993 and did not live to see her three grandchildren, "Lexie," Zackary, and Sam. (Courtesy of Elaine McAlister Dellinger.)

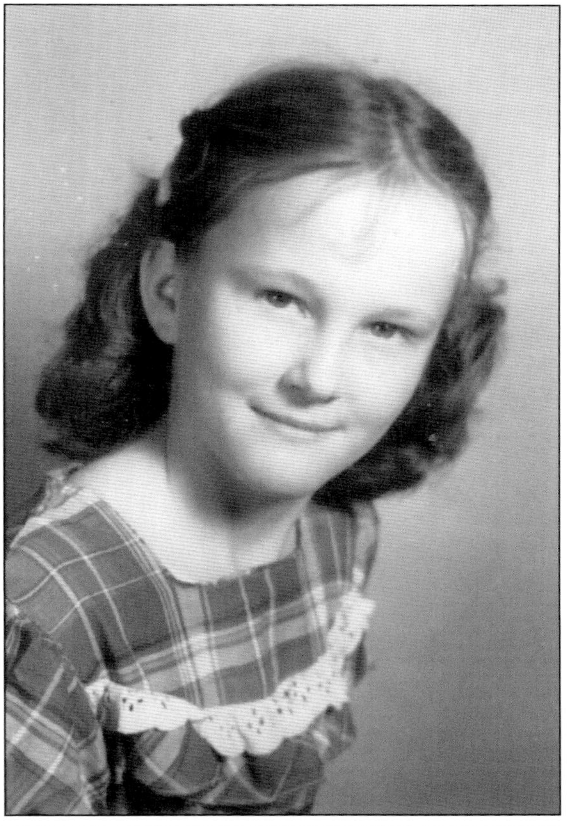

This 1917 photograph shows students of Browns Creek School, a two-room schoolhouse in Celo. (Courtesy of Mildred Gibbs Harris.)

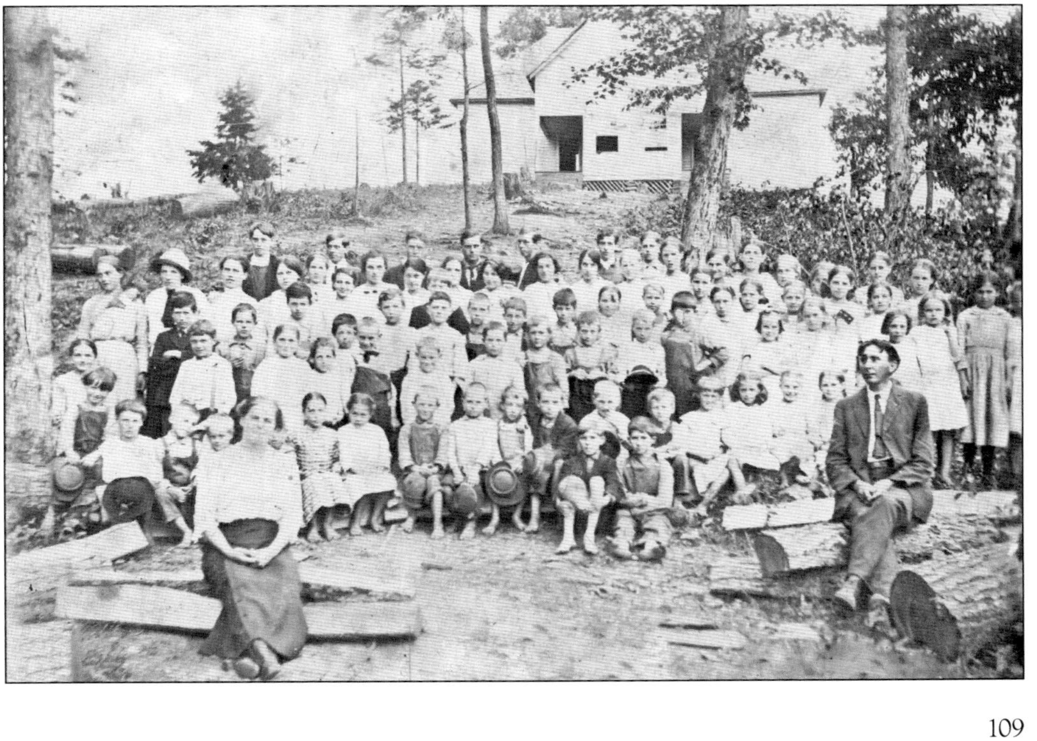

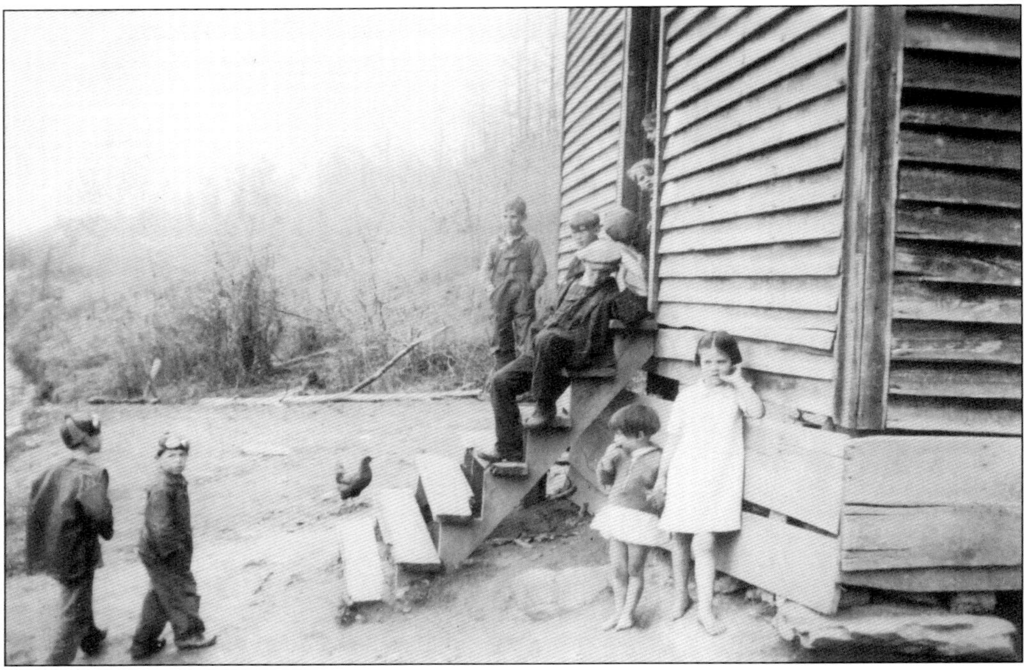

At the beginning of the 20th century, children play at Baker's Creek School during a recess between lessons. (Courtesy of Nancy Randolph Silvers.)

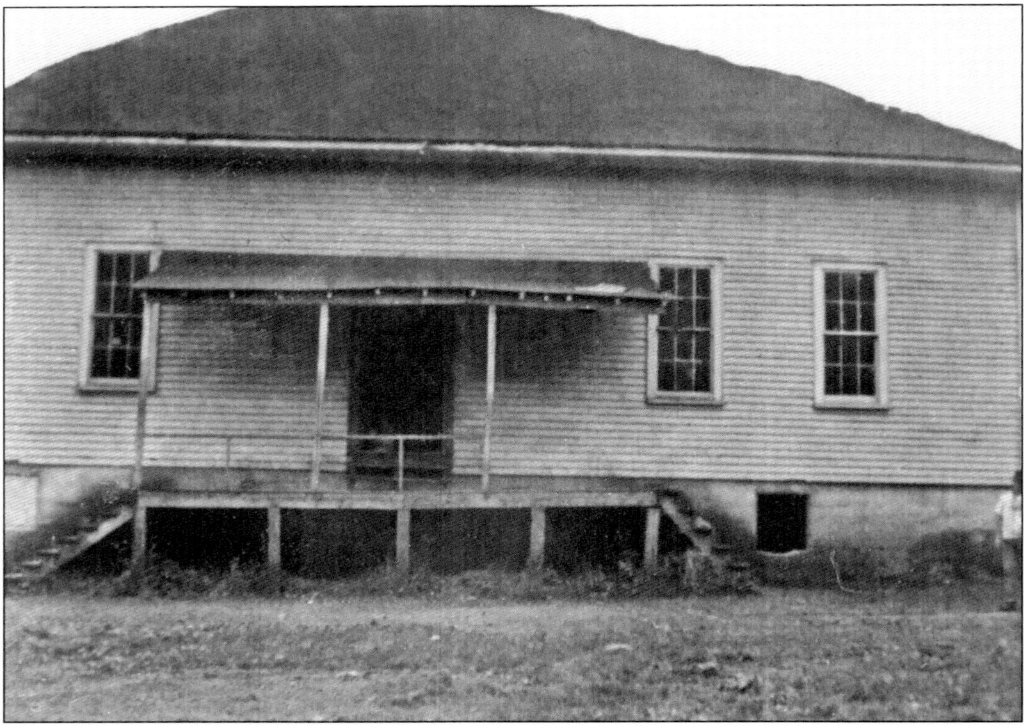

This earlier Bald Creek High School burned to the ground. (Courtesy of Sarah Woody Proffitt.)

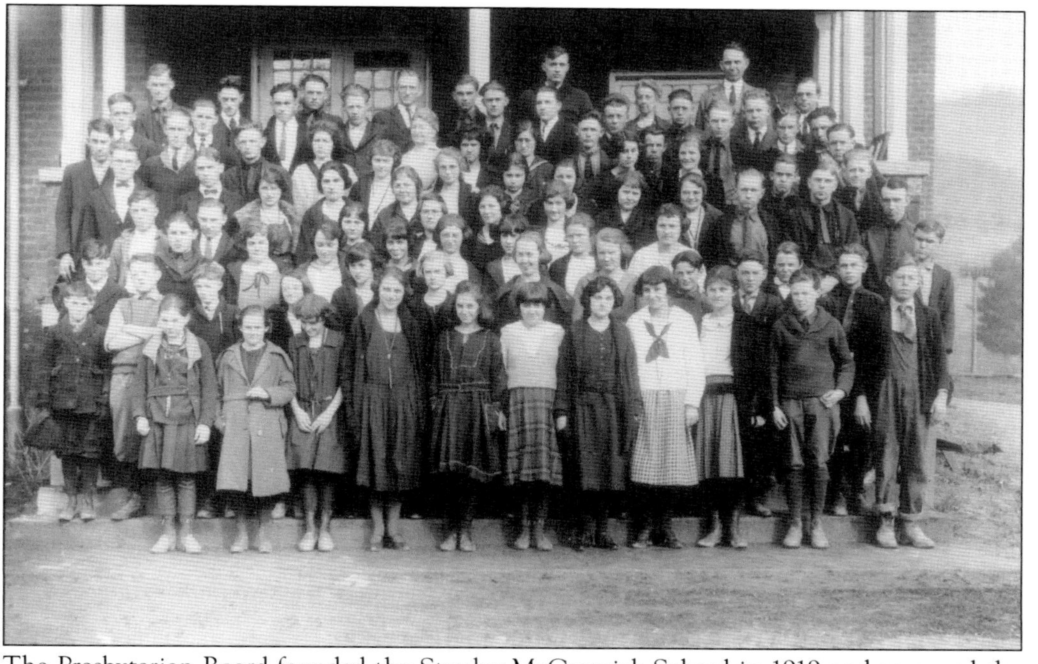

The Presbyterian Board founded the Stanley McCormick School in 1919 and arranged the curriculum according to the social and educational needs of the students. The many classmates here in the 1920s include (in no order): Troy Cooper, Vernie Wilson, Ralph and Claude Dellinger, Lena Tilson, Fairy Willhite, Lena Banks, Alma Banks, and many others. The school became the Carolina New College and closed in 1928. (Courtesy of Charles Lee Dellinger.)

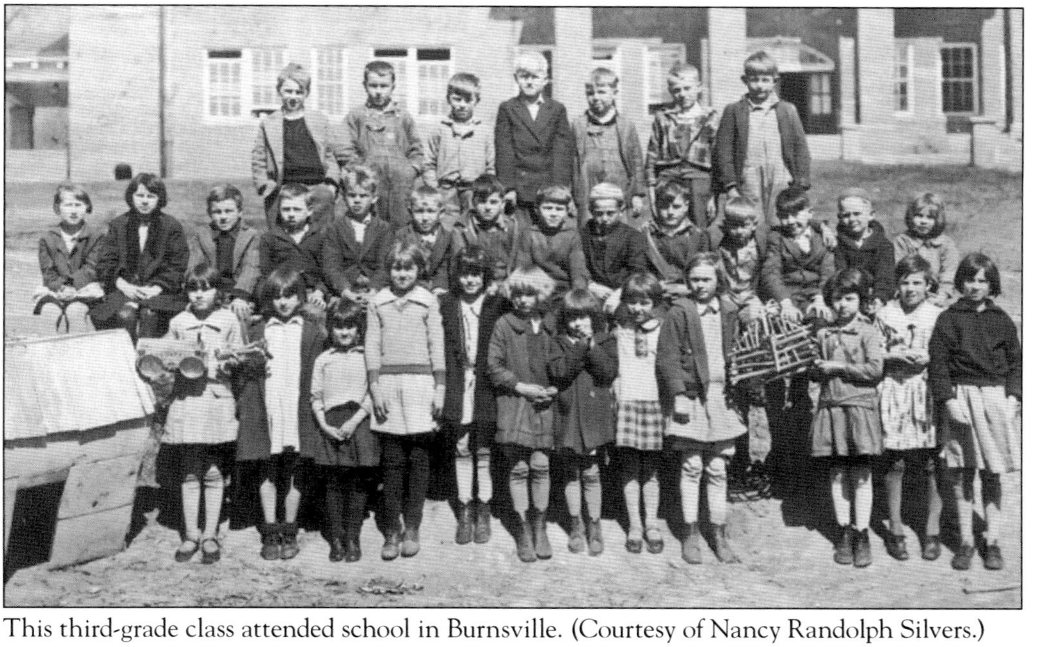

This third-grade class attended school in Burnsville. (Courtesy of Nancy Randolph Silvers.)

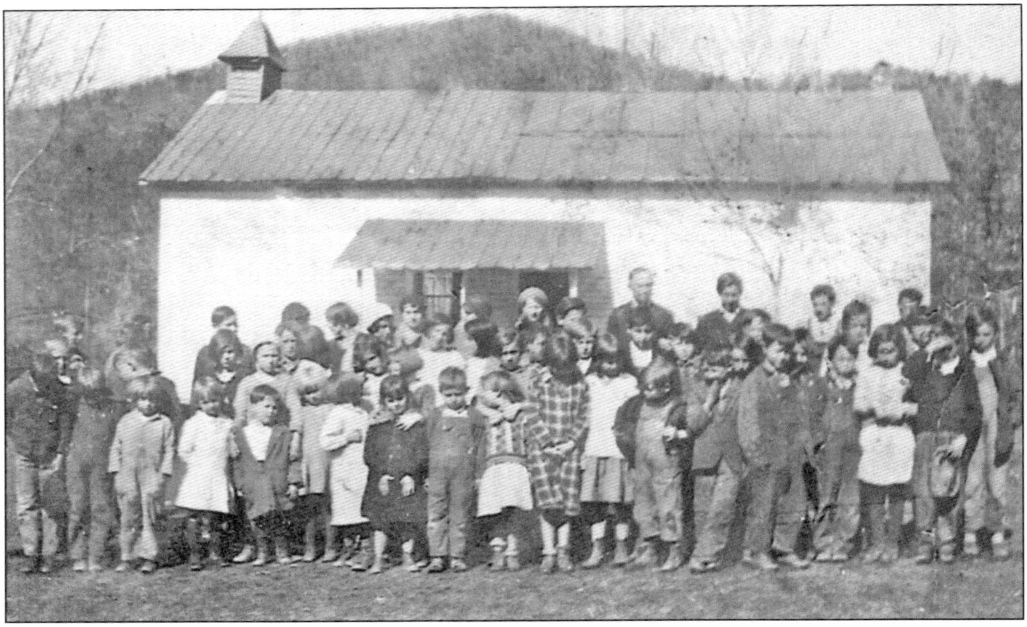

In the 1930s, the Busick School provided a multi-age education to students from South Toe River Road, near the Busick Forest Service Work Center. (Courtesy of Regina Wilson.)

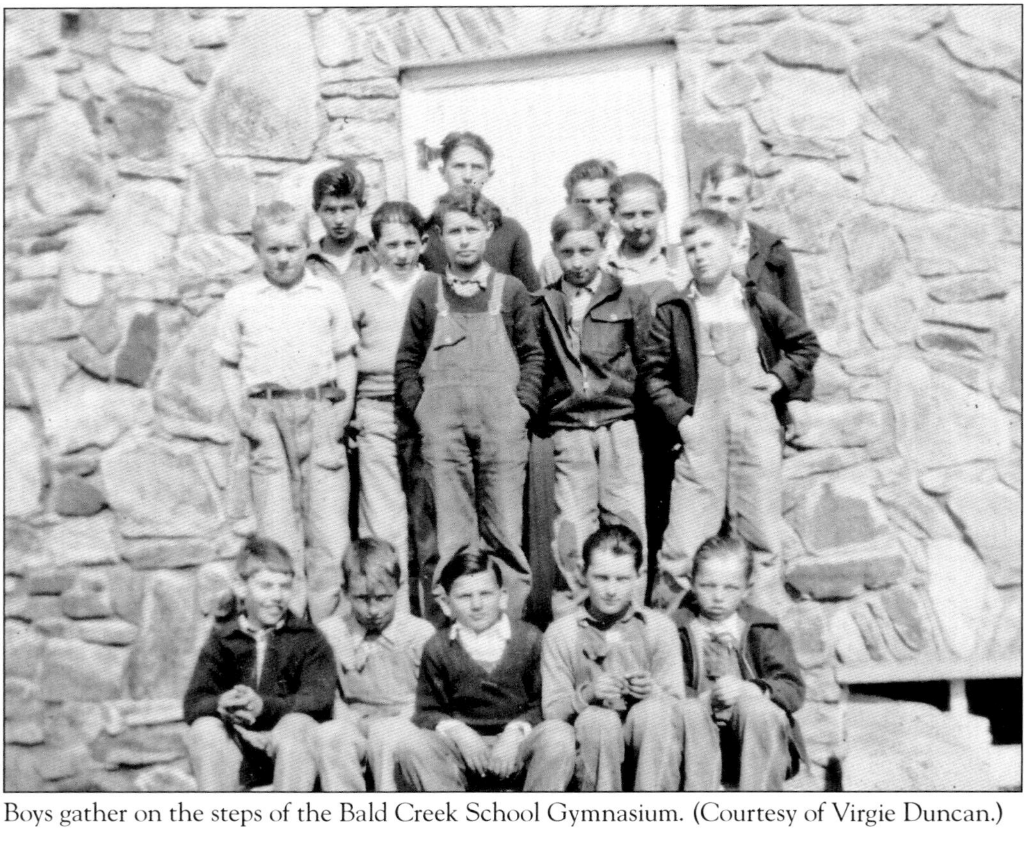

Boys gather on the steps of the Bald Creek School Gymnasium. (Courtesy of Virgie Duncan.)

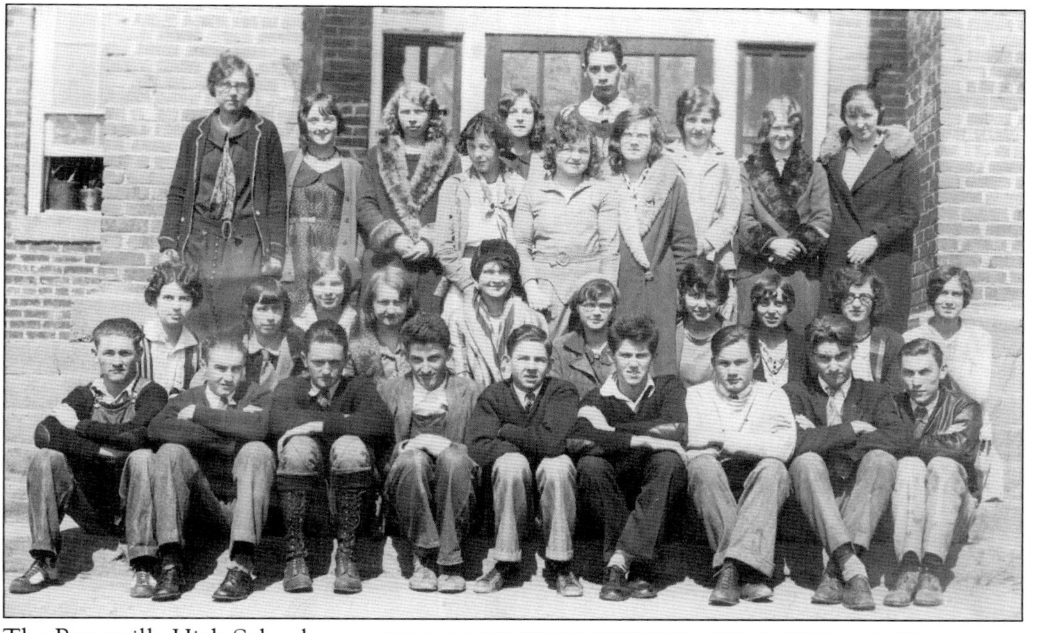

The Burnsville High School class of 1929–1930 included, from left to right, (first row) unidentified, Ottis Gibbs, David Chase, Charles Hyatt, Joe Pollard, Clyde Ayers, Mack Thompson, Mack Wilson, and Rush Wray; (second row) Elizabeth Bennett, unidentified, Avis Smith, Elizabeth Evans, Alma Briggs, Lucille Chase, unidentified, Robbie Hensley and Katherine Watson; (third row center) Helen Angel, Pauline Bailey, and unidentified; (fourth row) Corinne Green, Maphra Riddle, Celia King, Georgia Nichols, O. Nichols, Mary Lou Butner, Mamie Evans, and Nora Wilson. (Courtesy of Nancy Randolph Silvers.)

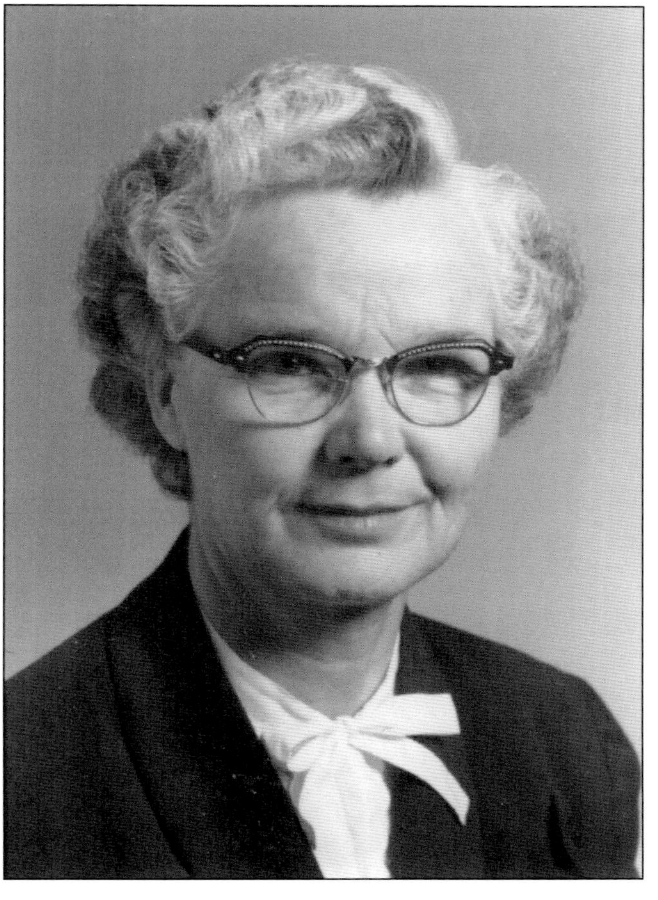

Hattie Phoenix taught school at Bald Creek for many years. She was the sister of Harvey Phoenix, and they were a longtime family in the area. (Courtesy of Virgie Duncan.)

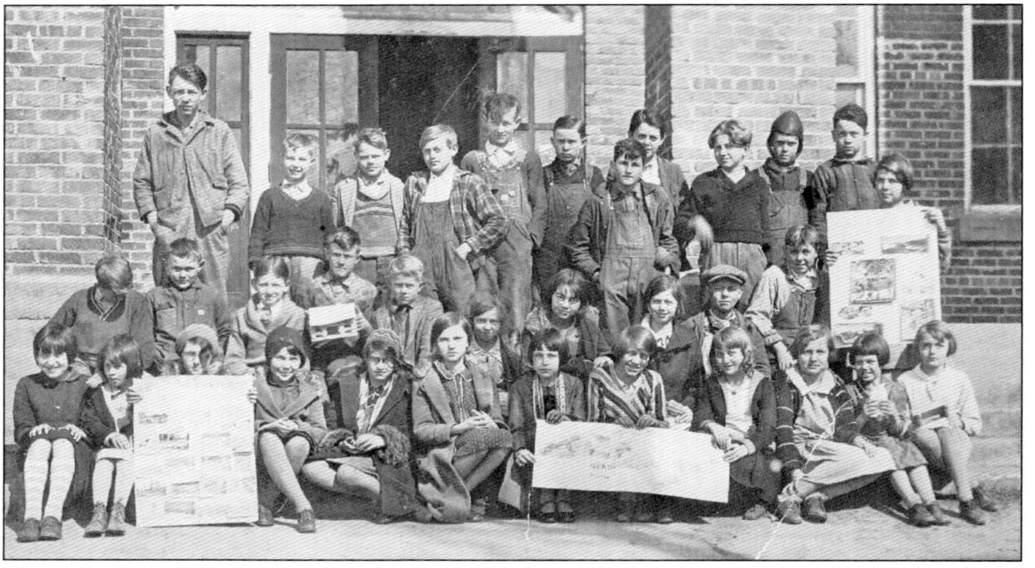

The fifth-grade class at Burnsville consisted of, from left to right, (first row) Lucille Reynolds, Jeannette Penland, Maude Westall, Sarah Woody, Olive Briggs, Mildred Bodford, Margaret English, Willie Mae Ayers, Mary Epps Anglin, June Murphy, Eula Mae Riddle, and Johnnie Marie Anglin; (second row) Clyde Williams, Arthur Janch, Ward Bennett, Charles Detty, Luther Ray, Badis Riddle, Ola Evans, Marie Brinkley, Edgar Wheeler, Woodrow Ayers, and Lillian Arrowood; (third row) Lewis Butner, Richard Peterson, Edd Hensley, John Cooper, Bill Autrey, Arnold Smith, Charles Black, Yates King, Hubert McIntosh, Leo McLaughlin, and Merritt Robertson. (Courtesy of Nancy Randolph Silvers.)

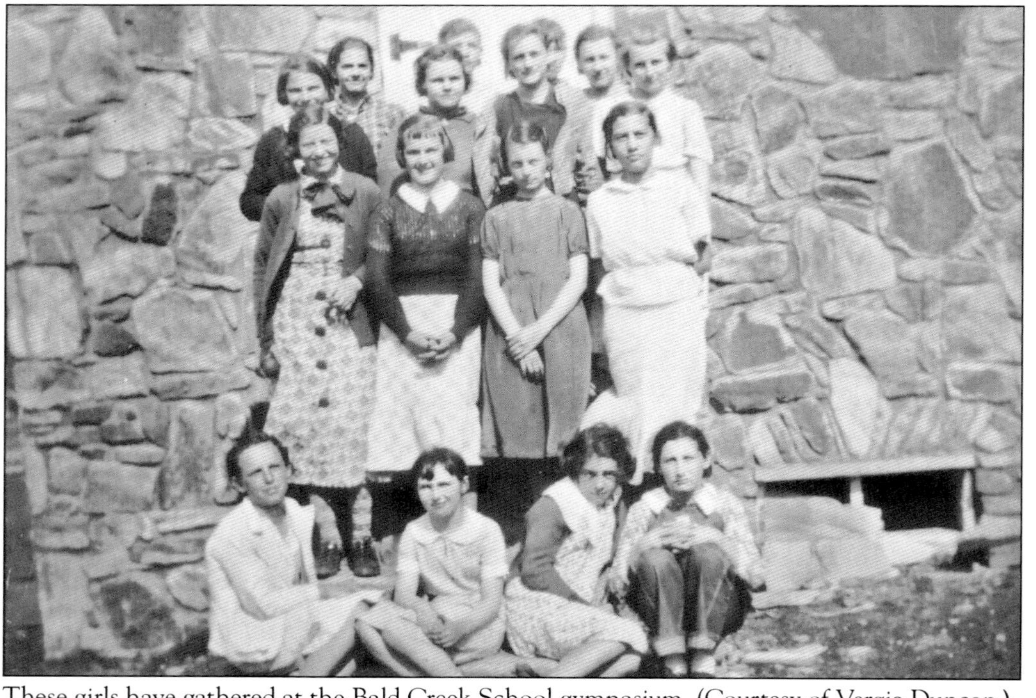

These girls have gathered at the Bald Creek School gymnasium. (Courtesy of Vergie Duncan.)

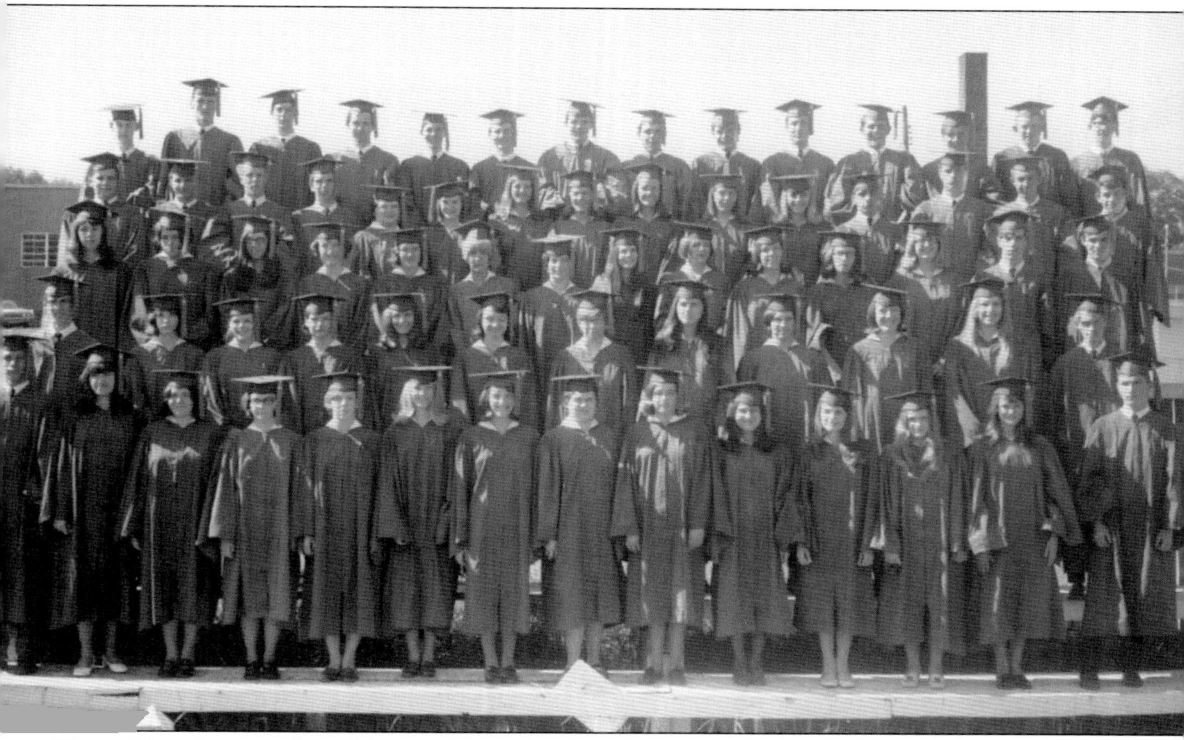

These 66 students graduated from Cane River High School in 1970. The school chose the rebel as its mascot, and the annual yearbook was called the *Confederate*, complete with the Southern Cross flag and kepi (hat) on the cover. The building has since become Cane River Middle School. (Courtesy of Elaine McAlister Dellinger.)

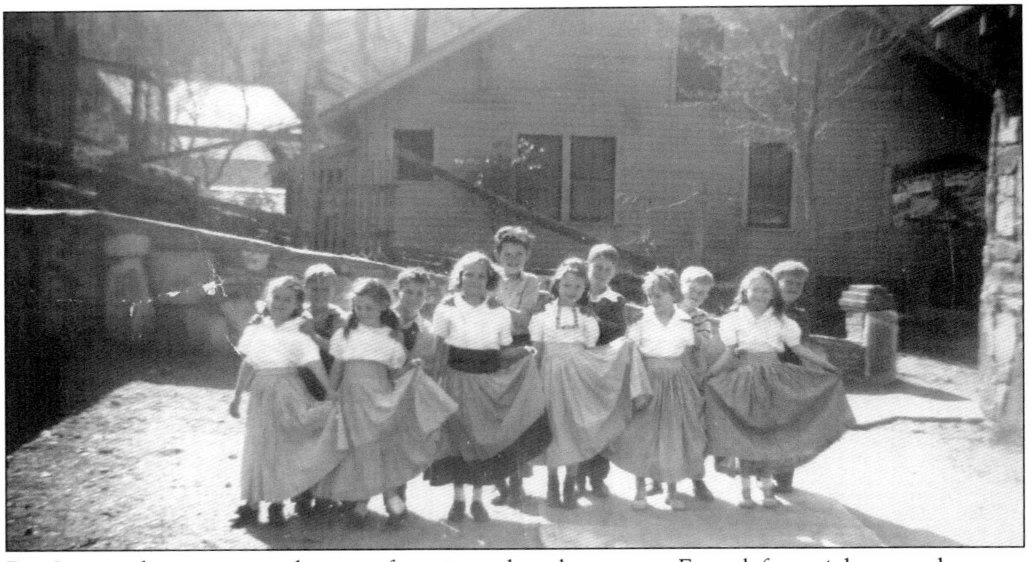

Bee Log students pose ready to perform in a chapel program. From left to right, seen here are (first row) Wanda Adkins, ? Miller, Maxine Wilson, Mary Anne Buchanan, Alice Ramsey, and Imogene Ramsey; (second row) two unidentified students, Kenneth Byrd, Scotty Ledford, Carleton Higgins, and unidentified. (Courtesy of Nancy Randolph Silvers.)

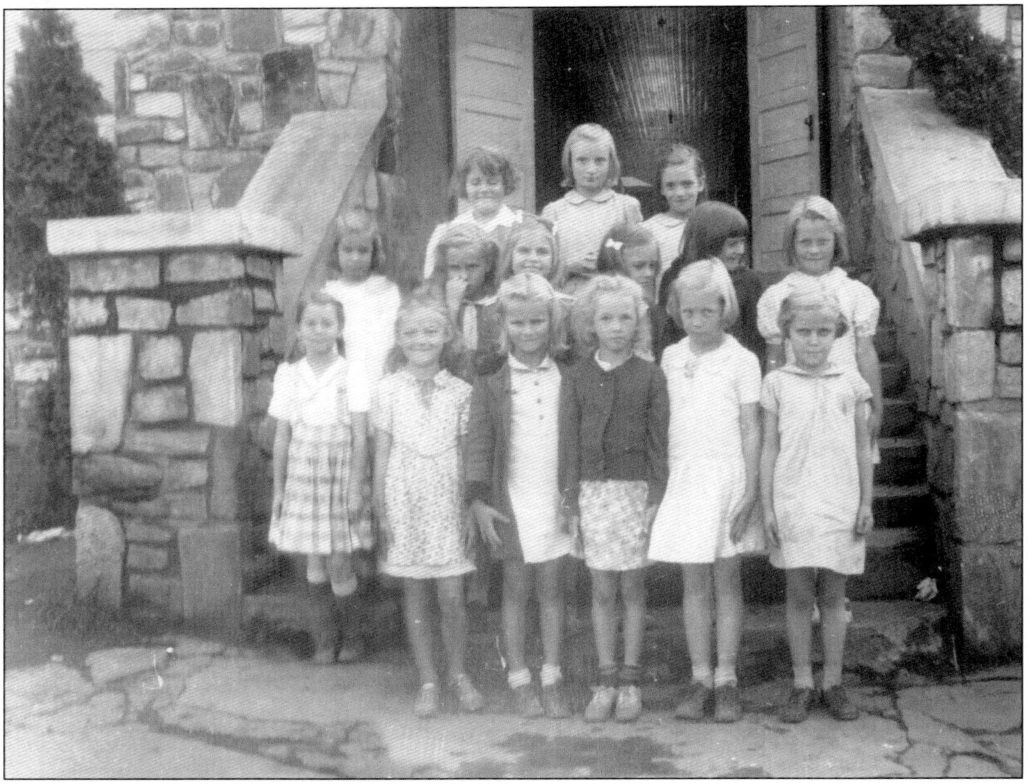

These girls stand on the steps of the Bald Creek School in the 1930s. (Courtesy of Nancy Randolph Silvers.)

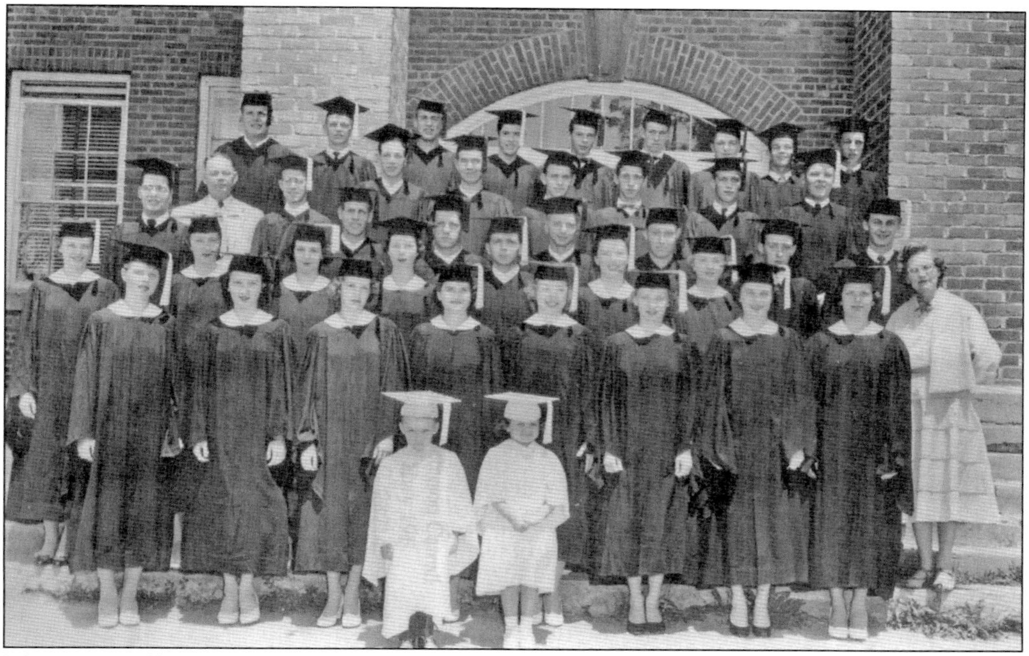

The Burnsville High School class of 1955 celebrates its graduation. (Courtesy of Charles Lee Dellinger.)

The Burnsville Class of 1955 is shown here in 1995 at Burnsville High School. From left to right, seen here are (first row) Claudette Peterson, Barbara Jean Allen, Bobby Styles, and Teddy Styles; (second row) Dee Smith, Aubrey Duncan, Clarence Harris, and Glenn Fox; (third row) L.G. Deyton, Arnold Melton, and Bobby Proffitt; (fourth row) Charles Robinson, Tommy Higgins, Clifford Silvers, and Gayle Hall; (fifth row) Jimmy Curtis, Bobby King, and Charles Lee Dellinger; (sixth row) James Riddle and Bryan Evans. (Courtesy of Charles Lee Dellinger.)

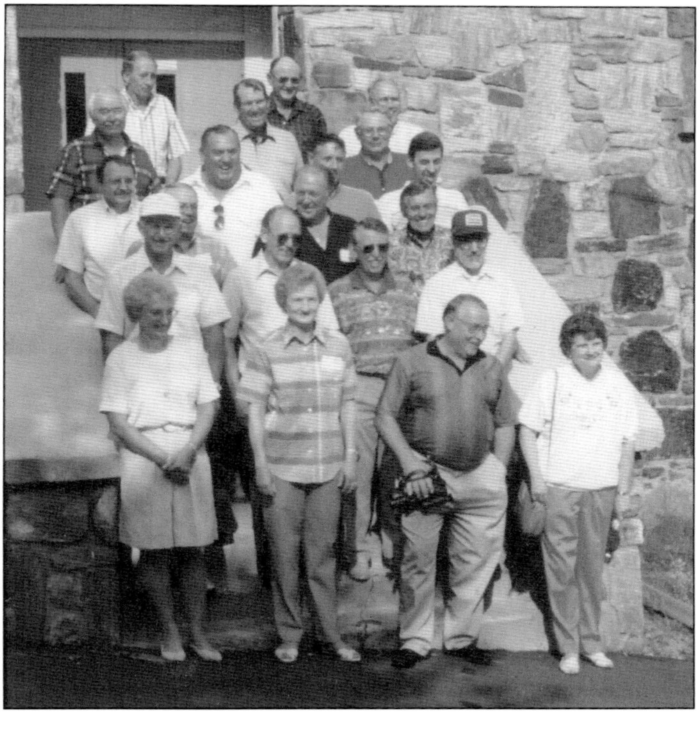

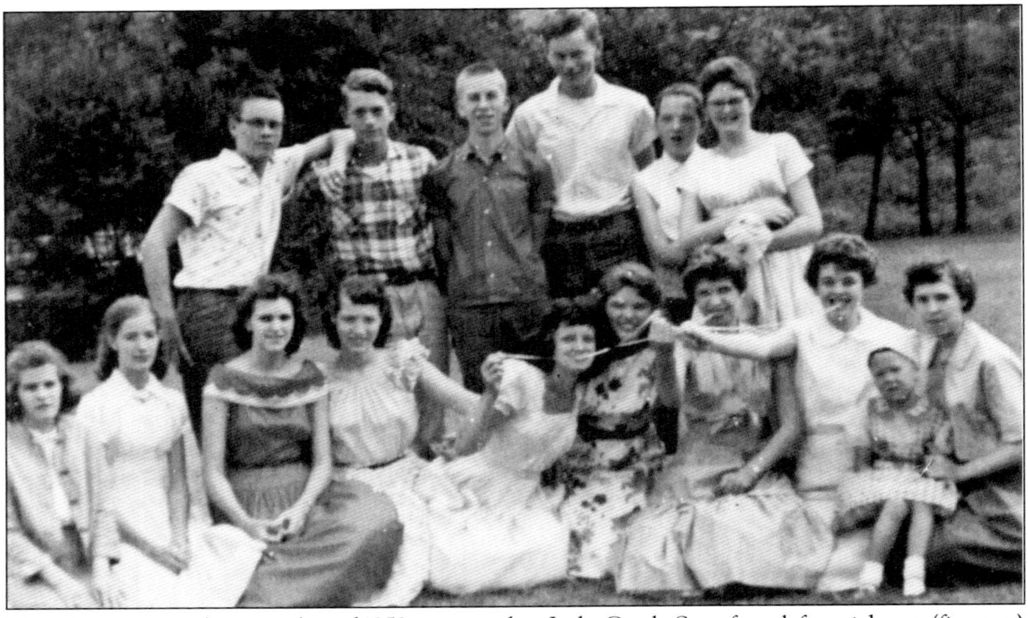

The Clearmont High junior class of 1958 is pictured on Jacks Creek. Seen from left to right are (first row) Mildred Tipton, Linda Willis, Mary Evelyn Hughes, Hope Deyton, Helen Silvers, Arlene Grindstaff, Kay Bennett, Barbara Ann Bailey, and Frances Higgins; (second row) Joe Bailey, Earl Webb, James Byrd, Craig McCurry, Erma Jean Deyton, and Ann Letterman. (Courtesy of Earl Webb.)

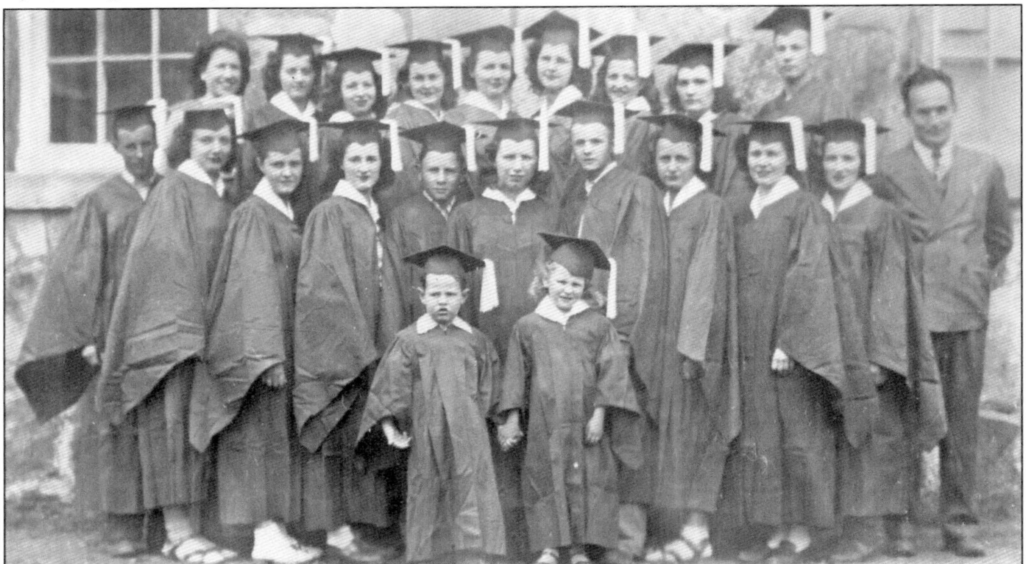

Here stand the 1944 graduates of Micaville High School minus Harold Silver (who had to go to war right before graduation). Mascots are Johnny Boone (left) and Nina Gibbs. Seen from left to right are (first row) Bruce Smith, Edith Westall, Cordy Rector, Ruth Ballew, Perry Wilson, Harriet Elliott, Dewey Hall, A Rector, Irene ?, Mildred Gibbs, and principal Hubert Justice; (second row) teacher Miss Hensley, Nell Edge, Maxine Buchanan, Genevieve Robinson, Jean Hall, Geneva Thomas, Marie Gouge, Irene Ballew, and Carl Silvers Jr. Bruce Smith went on to become the Burnsville postmaster. (Courtesy of Mildred Gibbs Harris.)

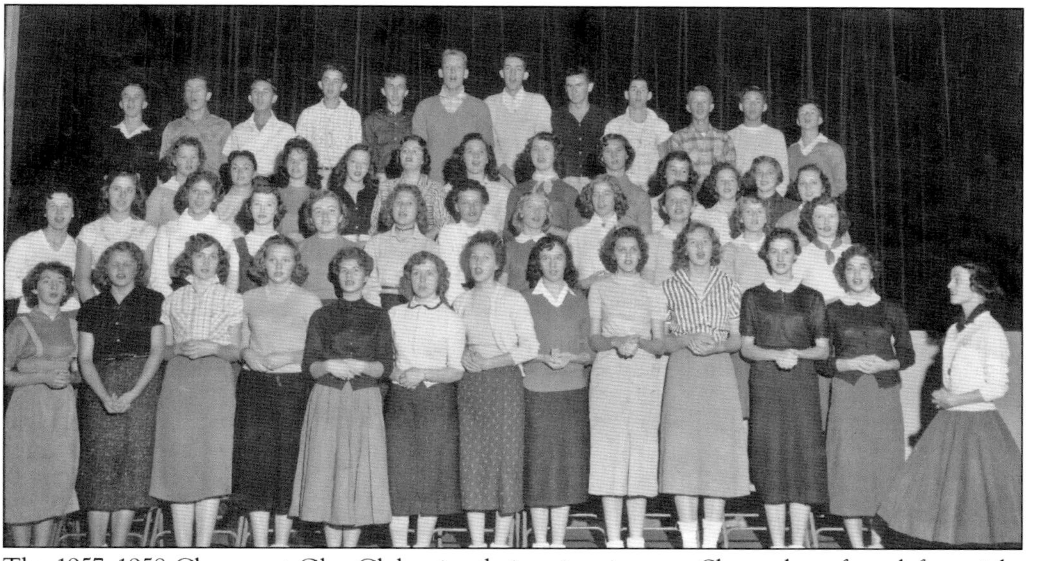

The 1957–1958 Clearmont Glee Club raise their voices in song. Shown here from left to right are (first row) Betty Lou Peterson, Arlene Grindstaff, Laura Phillips, Verna Peterson, Eloise Tipton, Anna Deyton, Frances Higgins, Rachel Ann Fox, Mary E. Hughes, Nadine Whitson, Betty Young, Stella Deyton and Janet Granta; (second row) Barbara Hughes, Shirley Miller, Edna Tipton, Mary E. Connelly, Elizabeth Wheeler, Maybelle Robinson, Helen Silvers, Diana Evans, Linda Willis, Verlene Silvers, Charlotte Edwards, and Laura Randolph; (third row) Evelyn Ayers, Martha Williams, Jolene Woody, Hope Deyton, Mary Ann Letterman, Helen Gortney, Bobbie Ayers, Beatrice Freeman, Lois Gortney, Peggy Deyton, Wanda Hope Laughrun, and Lodella Duncan; (fourth row) James Byrd, Ivan Woody, Lester Miller, Bill Young, Theron Woody, Junior Robinson, U.B. Deyton, Gerald Garland, Edgar Byrd, Jim Evans, A.J. Laws, and Robert Deyton. (Courtesy of Charlotte Anglin.)

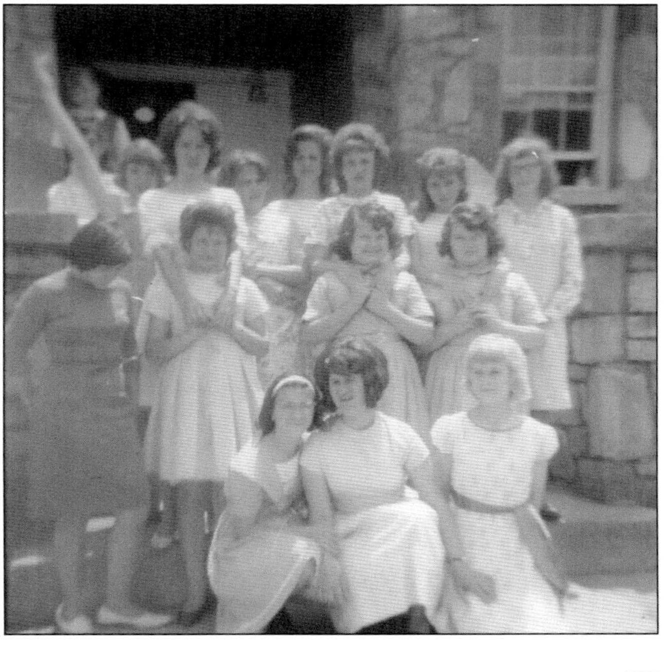

This seventh-grade class of 1964–1965 attended Bald Creek School. Among those pictured are Joyce Banks, Betty Ann Austin, Karen Burleson, Wanda Penland, Elaine McAlister, Geraldine Hall, Anita and Norita Edwards, Avis Banks, Christine Edwards, Dona Buckner, and Nancy Ruth Randolph. (Courtesy of Nancy Randolph Silvers.)

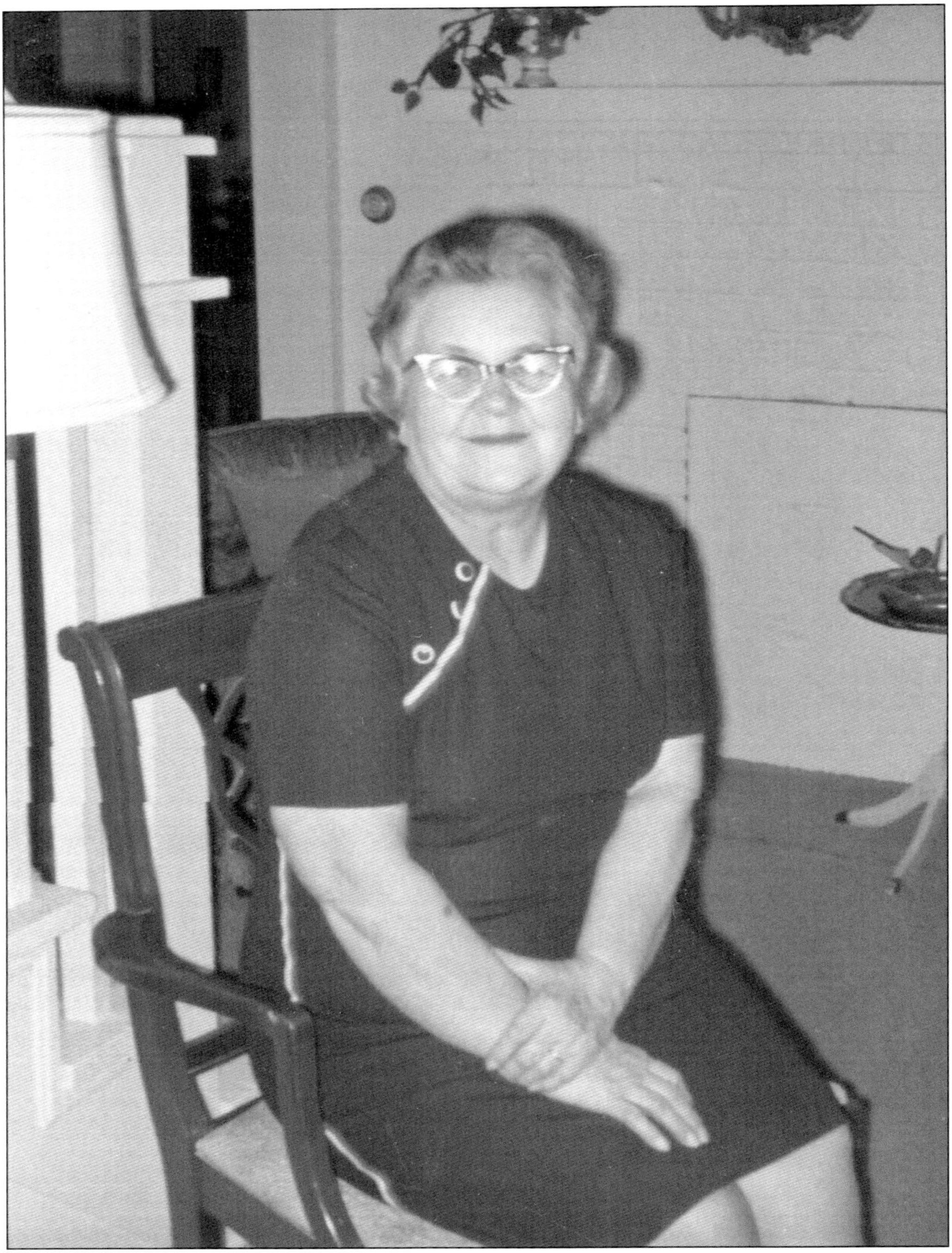

A most-beloved Pauline Bailey Hensley taught home economics at both the Bald Creek and Cane River High Schools. She touched many young women's lives by teaching them how to make a house a home through sewing, cooking, canning, freezing, and gardening. (Courtesy of Elaine McAlister Dellinger.)

Ten

A Backward Glance

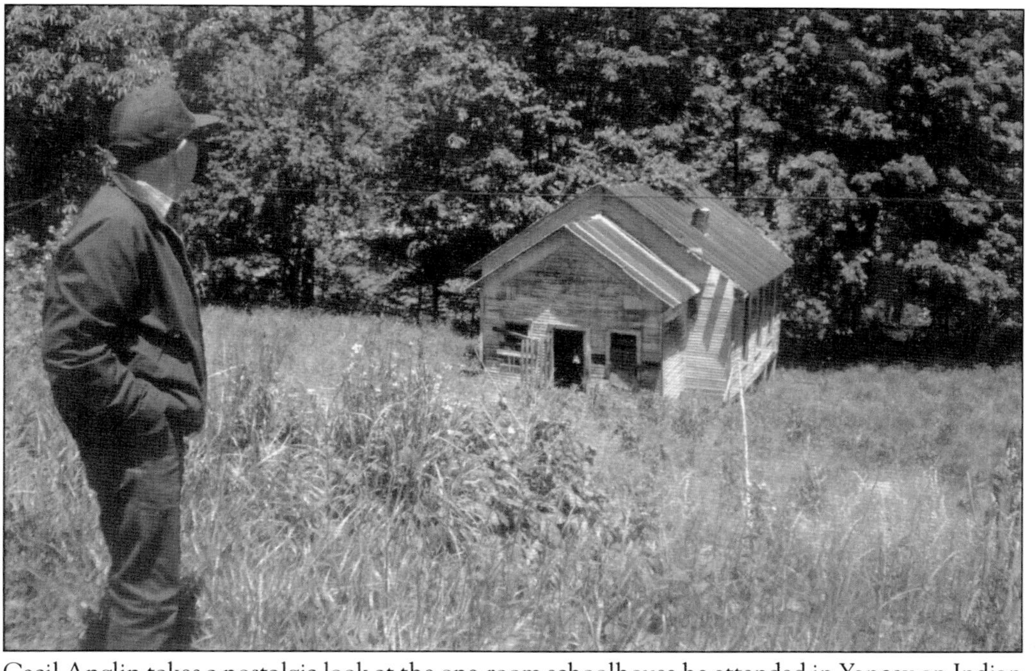

Cecil Anglin takes a nostalgic look at the one-room schoolhouse he attended in Yancey on Indian Creek, remembering his and his two sisters' three-mile walk from Metcalf Creek in Madison County to this, the closest school. The schoolhouse was built in the early 1900s and burned down in 2005. (Courtesy of Roy Lee Anglin.)

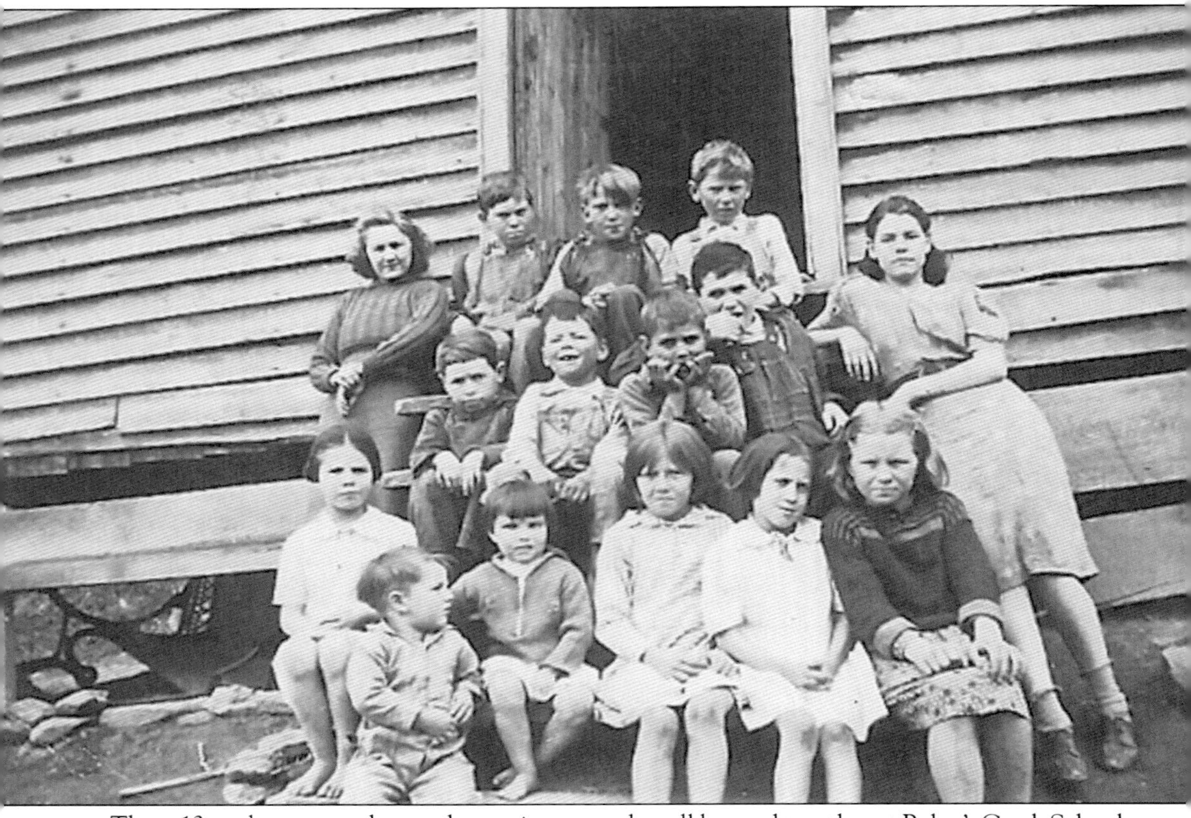

These 13 students, a teacher, and an assistant teacher all learned together at Baker's Creek School. (Courtesy of Roy Lee Anglin.)

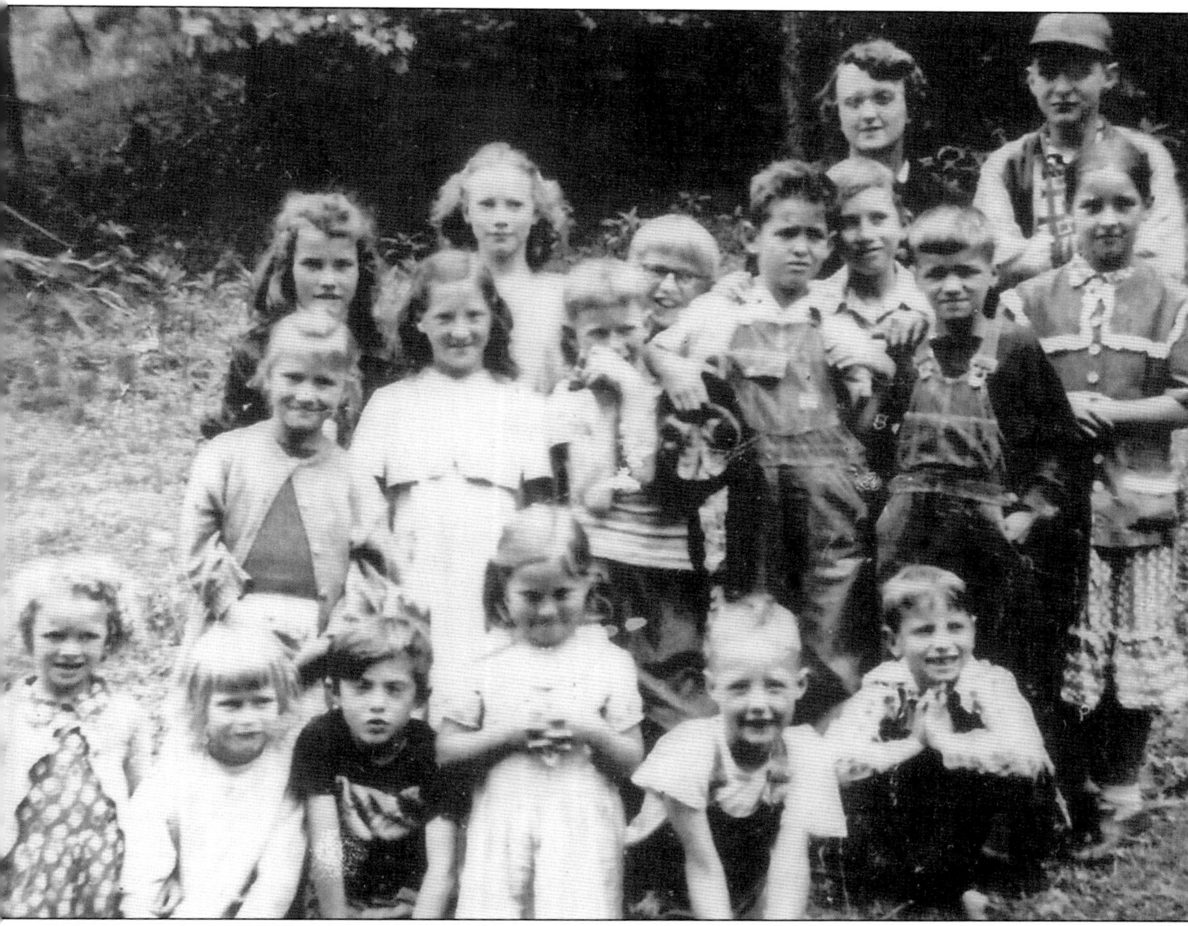

The 1949 class at Baker's Creek School included, from left to right: (first row) Shirley Black, Genette King, Glenn Roland, Barbara Melton, Gene Elkins, and Earnest Ayers; (second row) Genella Anglin, Ivory Melton, Dean King, Charles Roland, Arville Baker, Howard Roland, Jeralene Byrd, and Roy Anglin; (third row) Nadine McIntosh, Evalee King, Maphria Wilson, and Norris McCandless. The Baker's Creek Baptist Church housed the school. (Courtesy of Roy Lee Anglin.)

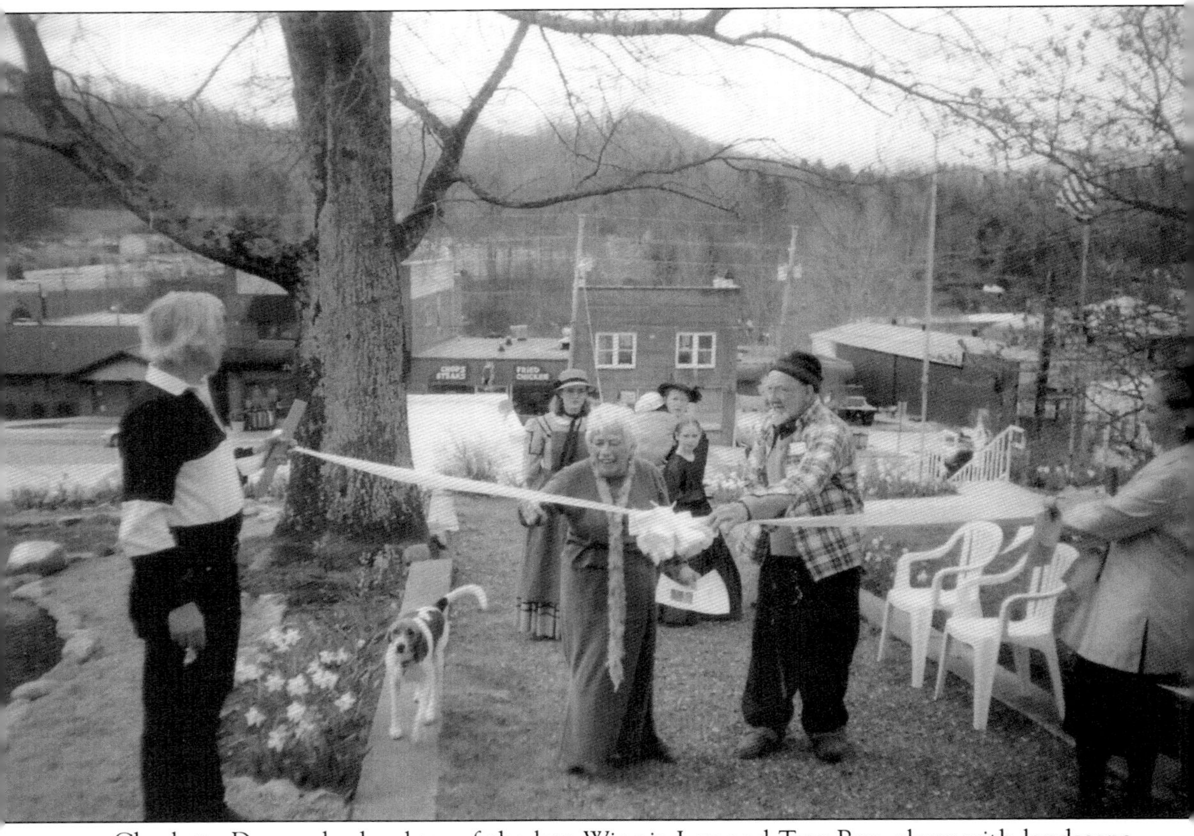

Charlotte Derrough, daughter of the late Winnie Lou and Troy Ray, along with landscape designer and local historian Grant Ward, cut the ribbon at the dedication of the Winnie Lou Memorial Flower Garden. Winnie Lou and Troy Ray were the last residents of the house that became the Rush Wray Museum. Pictured also are then-members of the board of directors for Yancey History Association James Cochrane (president, at left), Sara Cochrane (secretary of the board, at right), Collette Blankenship (museum manager, background at left) and Judy Lackey (board member, background at right) with her children Kyle and Katie. (Courtesy of Elaine McAlister Dellinger.)

Archaeology student Elaine McAlister Dellinger excavated the well of the McElroy House—now the Rush Wray Museum of Yancey History. Elaine suffered a tragic accident during the project in 2004, when the well's false bottom gave way, causing her to fall 40 feet. She suffered major injuries to her back and spine but survived to continue serving on the museum's board of directors. (Courtesy of Elaine McAlister Dellinger.)

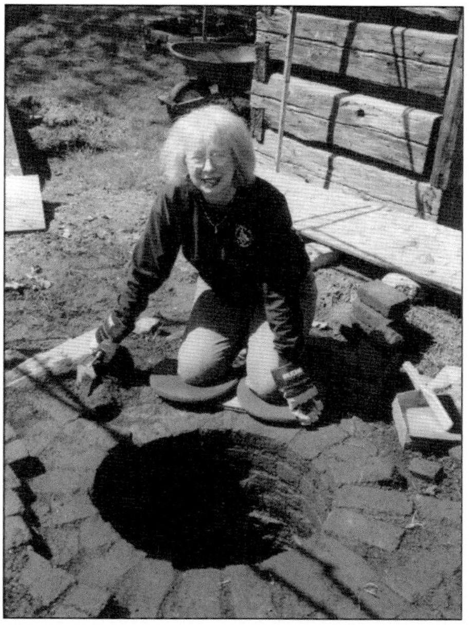

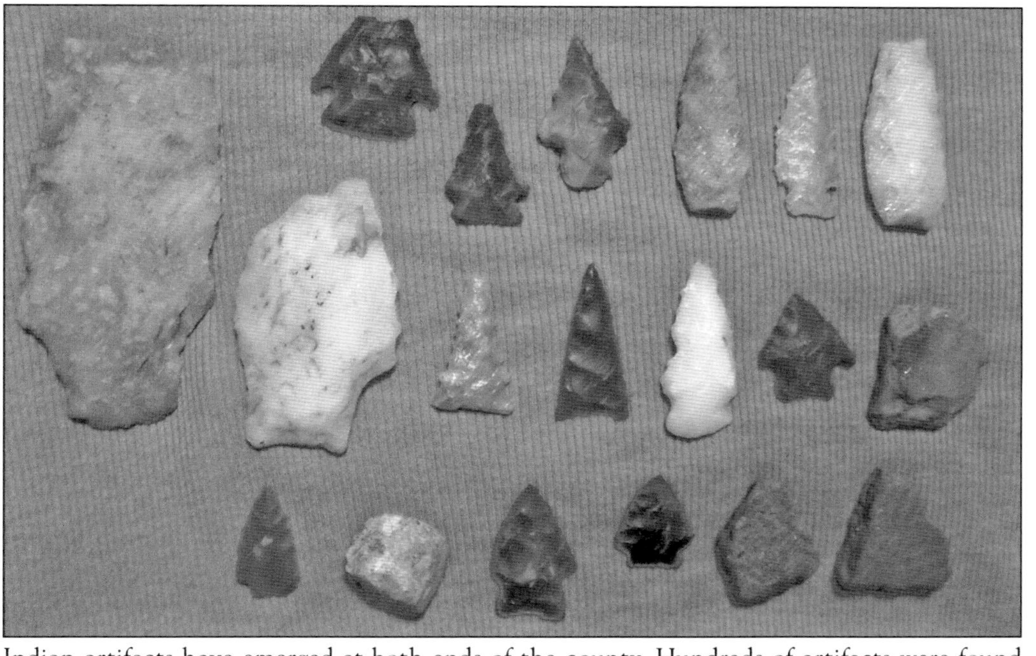

Indian artifacts have emerged at both ends of the county. Hundreds of artifacts were found while a couple was adding a greenhouse to their home back in 2002–2003 in the Brush Creek area, including arrowheads and spear points of jasper and quartzite, which were thought to date from the Paleo-Archaic to the Woodland Periods (8000 BC to 1600 AD). Indian artifacts from the Cane River Valley near Proffitt Branch include projectile points such as Palmer, Guilford Lancets, early Savannah River, Caraway, and Randolph; Woodland Period ceramic pottery; and points reworked to be used as scrapers and knives. The dates for these artifacts are believed to range from 10,000 BC to 1800 AD. This photograph brings the reader back to the earliest-known inhabitants of the region. (Courtesy of Elaine McAlister Dellinger.)

Index of Contributors

Bibliography

Branon's North Carolina Business Directory for 1869. Raleigh: J.A. Jones, 1884.

Dellinger, Elaine McAlister and Gwen Bodford. *Yancey County NC Cemeteries by Township*. Burnsville, NC: Mike and Toni Shelton, 2009.

Dugger, Shepherd M. *War Trails of the Blue Ridge*. Banner Elk, NC: Shepherd Dugger, 1932.

Garren, Terrell T. *Mountain Myth: Unionism in Western North Carolina*. Spartanburg, SC: Reprint Company, 2006.

Hardy, Michael C. *McElroy House*. Virginia Beach: Downing Company, 2004.

Inscoe, John C. and Gordon B. McKinney. *The Heart of Confederate Appalachia: Western North Carolina in the Civil War*. Chapel Hill: UNC Press, 2000.

Jackson, Leroy F. "The Social Program of the Stanley McCormick School." *Journal of Social Forces*, 1923; reprinted in *Social Forces*, UNC Press.

Kardulis, Paul E. 1850 Yancey County Census (NC), 1860 Yancey County Census (NC), 1870 Yancey County Census (NC).

Merschat, Carl E. *Geology of Yancey County, Geologic Note 5*. Raleigh: North Carolina Geologic Survey, Division of Land Resources, 1997.

http://files.usgwarchives.org/nc/yancey/census/1850/yancey50.txt

Teacher Training Class of Burnsville 1930. *History and Geography of Yancey County*.

Yancey County, NC 1850 & 1860 Agricultural Census.